D0621726

The
Reference Shelf®

The Politics of
the Oceans

Edited by

Kenneth Partridge

The Reference Shelf
Volume 83 • Number 5
H. W. Wilson
A Division of EBSCO Publishing, Inc.
Ipswich, Massachusetts
2011

The Reference Shelf

The books in this series contain reprints of articles, excerpts from books, addresses on current issues, and studies of social trends in the United States and other countries. There are six separately bound numbers in each volume, all of which are usually published in the same calendar year. Numbers one through five are each devoted to a single subject, providing background information and discussion from various points of view and concluding with a subject index and comprehensive bibliography that lists books, pamphlets, and abstracts of additional articles on the subject. The final number of each volume is a collection of recent speeches, and it contains a cumulative speaker index. Books in the series may be purchased individually or on subscription.

Library of Congress has cataloged this serial title as follows:

Partridge, Kenneth, 1980-
  The politics of the oceans / edited by Kenneth Partridge.
    p. cm. -- (The reference shelf ; v. 83, no. 5)
  Includes bibliographical references and index.
  ISBN 978-0-8242-1111-0 (alk. paper)
  1. Ocean--Political aspects. 2. Law of the sea. 3. Territorial waters. 4. Ocean--Environmental aspects. I. Title.
  JZ3690.P38 2011
  341.4'5--dc23

2011031934

Cover: NEW ORLEANS—Fire boat response crews battle the blazing remnants of the offshore oil rig *Deepwaer Horizon* on April 21, 2010. A Coast Guard MH-65C Dolphin rescue helicopter and crew document the fire aboard the *Deepwater Horizon* while searching for survivors. Multiple Coast Guard helicopters, planes, and cutters responded to rescue the *Deepwater Horizon*'s 126 person crew. (Courtesy of the United States Coast Guard)

Copyright © 2011, by H. W. Wilson, A Division of EBSCO Publishing, Inc.

All rights in this book are reserved. No part of this work may be used or reproduced in any manner whatsoever or transmitted in any form or by any means, electronic or mechanical, including photocopy, recording, or any information storage and retrieval system, without written permission from the copyright owner. For information, contact the publisher, EBSCO Publishing, 10 Estes Street, Ipswich, MA 01938.

Visit H. W. Wilson's Web site: www.hwwilson.com

Printed in the United States of America

Contents

Preface

For much of human history, the oceans were politics-free zones. Thanks to an unwritten law known as the "freedom of the seas" doctrine, nations laid claim only to waters just off their coastlines, leaving the rest in common. Until a few years ago, the Arctic was frozen solid, meaning no one was angling for trade routes at the top of the world. Before cars and airplanes, there was relatively little demand for oil, hence no contentious offshore drilling or devastating spills. Fishing was done with lines and simple nets, not today's brutally efficient trawlers and helicopter-guided purse seines—massive nets designed to sweep up huge amounts of fish—and while there have always been pirates, they used to arm themselves with swords and cannons, not the AK-47s favored by the modern-day Blackbeards causing trouble off the Horn of Africa.

Clearly, a great deal has changed in the last 100 years. "We live in a political world," as Bob Dylan sang on the 1989 album *Oh Mercy*, and our world is three-quarters water. In this edition of The Reference Shelf, we examine "The Politics of the Oceans" and consider humanity's evolving relationship with the sea. Although we remain very much at its mercy—as was proved most recently by the tsunami that struck Japan in March 2011—we've found ways to pollute, overfish, and fight for control of that which we'll never tame.

The book opens with "LOST at Sea: Debating the Law of the Sea Treaty," a chapter devoted to a United Nations (UN) agreement the United States signed in 1994 but has never put before the U.S. Senate for an official vote. Because ratifying the treaty would force American ships—be they military or civilian—to follow rules set forth by an international body, as well as pay royalties on oil and gas mined from the continental shelf, many lawmakers are staunchly opposed. "If joining the treaty were really in the interest of the United States, one would have thought the Senate would have ratified it long ago," James Carafano writes in the piece "LOST Would Be a Loser for the U.S." LOST supporters, meanwhile, insist that ratification would help America claim a piece of the rapidly thawing, potentially lucrative Arctic Ocean.

Entries in the second chapter, "Lines in the Water: Territorial Disputes in the Arctic and Beyond," look at how nations are vying for control of not only the Arctic Ocean, but also the Pacific and Indian. In the latter case, a confluence of Middle

Eastern, African, and Asian interests has made for a great deal of political intrigue, much of it related to China's race with India to dominate the regional economy.

Selections in the third chapter, "Trouble in the Gulf: The BP Oil Spill," consider who is to blame for the ecological disaster touched off on April 20, 2010, when the *Deepwater Horizon* drilling rig exploded in the Gulf of Mexico, killing 11 and opening a gusher 5,000 feet below the surface. While scientists continue to debate the impact of the spill, which has been called the largest in history, the Gulf Coast fishing and tourism industries have been hard hit, and critics accuse BP of improperly distributing compensatory funds to victims.

Sadly, oil isn't the only substance mucking up our oceans. While oceanographers dispute the existence of the "Great Pacific Garbage Patch"—a floating mound of refuse said to be twice the size of Texas—tests show that microscopic plastic particles are abundant in waters around the world. When these toxic specks make their way into the food chain, researchers warn, humans are at risk for serious illness. Entries in the fourth chapter, "Pollution and the Island of Trash," explain why— garbage patch or not—plastic is a real problem.

In the fifth chapter, "Scourge of the Seas: Piracy," the selections center on a type of violent crime that's become increasingly prevalent in recent years, particularly off the coast of Somalia. While the original Somali pirates of the 1990s were fishermen fighting against the foreign companies they blamed for encroaching on their waters and stealing their jobs, Ishaan Tharoor explains in a piece for *Time*, the men who today don ski masks and wield machine guns tend to lack an ideological motive for their crimes. According to the consulting firm Geopolicity, the annual cost of Indian Ocean piracy has topped $12 billion, and some fear it could hit $15 billion by 2015.

Articles in the sixth and final chapter, "The End of Seafood? Overfishing Around the World," consider what can be done to replenish dwindling fish stocks. As reported in the opening piece, marine biologist Boris Worm warned in 2006 that, barring a major "change in the way we manage all the oceans species together, as working ecosystems," seafood could disappear from our plates by 2048. While efforts in the United States have been largely successful—at least according to Michael Conathan, who's represented here with a pair of "Fish on Friday" columns— the book's final piece, "Something Fishy," explains why Canadian environmentalists are less than satisfied with their country's Maritime Stewardship Council, a private charity that identifies sustainable fisheries for the benefit of consumers.

In conclusion, I'd like to thank the many authors and publications who granted us permission to reprint the articles included in this volume. I'm also grateful to have once again worked with Paul McCaffrey and Rich Stein, fellow H.W. Wilson editors who collect knowledge much as the North Pacific Gyre does discarded soda bottles. Thanks, too, to my wife, Lindsey, with whom I'd gladly retire to a secluded tropical island, plastic or otherwise.

Kenneth Partridge
October 2011

1

LOST at Sea:
Debating the Law of the Sea Treaty

Courtesy of the Library of Congress

President Harry S. Truman declared in 1945 that the United States had jurisdiction over its continental shelf, a move that kickstarted a new era in ocean politics.

Courtesy of Stefano Corso

The United Nations (UN) Headquarters in New York City. Many opponents of the Law of the Sea Treaty (LOST) believe the agreement would cede American sovereignty to the UN.

Editor's Introduction

For roughly 400 years, from the 17th century to the dawn of the Cold War, oceangoing nations around the world subscribed to the "freedom of the seas" doctrine, an unwritten code that gave countries jurisdiction over narrow stretches of water just off their shores. Beyond these buffers—three miles, in most cases—the ocean belonged to no one and was essentially up for grabs. Like many international agreements made before World War II, "freedom of the seas" became obsolete in the mid-20th century, as emerging geopolitical realities and advances in shipping, fishing, and drilling made control of the Earth's waterways a prerequisite for both economic prosperity and national security.

President Harry S. Truman was quick to realize this, and in September 1945, he asserted America's right to harvest all natural resources on the country's continental shelf. This extended U.S. sovereignty well beyond the traditional three-mile zone, and by the end of the decade, a number of South American countries, including Argentina, Chile, and Peru, had made similar claims on their coastal waters. On the other side of the world, Egypt, Saudi Arabia, and Ethiopia established 12-mile territorial zones, as did several Eastern European nations, further eradicating the system that had been in place since the days of cannonballs and wooden ships.

As the century progressed, competition for resources only grew fiercer. Offshore oil drilling became big business, causing disputes in such places as the North Sea, where Denmark, Great Britain, and Germany all laid claim to the continental shelf. The same went for fishing, as fleets from different countries congregated in the same hot spots, vying for diminishing stocks of cod, tuna, and other species. In addition to overfishing, pollution became a major environmental concern, especially as oil tankers proved prone to spills.

Alarmed by these and other trends, Arvid Pardo, Malta's ambassador to the United Nations (UN), addressed the General Assembly on November 1, 1967, calling for the creation of an "effective international regime over the seabed and the ocean floor beyond a clearly defined national jurisdiction." As Pardo saw it, cooperation between countries was the only way to prevent violent conflict and further degradation of marine ecosystems. Some five years later, in 1973, the Third United Nations Conference on the Law of the Sea convened in New York City. In 1982, having spent nearly a decade consulting with representatives from 160 sovereign states, the Conference adopted the United Nations Convention on the Law of the Sea Treaty (LOST), the subject of the articles in this chapter.

The chapter opens with a history of LOST prepared by the UN Division for Ocean Affairs and the Law of the Sea. The selection explains how the treaty defines such key concepts as "territorial seas" and "exclusive economic zones," regulates fishing and the collection of other natural resources, ensures fairness for landlocked countries, and mediates conflicts between signees. While the United States signed LOST in 1994 and adheres to many of its rules, the Senate has never officially ratified the treaty. There are a number of reasons for this, and in the subsequent four articles, LOST supporters and detractors make the case for and against adopting the treaty.

In "LOST Would Be a Loser for the U.S.," James Carafano blasts President Barack Obama for supporting the treaty. Carafano's main objections have to do with provisions that would force U.S. companies to pay royalties on money made mining oil and gas on the continental shelf. "We already have the right to those resources," he writes. "Why pay an international bureaucracy for what's already ours?" He also worries Obama will use LOST "as another excuse to gut the armed forces." Carafano believes that a strong U.S. Navy is all that is needed to preserve freedom of the seas.

In *The New York Times* editorial that follows, a LOST proponent argues that ratifying the treaty makes good economic sense, since it would help the United States claim valuable natural resources—oil and gas, in particular—thought to exist under the thawing Arctic ice. Russia, Canada, and Denmark have already begun competing for drilling rights, and according to the editorial, "the United States will have a hard time pressing those claims unless it ratifies the treaty and gets a seat at the negotiating table."

In the next piece, *U.S. Report* writer Chris Carter interviews *Accuracy in Media Report* editor Cliff Kincaid, another LOST critic wary of forfeiting American naval superiority. Rather than focus on the treaty, Kincaid says, the U.S. government should bolster its fleet and build the 600-ship navy once envisioned by President Ronald Reagan. "LOST grants us no right that we do not already have," he concludes. "We have everything to lose and nothing to gain."

As Andrew Jensen reports in the final selection, "Sea Treaty Has Broad Support, But Little Chance of Ratification," some lawmakers beg to differ. Alaska senators Lisa Murkowski and Mark Begich, a Republican and Democrat, respectively, support the treaty, since it would pave the way for oil exploration in the Arctic. Although many environmental groups have joined energy companies in backing the treaty, it's unlikely the Senate will take up the measure anytime soon.

The United Nations Convention on the Law of the Sea[*]

(A Historical Perspective)

The United Nations
Division for Ocean Affairs and the Law of the Sea, 1998

A HISTORICAL PERSPECTIVE

The oceans had long been subject to the freedom-of-the-seas doctrine—a principle put forth in the seventeenth century essentially limiting national rights and jurisdiction over the oceans to a narrow belt of sea surrounding a nation's coastline. The remainder of the seas was proclaimed to be free to all and belonging to none. While this situation prevailed into the twentieth century, by mid-century there was an impetus to extend national claims over offshore resources. There was growing concern over the toll taken on coastal fish stocks by long-distance fishing fleets and over the threat of pollution and wastes from transport ships and oil tankers carrying noxious cargoes that plied sea routes across the globe. The hazard of pollution was ever present, threatening coastal resorts and all forms of ocean life. The navies of the maritime powers were competing to maintain a presence across the globe on the surface waters and even under the sea.

A tangle of claims, spreading pollution, competing demands for lucrative fish stocks in coastal waters and adjacent seas, growing tension between coastal nations' rights to these resources and those of distant-water fishermen, the prospects of a rich harvest of resources on the sea floor, the increased presence of maritime powers and the pressures of long-distance navigation and a seemingly outdated, if not inherently conflicting, freedom-of-the-seas doctrine—all these were threatening to transform the oceans into another arena for conflict and instability.

In 1945, President Harry S. Truman, responding in part to pressure from domestic oil interests, unilaterally extended United States jurisdiction over all natural resources on that nation's continental shelf—oil, gas, minerals, etc. This was the

---

[*] Prepared by the Division for Ocean Affairs and the Law of the Sea, Office of Legal Affairs, United Nations. All rights reserved.

first major challenge to the freedom-of-the-seas doctrine. Other nations soon followed suit.

In October 1946, Argentina claimed its shelf and the epicontinental sea above it. Chile and Peru in 1947, and Ecuador in 1950, asserted sovereign rights over a 200-mile zone, hoping thereby to limit the access of distant-water fishing fleets and to control the depletion of fish stocks in their adjacent seas.

Soon after the Second World War, Egypt, Ethiopia, Saudi Arabia, Libya, Venezuela and some Eastern European countries laid claim to a 12-mile territorial sea, thus clearly departing from the traditional three-mile limit.

Later, the archipelagic nation of Indonesia asserted the right to dominion over the water that separated its 13,000 islands. The Philippines did likewise. In 1970, Canada asserted the right to regulate navigation in an area extending for 100 miles from its shores in order to protect Arctic water against pollution.

From oil to tin, diamonds to gravel, metals to fish, the resources of the sea are enormous. The reality of their exploitation grows day by day as technology opens new ways to tap those resources.

In the late 1960s, oil exploration was moving further and further from land, deeper and deeper into the bedrock of continental margins. From a modest beginning in 1947 in the Gulf of Mexico, offshore oil production, still less than a million tons in 1954, had grown to close to 400 million tons. Oil drilling equipment was already going as far as 4,000 metres below the ocean surface.

The oceans were being exploited as never before. Activities unknown barely two decades earlier were in full swing around the world. Tin had been mined in the shallow waters off Thailand and Indonesia. South Africa was about to tap the Namibian coast for diamonds. Potato-shaped nodules, found almost a century earlier and lying on the seabed some five kilometres below, were attracting increased interest because of their metal content.

And then there was fishing. Large fishing vessels were roaming the oceans far from their native shores, capable of staying away from port for months at a time. Fish stocks began to show signs of depletion as fleet after fleet swept distant coastlines. Nations were flooding the richest fishing waters with their fishing fleets virtually unrestrained: coastal States setting limits and fishing States contesting them. The so-called "Cod War" between Iceland and the United Kingdom had brought about the spectacle of British Navy ships dispatched to rescue a fishing vessel seized by Iceland for violating its fishing rules.

Offshore oil was the centre of attraction in the North Sea. Britain, Denmark and Germany were in conflict as to how to carve up the continental shelf, with its rich oil resources.

It was late 1967 and the tranquility of the sea was slowly being disrupted by technological breakthroughs, accelerating and multiplying uses, and a super-Power rivalry that stood poised to enter man's last preserve—the seabed.

It was a time that held both dangers and promises, risks and hopes. The dangers were numerous: nuclear submarines charting deep waters never before explored; designs for antiballistic missile systems to be placed on the seabed; supertankers ferrying oil from the Middle East to European and other ports, passing through congested straits and leaving behind a trail of oil spills; and rising tensions between nations over conflicting claims to ocean space and resources.

The oceans were generating a multitude of claims, counterclaims and sovereignty disputes.

The hope was for a more stable order, promoting greater use and better management of ocean resources and generating harmony and goodwill among States that would no longer have to eye each other suspiciously over conflicting claims.

THIRD UNITED NATIONS CONFERENCE ON THE LAW OF THE SEA

On 1 November 1967, Malta's Ambassador to the United Nations, Arvid Pardo, asked the nations of the world to look around them and open their eyes to a looming conflict that could devastate the oceans, the lifeline of man's very survival. In a speech to the United Nations General Assembly, he spoke of the super-Power rivalry that was spreading to the oceans, of the pollution that was poisoning the seas, of the conflicting legal claims and their implications for a stable order and of the rich potential that lay on the seabed.

Pardo ended with a call for "an effective international regime over the seabed and the ocean floor beyond a clearly defined national jurisdiction". "It is the only alternative by which we can hope to avoid the escalating tension that will be inevitable if the present situation is allowed to continue", he said.

Pardo's urging came at a time when many recognized the need for updating the freedom-of-the-seas doctrine to take into account the technological changes that had altered man's relationship to the oceans. It set in motion a process that spanned 15 years and saw the creation of the United Nations Seabed Committee, the signing of a treaty banning nuclear weapons on the seabed, the adoption of the declaration by the General Assembly that all resources of the seabed beyond the limits of national jurisdiction are the common heritage of mankind and the convening of the Stockholm Conference on the Human Environment. What started as an exercise to regulate the seabed turned into a global diplomatic effort to regulate and write rules for all ocean areas, all uses of the seas and all of its resources. These were some of the factors that led to the convening of the Third United Nations Conference on the Law of the Sea, to write a comprehensive treaty for the oceans.

The Conference was convened in New York in 1973. It ended nine years later with the adoption in 1982 of a constitution for the seas—the United Nations Convention on the Law of the Sea. During those nine years, shuttling back and forth between New York and Geneva, representatives of more than 160 sovereign States sat down and discussed the issues, bargained and traded national rights and obligations in the course of the marathon negotiations that produced the Convention.

THE CONVENTION

Navigational rights, territorial sea limits, economic jurisdiction, legal status of resources on the seabed beyond the limits of national jurisdiction, passage of ships through narrow straits, conservation and management of living marine resources, protection of the marine environment, a marine research regime and, a more unique feature, a binding procedure for settlement of disputes between States— these are among the important features of the treaty. In short, the Convention is an unprecedented attempt by the international community to regulate all aspects of the resources of the sea and uses of the ocean, and thus bring a stable order to mankind's very source of life.

"Possibly the most significant legal instrument of this century" is how the United Nations Secretary-General described the treaty after its signing. The Convention was adopted as a "Package deal", to be accepted as a whole in all its parts without reservation on any aspect. The signature of the Convention by Governments carries the undertaking not to take any action that might defeat its objects and purposes. Ratification of, or accession to, the Convention expresses the consent of a State to be bound by its provisions. The Convention came into force on 16 November 1994, one year after Guyana became the 60th State to adhere to it.

Across the globe, Governments have taken steps to bring their extended areas of adjacent ocean within their jurisdiction. They are taking steps to exercise their rights over neighbouring seas, to assess the resources of their waters and on the floor of the continental shelf. The practice of States has in nearly all respects been carried out in a manner consistent with the Convention, particularly after its entry into force and its rapid acceptance by the international community as the basis for all actions dealing with the oceans and the law of the sea.

The definition of the territorial sea has brought relief from conflicting claims. Navigation through the territorial sea and narrow straits is now based on legal principles. Coastal States are already reaping the benefits of provisions giving them extensive economic rights over a 200-mile wide zone along their shores. The right of landlocked countries of access to and from the sea is now stipulated unequivocally. The right to conduct marine scientific research is now based on accepted principles and cannot be unreasonably denied. Already established and functioning are the International Seabed Authority, which organize and control activities in the deep seabed beyond national jurisdiction with a view to administering its resources; as well as the International Tribunal for the Law of the Sea, which has competence to settle ocean related disputes arising from the application or interpretation of the Convention.

Wider understanding of the Convention will bring yet wider application. Stability promises order and harmonious development. However, Part XI, which deals with mining of minerals lying on the deep ocean floor outside of nationally regulated ocean areas, in what is commonly known as the international seabed area, had raised many concerns especially from industrialized States. The Secretary-General, in an attempt to achieve universal participation in the Convention, initiated a series of informal consultations among States in order to resolve those areas of concern. The consultations successfully achieved, in July 1998, an Agreement Related to the Implementation of Part XI of the Convention. The Agreement, which is part of the Convention, is now deemed to have paved the way for all States to become parties to the Convention.

SETTING LIMITS

The dispute over who controls the oceans probably dates back to the days when the Egyptians first plied the Mediterranean in papyrus rafts. Over the years and centuries, countries large and small, possessing vast ocean-going fleets or small fishing flotillas, husbanding rich fishing grounds close to shore or eyeing distant harvests, have all vied for the right to call long stretches of oceans and seas their own.

Conflicting claims, even extravagant ones, over the oceans were not new. In 1494, two years after Christopher Columbus' first expedition to America, Pope Alexander VI met with representatives of two of the great maritime Powers of the day—Spain and Portugal—and neatly divided the Atlantic Ocean between them. A Papal Bull gave Spain everything west of the line the Pope drew down the Atlantic and Portugal everything east of it. On that basis, the Pacific and the Gulf of Mexico were acknowledged as Spain's, while Portugal was given the South Atlantic and the Indian Ocean.

Before the Convention on the Law of the Sea could address the exploitation of the riches underneath the high seas, navigation rights, economic jurisdiction, or any other pressing matter, it had to face one major and primary issue—the setting of limits. Everything else would depend on clearly defining the line separating national and international waters. Though the right of a coastal State to complete control over a belt of water along its shoreline—the territorial sea—had long been recognized in international law, up until the Third United Nations Conference on the Law of the Sea, States could not see eye to eye on how narrow or wide this belt should be.

At the start of the Conference, the States that maintained the traditional claims to a three-mile territorial sea had numbered a mere 25. Sixty-six countries had by then claimed a 12-mile territorial sea limit. Fifteen others claimed between 4 and 10 miles, and one remaining major group of eight States claimed 200 nautical miles.

Traditionally, smaller States and those not possessing large, ocean-going navies or merchant fleets favoured a wide territorial sea in order to protect their coastal waters from infringements by those States that did. Naval and maritime Powers, on the other hand, sought to limit the territorial sea as much as possible, in order to protect their fleets' freedom of movement.

As the work of the Conference progressed, the move towards a 12-mile territorial sea gained wider and eventually universal acceptance. Within this limit, States are in principle free to enforce any law, regulate any use and exploit any resource.

The Convention retains for naval and merchant ships the right of "innocent passage" through the territorial seas of a coastal State. This means, for example, that a Japanese ship, picking up oil from Gulf States, would not have to make a 3,000-mile detour in order to avoid the territorial sea of Indonesia, provided passage is not detrimental to Indonesia and does not threaten its security or violate its laws.

In addition to their right to enforce any law within their territorial seas, coastal States are also empowered to implement certain rights in an area beyond the territorial sea, extending for 24 nautical miles from their shores, for the purpose of preventing certain violations and enforcing police powers. This area, known as the "contiguous zone", may be used by a coast guard or its naval equivalent to pursue and, if necessary, arrest and detain suspected drug smugglers, illegal immigrants and customs or tax evaders violating the laws of the coastal State within its territory or the territorial sea.

The Convention also contains a new feature in international law, which is the regime for archipelagic States (States such as the Philippines and Indonesia, which are made up of a group of closely spaced islands). For those States, the territorial sea is a 12-mile zone extending from a line drawn joining the outermost points of the outermost islands of the group that are in close proximity to each other. The waters between the islands are declared archipelagic waters, where ships of all States enjoy the right of innocent passage. In those waters, States may establish sea lanes and air routes where all ships and aircraft enjoy the right of expeditious and unobstructed passage.

NAVIGATION

Perhaps no other issue was considered as vital or presented the negotiators of the Convention on the Law of the Sea with as much difficulty as that of navigational rights.

Countries have generally claimed some part of the seas beyond their shores as part of their territory, as a zone of protection to be patrolled against smugglers, warships and other intruders. At its origin, the basis of the claim of coastal States to a belt of the sea was the principle of protection; during the seventeenth and eighteenth centuries another principle gradually evolved: that the extent of this belt should be measured by the power of the littoral sovereign to control the area.

In the eighteenth century, the so-called "cannon-shot" rule gained wide acceptance in Europe. Coastal States were to exercise dominion over their territorial seas as far as projectiles could be fired from a cannon based on the shore. According to some scholars, in the eighteenth century the range of land-based cannons was approximately one marine league, or three nautical miles. It is believed that on the basis of this formula developed the traditional three-mile territorial sea limit.

By the late 1960s, a trend to a 12-mile territorial sea had gradually emerged throughout the world, with a great majority of nations claiming sovereignty out to that seaward limit. However, the major maritime and naval Powers clung to a three-mile limit on territorial seas, primarily because a 12-mile limit would effectively close off and place under national sovereignty more than 100 straits used for international navigation.

A 12-mile territorial sea would place under national jurisdiction of riparian States strategic passages such as the Strait of Gibraltar (8 miles wide and the only open access to the Mediterranean), the Strait of Malacca (20 miles wide and the main sea route between the Pacific and Indian Oceans), the Strait of Hormuz (21 miles wide and the only passage to the oil-producing areas of Gulf States) and Bab el Mandeb (14 miles wide, connecting the Indian Ocean with the Red Sea).

At the Third United Nations Conference on the Law of the Sea, the issue of passage through straits placed the major naval Powers on one side and coastal States controlling narrow straits on the other. The United States and the Soviet Union insisted on free passage through straits, in effect giving straits the same legal status as the international waters of the high seas. The coastal States, concerned that passage of foreign warships so close to their shores might pose a threat to their national security and possibly involve them in conflicts among outside Powers, rejected this demand.

Instead, coastal States insisted on the designation of straits as territorial seas and were willing to grant to foreign warships only the right of "innocent passage", a term that was generally recognized to mean passage "not prejudicial to the peace, good order or security of the coastal State". The major naval Powers rejected this concept, since, under international law, a submarine exercising its right of innocent passage, for example, would have to surface and show its flag—an unacceptable security risk in the eyes of naval Powers. Also, innocent passage does not guarantee the aircraft of foreign States the right of overflight over waters where only such passage is guaranteed.

In fact, the issue of passage through straits was one of the early driving forces behind the Third United Nations Conference on the Law of the Sea, when, in early 1967, the United States and the Soviet Union proposed to other Member countries of the United Nations that an international conference be held to deal specifically with the entangled issues of straits, overflight, the width of the territorial sea and fisheries.

The compromise that emerged in the Convention is a new concept that combines the legally accepted provisions of innocent passage through territorial waters and freedom of navigation on the high seas. The new concept, "transit passage", required concessions from both sides.

The regime of transit passage retains the international status of the straits and gives the naval Powers the right to unimpeded navigation and overflight that they had insisted on. Ships and vessels in transit passage, however, must observe international regulations on navigational safety, civilian air-traffic control and prohibition of vessel-source pollution and the conditions that ships and aircraft proceed without delay and without stopping except in distress situations and that they refrain from any threat or use of force against the coastal State. In all matters other than such transient navigation, straits are to be considered part of the territorial sea of the coastal State.

EXCLUSIVE ECONOMIC ZONE

The exclusive economic zone (EEZ) is one of the most revolutionary features of the Convention, and one which already has had a profound impact on the management and conservation of the resources of the oceans. Simply put, it recognizes the right of coastal States to jurisdiction over the resources of some 38 million square nautical miles of ocean space. To the coastal State falls the right to exploit, develop, manage and conserve all resources—fish or oil, gas or gravel, nodules or sulphur—to be found in the waters, on the ocean floor and in the subsoil of an area extending 200 miles from its shore.

The EEZs are a generous endowment indeed. About 87 per cent of all known and estimated hydrocarbon reserves under the sea fall under some national jurisdiction as a result. So too will almost all known and potential offshore mineral resources, excluding the mineral resources (mainly manganese nodules and metallic crusts) of the deep ocean floor beyond national limits. And whatever the value of the nodules, it is the other non-living resources, such as hydrocarbons, that represent the presently attainable and readily exploitable wealth.

The most lucrative fishing grounds too are predominantly the coastal waters. This is because the richest phytoplankton pastures lie within 200 miles of the continental masses. Phytoplankton, the basic food of fish, is brought up from the deep by currents and ocean streams at their strongest near land, and by the upwelling of cold waters where there are strong offshore winds.

The desire of coastal States to control the fish harvest in adjacent waters was a major driving force behind the creation of the EEZs. Fishing, the prototypical cottage industry before the Second World War, had grown tremendously by the 1950s and 1960s. Fifteen million tons in 1938, the world fish catch stood at 86 million tons in 1989. No longer the domain of a lone fisherman plying the sea in a wooden dhow, fishing, to be competitive in world markets, now requires armadas of factory-fishing vessels, able to stay months at sea far from their native shores, and carrying sophisticated equipment for tracking their prey.

The special interest of coastal States in the conservation and management of fisheries in adjacent waters was first recognized in the 1958 Convention on Fishing and Conservation of the Living Resources of the High Seas. That Convention allowed coastal States to take "unilateral measures" of conservation on what was then the high seas adjacent to their territorial waters. It required that if six months of prior negotiations with foreign fishing nations had failed to find a formula for sharing, the coastal State could impose terms. But still the rules were disorderly, procedures undefined, and rights and obligations a web of confusion. On the whole, these rules were never implemented.

The claim for 200-mile offshore sovereignty made by Peru, Chile and Ecuador in the late 1940s and early 1950s was sparked by their desire to protect from foreign fishermen the rich waters of the Humboldt Current (more or less coinciding with the 200-mile offshore belt). This limit was incorporated in the Santiago Declaration of 1952 and reaffirmed by other Latin American States joining the three in the Montevideo and Lima Declarations of 1970. The idea of sovereignty over coastal-area resources continued to gain ground.

As long-utilized fishing grounds began to show signs of depletion, as long-distance ships came to fish waters local fishermen claimed by tradition, as competition increased, so too did conflict. Between 1974 and 1979 alone there were some 20 disputes over cod, anchovies or tuna and other species between, for example, the United Kingdom and Iceland, Morocco and Spain, and the United States and Peru.

And then there was the offshore oil.

The Third United Nations Conference on the Law of the Sea was launched shortly after the October 1973 Arab-Israeli war. The subsequent oil embargo and skyrocketing of prices only helped to heighten concern over control of offshore oil reserves. Already, significant amounts of oil were coming from offshore facilities: 376 million of the 483 million tons produced in the Middle East in 1973; 431 million barrels a day in Nigeria, 141 million barrels in Malaysia, 246 million barrels in Indonesia. And all of this with barely 2 per cent of the continental shelf explored. Clearly, there was hope all around for a fortunate discovery and a potential to be protected.

Today, the benefits brought by the EEZs are more clearly evident. Already 86 coastal States have economic jurisdiction up to the 200-mile limit. As a result, almost 99 per cent of the world's fisheries now fall under some nation's jurisdiction. Also, a large percentage of world oil and gas production is offshore. Many other marine resources also fall within coastal-State control. This provides a long-needed opportunity for rational, well-managed exploitation under an assured authority.

Figures on known offshore oil reserves now range from 240 to 300 billion tons. Production from these reserves amounted to a little more than 25 per cent of total world production in 1996. Experts estimate that of the 150 countries with offshore jurisdiction, over 100, many of them developing countries, have medium to excellent prospects of finding and developing new oil and natural gas fields.

It is evident that it is archipelagic States and large nations endowed with long coastlines that naturally acquire the greatest areas under the EEZ regime. Among the major beneficiaries of the EEZ regime are the United States, France, Indonesia, New Zealand, Australia and the Russian Federation.

But with exclusive rights come responsibilities and obligations. For example, the Convention encourages optimum use of fish stocks without risking depletion through overfishing. Each coastal State is to determine the total allowable catch for each fish species within its economic zone and is also to estimate its harvest capacity and what it can and cannot itself catch. Coastal States are obliged to give access to others, particularly neighbouring States and land-locked countries, to the surplus of the allowable catch. Such access must be done in accordance with the conservation measures established in the laws and regulations of the coastal State.

Coastal States have certain other obligations, including the adoption of measures to prevent and limit pollution and to facilitate marine scientific research in their EEZs.

CONTINENTAL SHELF

In ancient times, navigation and fishing were the primary uses of the seas. As man progressed, pulled by technology in some instances and pushing that technology at other times in order to satisfy his needs, a rich bounty of other resources and uses were found underneath the waves on and under the ocean floor—minerals, natural gas, oil, sand and gravel, diamonds and gold. What should be the extent of a coastal State's jurisdiction over these resources? Where and how should the lines demarcating their continental shelves be drawn? How should these resources be exploited? These were among the important questions facing lawyers, scientists and diplomats as they assembled in New York in 1973 for the Third Conference.

Given the real and potential continental shelf riches, there naturally was a scramble by nations to assert shelf rights. Two difficulties quickly arose. States with a naturally wide shelf had a basis for their claims, but the geologically disadvantaged might have almost no shelf at all. The latter were not ready to accept geological discrimination. Also, there was no agreed method on how to define the shelf's outer limits, and there was a danger of the claims to continental shelves being overextended—so much so as to eventually divide up the entire ocean floor among such shelves.

Although many States had started claiming wide continental-shelf jurisdiction since the Truman Proclamation of 1945, these States did not use the term "continental shelf" in the same sense. In fact, the expression became no more than a convenient formula covering a diversity of titles or claims to the seabed and subsoil adjacent to the territorial seas of States. In the mid-1950s the International Law Commission made a number of attempts to define the "continental shelf" and coastal State jurisdiction over its resources.

In 1958, the first United Nations Conference on the Law of the Sea accepted a definition adopted by the International Law Commission, which defined the continental shelf to include "the seabed and subsoil of the submarine areas adjacent to the coast but outside the area of the territorial sea, to a depth of 200 metres, or, beyond that limit, to where the depth of the superjacent waters admits of the exploitation of the natural resources of the said areas".

Already, as the Third United Nations Conference on the Law of the Sea got under way, there was a strong consensus in favour of extending coastal-State control over ocean resources out to 200 miles from shore so that the outer limit coincides with that of the EEZ. But the Conference had to tackle the demand by States with a geographical shelf extending beyond 200 miles for wider economic jurisdiction.

The Convention resolves conflicting claims, interpretations and measuring techniques by setting the 200-mile EEZ limit as the boundary of the continental shelf for seabed and subsoil exploitation, satisfying the geologically disadvantaged. It satisfied those nations with a broader shelf—about 30 States, including Argentina, Australia, Canada, India, Madagascar, Mexico, Sri Lanka and France with respect to its overseas possessions—by giving them the possibility of establishing a boundary going out to 350 miles from their shores or further, depending on certain geological criteria.

Thus, the continental shelf of a coastal State comprises the seabed and its subsoil that extend beyond the limits of its territorial sea throughout the natural prolongation of its land territory to the outer edge of the continental margin, or to a distance of 200 miles from the baselines from which the territorial sea is measured, where the outer edge of the continental margin does not extend up to that distance.

In cases where the continental margin extends further than 200 miles, nations may claim jurisdiction up to 350 miles from the baseline or 100 miles from the 2,500 metre depth, depending on certain criteria such as the thickness of sedimentary deposits. These rights would not affect the legal status of the waters or that of the airspace above the continental shelf.

To counterbalance the continental shelf extensions, coastal States must also contribute to a system of sharing the revenue derived from the exploitation of mineral resources beyond 200 miles. These payments or contributions—from which developing countries that are net importers of the mineral in question are exempt—are to be equitably distributed among States parties to the Convention through the International Seabed Authority.

To control the claims extending beyond 200 miles, the Commission on the Limits of the Continental Shelf was established to consider the data submitted by the coastal States and make recommendations.

DEEP SEABED MINING

Deep seabed mining is an enormous challenge that has been compared to standing atop a New York City skyscraper on a windy day, trying to suck up marbles off the street below with a vacuum cleaner attached to a long hose.

Mining will take place at a depth of more than fifteen thousand feet of open ocean, thousands of miles from land. Mining ships are expected to remain on station five years at a time, working without a stop, and to transfer the seabed minerals they bring up to auxiliary vessels.

At the centre of the controversy were potato-sized manganese nodules found on the deep ocean floor and containing a number of important metals and minerals.

On 13 March 1874, somewhere between Hawaii and Tahiti, the crew of the British research vessel HMS Challenger, on the first great oceanographic expedition of modern times, hauled in from a depth of 15,600 feet a trawl containing the first known deposits of manganese nodules. Analysis of the samples in 1891 showed the Pacific Ocean nodules to contain important metals, particularly nickel, copper and cobalt. Subsequent sampling demonstrated that nodules were abundant throughout the deep regions of the Pacific.

In the 1950s, the potential of these deposits as sources of nickel, copper and cobalt ore was finally appreciated. Between 1958 and 1968, numerous companies began serious prospecting of the nodule fields to estimate their economic potential. By 1974, 100 years after the first samples were taken, it was well established that a broad belt of sea floor between Mexico and Hawaii and a few degrees north of the equator (the so-called Clarion Clipperton zone) was literally paved with nodules over an area of more than 1.35 million square miles.

In 1970 the United Nations General Assembly declared the resources of the seabed beyond the limits of national jurisdiction to be "the common heritage of mankind". For 12 years from then, up to 1982 when the Convention on the Law of the Sea was adopted, nothing tested so sorely the ability of diplomats from various corners of the world to reach common ground than the goal of conserving that common heritage and profiting from it at the same time.

THE EXPLOITATION REGIME

Having established that the resources of the seabed beyond the limits of national jurisdiction are the common heritage of mankind, the framers of the treaty faced the question of who should mine the minerals and under what rules. The developed countries took the view that the resources should be commercially exploited by mining companies in consortia and that an international authority should grant licenses to those companies. The developing countries objected to this view on the grounds that the resource was unique and belonged to the whole of mankind, and that the most appropriate way to benefit from it was for the international community to establish a public enterprise to mine the international seabed area.

Thus, the gamut of proposals ran from a "weak" international authority, noting claims and collecting fees, to a "strong" one with exclusive rights to mine the common heritage area, involving States or private groups only as it saw fit. The solution found was to make possible both the public and private enterprises on one hand and the collective mining on the other—the so-called "parallel system".

This complex system, though simplified to a great degree by the Agreement on Part XI, is administered by the International Seabed Authority, headquartered in Jamaica. The Authority is divided into three principal organs, an Assembly, made up of all members of the Authority with power to set general policy, a council, with powers to make executive decisions, made up of 36 members elected from among the members of the Authority, and a secretariat headed by a secretary-general.

TECHNOLOGICAL PROSPECTS

Unfortunately, the road to the market is long, hard and expensive. The nodules lie two to three miles—about 5 kilometres—down, in pitch-black water where pressures exceed 7,000 pounds per square inch and temperatures are near freezing. Many of the ocean floors are filled with treacherous hills and valleys. Appropriate deep-sea mining technology must be developed to accommodate this environment.

Many mining systems have been tried, and some have appeared more promising than others. For a while, hydraulic suction dredge airlifts and a continuous-line bucket system were thought to be a promising answer to the mining dilemma. Another system, the so-called shuttle system, involves sending down a remotely operated, Jules Verne-like vehicle, with television "eyes" and powerful lights, to crawl over the ocean floor, gobble up and crush nodules and resurface with its catch.

Today, the continuous-line bucket system, where empty buckets are lowered to the bottom of the ocean and later raised, partially filled with nodules, has been discarded because of low recovery rates. The shuttle system has been shelved because its operational and investment costs far exceeded the costs of more conventional approaches. However, this system is thought to be the technology of the future. Thus, the current focus is on the hydraulic suction and dredge method. But there are a number of technological problems to be worked out before it will be ready for commercial application.

Keeping a steady ship position, since a vessel cannot anchor 5 kilometres above the sea floor and making sure that the pipe does not snap or that the recovery vehicle is not lost or permanently stuck on the ocean floor are among the many headaches involved in developing the necessary technology for commercial exploitation.

Extracting metals from the nodules is another task altogether. All agree that this phase will be the most expensive, even if only at the initial investment stage. Technologically, however, processing does not pose as much of a challenge as the recovery of manganese nodules. That is because it is thought that the two processing techniques applied to land-derived ores—heat and chemical separation of the metals—will apply just as well to the seabed resources.

Because of their porous nature, recovered nodules retain a great deal of water. Heat processing would therefore require a great amount of energy in order to dry the nodules prior to extracting the metals. It is for that reason that some believe that chemical techniques will prove to be the most efficient and least costly.

Moreover, processing would involve such waste that special barren sites would have to be found to carry out operations. Yet, others believe that the economic viability of seabed mining would be greatly enhanced if a method is devised to process the nodules at sea, saving enormous energy costs involved in the transfer of nodules to land-based processing plants.

THE QUESTION OF UNIVERSAL PARTICIPATION IN THE CONVENTION

Prospects for seabed mining depend to a large degree on the market conditions for the metals to be produced from seabed nodules. While one of the driving forces behind the Convention on the Law of the Sea was the prevailing belief in the 1970s that commercial seabed mining was imminent, today the prospects for the inherently expensive process of mining the seabed have greatly receded with changing economic and other conditions since the early 1980s. Indeed, some experts predict that commercial mining operations are not likely to begin until well after the year 2000.

A number of important political and economic changes have taken place in the 10 years that have elapsed since the adoption of the Convention, some directly affecting the deep seabed mining provisions of the Convention, others affecting international relations in general. In the meantime, the prevailing economic prognosis on which the seabed mining regime was built has not been realized.

The Convention on the Law of the Sea holds out the promise of an orderly and equitable regime or system to govern all uses of the sea. But it is a club that one must join in order to fully share in the benefits. The Convention—like other treaties—creates rights only for those who become parties to it and thereby accept its obligations, except for the provisions which apply to all States because they either merely confirm existing customary law or are becoming customary law.

However, as its preamble states, the Convention starts from the premise that the problems of ocean space are closely interrelated and need to be considered as a whole. The desire for a comprehensive Convention arose from the recognition that traditional sea law was disintegrating and that the international community could not be expected to behave in a consistent manner without dialogue, negotiations and agreement.

In this context, it must be underscored that the Convention was adopted as a "package deal", with one aim above all, namely universal participation in the Convention. No State can claim that it has achieved quite all it wanted. Yet every State benefits from the provisions of the Convention and from the certainty that it has established in international law in relation to the law of the sea. It has defined rights while underscoring the obligations that must be performed in order to benefit from those rights. Any trend towards exercising those rights without complying with the corresponding obligations, or towards exercising rights inconsistent with the Convention, must be viewed as damaging to the universal regime that the Convention establishes.

The adoption of the Agreement on Part XI has eliminated this threat. With nearly all States now adhering, even on a provisional basis pending ratification or accession, to the Convention, the threat to the Convention has been eliminated. The Agreement has particularly removed those obstacles which had prevented the industrialized countries from adhering to the Convention. Those same countries have either ratified the Convention or submitted it for their internal legislative pro-

cedures. Even more important, is their active participation in the institutions created by the Convention and their strong support for the regime contained in it.

PIONEER INVESTORS

The Preparatory Commission for the International Seabed Authority and for the
International Tribunal for the Law of the Sea was established, prior to the entry
into force of the Convention, to prepare for the setting up of both institutions. The
Preparatory Commission proceeded with the implementation of an interim regime
adopted by the Third United Nations Conference on the Law of the Sea, designed
to protect those States or entities that have already made a large investment in
seabed mining. This so-called Pioneer Investor Protection regime allows a State, or
consortia of mining companies to be sponsored by a State, to be registered as a Pioneer Investor. Registration reserves for the Pioneer Investor a specific mine site in
which the registered Investor is allowed to explore for, but not exploit, manganese
nodules. Registered Investors are also obligated to explore a mine site reserved for
the Enterprise and undertake other obligations, including the provision of training
to individuals to be designated by the Preparatory Commission.

The Preparatory Commission had registered seven pioneer investors: China,
France, India, Japan, the Republic of Korea, and the Russian Federation, as well as
a consortium known as the Interoceanmetal Joint Organization (IMO). With the
Convention in force and the International Seabed Authority being functioning,
those pioneer investors will become contractors along the terms contained in the
Convention and the Agreement, as well as regulations established by the International Seabed Authority.

PROTECTION OF THE MARINE ENVIRONMENT

Thor Heyerdahl, sailing the Atlantic in his papyrus raft, Ra, found globs of
oil, tar and plastics stretching from the coast of Africa to South America. Parts of
the Baltic, Mediterranean and Black Sea are already so polluted that marine life
is severely threatened. And waste dumped in the Pacific and Atlantic Oceans has
washed up on the shores of Antarctica.

In the United States, long stretches of beaches are often closed because of medical and other waste washing up on shore. And every time an oil tanker is involved
in an accident, the world's pulse quickens a bit in fear of a major catastrophe. In
fact, every time a tanker cleans its tanks at sea, every time a factory channels toxic
residues to coastal waters or a city conveniently releases raw sewage into the sea,
every time a service station changes the oil of an automobile and pours the waste
oil into the sewers, the oceans become a little more polluted. Eventually, scientists
fear, the oceans' regenerative capacity will be overwhelmed by the amount of pollution it is subjected to by man. Signs of such catastrophe are clearly observed in

many seas—particularly along the heavily populated coasts and enclosed or semi-enclosed seas.

There are six main sources of ocean pollution addressed in the Convention: land-based and coastal activities; continental-shelf drilling; potential seabed mining; ocean dumping; vessel-source pollution; and pollution from or through the atmosphere.

The Convention lays down, first of all, the fundamental obligation of all States to protect and preserve the marine environment. It further urges all States to cooperate on a global and regional basis in formulating rules and standards and otherwise take measures for the same purpose.

Coastal States are empowered to enforce their national standards and anti-pollution measures within their territorial sea. Every coastal State is granted jurisdiction for the protection and preservation of the marine environment of its EEZ. Such jurisdiction allows coastal States to control, prevent and reduce marine pollution from dumping, land-based sources or seabed activities subject to national jurisdiction, or from or through the atmosphere. With regard to marine pollution from foreign vessels, coastal States can exercise jurisdiction only for the enforcement of laws and regulations adopted in accordance with the Convention or for "generally accepted international rules and standards". Such rules and standards, many of which are already in place, are adopted through the competent international organization, namely the International Maritime Organization (IMO).

On the other hand, it is the duty of the "flag State", the State where a ship is registered and whose flag it flies, to enforce the rules adopted for the control of marine pollution from vessels, irrespective of where a violation occurs. This serves as a safeguard for the enforcement of international rules, particularly in waters beyond the national jurisdiction of the coastal State, i.e., on the high seas.

Furthermore, the Convention gives enforcement powers to the "port State", or the State where a ship is destined. In doing so it has incorporated a method developed in other Conventions for the enforcement of treaty obligations dealing with shipping standards, marine safety and pollution prevention. The port State can enforce any type of international rule or national regulations adopted in accordance with the Convention or applicable international rules as a condition for the entry of foreign vessels into their ports or internal waters or for a call at their offshore terminals. This has already become a significant factor in the strengthening of international standards.

Finally, as far as the international seabed area is concerned, the International Seabed Authority, through its Council, is given broad discretionary powers to assess the potential environmental impact of a given deep seabed mining operation, recommend changes, formulate rules and regulations, establish a monitoring programme and recommend issuance of emergency orders by the Council to prevent serious environmental damage. States are to be held liable for any damage caused by either their own enterprise or contractors under their jurisdiction.

With the passage of time, United Nations involvement with the law of the sea has expanded as awareness increases that not only ocean problems but global problems as a whole are interrelated. Already, the 1992 United Nations Conference on Environment and Development (UNCED) held in Rio de Janeiro, Brazil in 1992, placed a great deal of emphasis on the protection and preservation of the oceans' environment in harmony with the rational use and development of their living resources, thus establishing the concept of "sustainable development" embodied in Agenda 21, the programme of action adopted at the Conference.

The necessity to combat the degradation and depletion of fish stocks, both in the zones under national jurisdiction and in the high seas and its causes, such as overfishing and excess fishing capacity, by-catch and discards, has been one of the recurrent topics in the process of implementation of the programme of action adopted in Rio de Janeiro.

In this respect, among the most important outputs of the Conference was the convening of an intergovernmental conference under United Nations auspices with a view to resolving the old conflict between coastal States and distant-water fishing States over straddling and highly migratory fish stocks in the areas adjacent to the 200 nautical-mile exclusive economic zones. This Conference adopted the 1995 Agreement on Straddling Fish Stocks and Highly Migratory Fish Stocks which introduces a number of innovative measures, particularly in the area of environmental and resource protection obliging States to adopt a precautionary approach to fisheries exploitation and giving expanded powers to port States to enforce proper management of fisheries resources.

MARINE SCIENTIFIC RESEARCH

With the extension of the territorial sea to 12 miles and the establishment of the new 200-mile EEZ, the area open to unrestricted scientific research was circumscribed. The Convention thus had to balance the concerns of major research States, mostly developed countries, which saw any coastal-state limitation on research as a restriction of a traditional freedom that would not only adversely affect the advancement of science but also deny its potential benefits to all nations in fields such as weather forecasting and the study of effects of ocean currents and the natural forces at work on the ocean floor.

On the other side, many developing countries had become extremely wary of the possibility of scientific expeditions being used as a cover for intelligence gathering or economic gain, particularly in relatively uncharted areas, [since] scientific research was yielding knowledge of potential economic significance.

The developing countries demanded "prior consent" of a coastal State to all scientific research on the continental shelf and within the EEZ. The developed countries offered to give coastal States "prior notification" of research projects to be carried out on the continental shelf and within the EEZ, and to share any data pertinent to offshore resources.

The final provisions of the Convention represent a concession on the part of developed States. Coastal State jurisdiction within its territorial sea remains absolute. Within the EEZ and in cases involving research on the continental shelf, the coastal State must give its prior consent. However, such consent for research for peaceful purposes is to be granted "in normal circumstances" and "shall not be delayed or denied unreasonably", except under certain specific circumstances identified in the Convention. In case the consent of the coastal State is requested and such State does not reply within six months of the date of the request, the coastal State is deemed to have implicitly given its consent. These last provisions were intended to circumvent the long bureaucratic delays and frequent burdensome differences in coastal State regulations.

SETTLEMENT OF DISPUTES

Provisions for the settlement of disputes arising out of an international treaty are often contained in a separate optional protocol. Parties to the treaty could choose to be bound by those provisions or not by accepting or not accepting the Protocol. The Convention on the Law of the Sea is unique in that the mechanism for the settlement of disputes is incorporated into the document, making it obligatory for parties to the Convention to go through the settlement procedure in case of a dispute with another party.

During the drafting of the Convention, some countries were opposed in principle to binding settlement to be decided by third party judges or arbitrators, insisting that issues could best be resolved by direct negotiations between States without requiring them to bring in outsiders. Others, pointing to a history of failed negotiations and long-standing disputes often leading to a use of force, argued that the only sure chance for peaceful settlement lay in the willingness of States to bind themselves in advance to accept the decisions of judicial bodies.

What emerged from the negotiations was a combination of the two approaches, regarded by many as a landmark in international law.

If direct talks between the parties fail, the Convention gives them a choice among four procedures—some new, some old: submission of the dispute to the International Tribunal for the Law of the Sea, adjudication by the International Court of Justice, submission to binding international arbitration procedures or submission to special arbitration tribunals with expertise in specific types of disputes. All of these procedures involve binding third-party settlement, in which an agent other than the parties directly involved hands down a decision that the parties are committed in advance to respect.

The only exception to these provisions is made for sensitive cases involving national sovereignty. In such circumstances, the parties are obliged to submit their dispute to a conciliation commission, but they will not be bound by any decision or finding of the commission. The moral pressure resulting was argued as being persuasive and adequate to ensure compliance with the findings. The Convention also contains so-called "optional exceptions", which can be specified at the time a country signs, ratifies or accedes to the Convention or at any later time. A State may declare that it chooses not to be bound by one or more of the mandatory procedures if they involve existing maritime boundary disputes, military activities or issues under discussion in the United Nations Security Council.

Disputes over seabed activities will be arbitrated by an 11-member Seabed Disputes Chamber, within the International Tribunal for the Law of the Sea. The Chamber has compulsory jurisdiction over all such conflicts, whether involving States, the International Seabed Authority or companies or individuals having seabed mining contracts.

THE UNITED NATIONS AND THE LAW OF THE SEA

Throughout the years, beginning with the work of the Seabed Committee in 1968 and later during the nine-year duration of the Third United Nations Conference on the Law of the Sea, the United Nations has been actively engaged in encouraging and guiding the development and eventual adoption of the Law of the Sea Convention. Today, it continues to be engaged in this process, by monitoring developments as they relate to the Convention and providing assistance to States, when called for, in either the ratification or the implementation process.

The goal of the Organization is to help States to better understand and implement the Convention in order to utilize their marine resources in an environment relatively free of conflict and conducive to development, safeguarding the rule of law in the oceans.

In this context, the Division for Ocean Affairs and the Law of the Sea (DOA-LOS) of the United Nations Office of Legal Affairs helps to coordinate the Organization's activities and programmes in the area of marine affairs. It is active in assisting and advising States in the integration of the marine sector in their development planning. It also responds to requests for information and advice on the legal, economic and political aspects of the Convention and its implications for States. Such information is used by States during the ratification process, in the management of the marine sector of their economies and in the development of a national sea-use policy.

The United Nations also gives assistance to the two newly created institutions— the International Seabed Authority and the International Tribunal for the Law of the Sea.

THE FUTURE

The entry into force of the Convention, together with extended jurisdiction, new fields of activity and increased uses of the oceans, will continue to confront all States with important challenges. These challenges will include how to apply the new provisions in accordance with the letter and spirit of the Convention, how to harmonize national legislation with it and how to fulfil the obligations incumbent upon States under the Convention.

Another major challenge will be to provide the necessary assistance, particularly to developing States, in order to allow them to benefit from the rights they have acquired under the new regime. For example, a great many of the States that have established their EEZs are not at present in a position to exercise all their rights and perform duties under the Convention. The delimitation of EEZ, the surveying of its area, its monitoring, the utilization of its resources and, generally speaking, its management and development are long-term endeavours beyond the present and possibly near-term capabilities of most developing countries.

The United Nations will continue to play a major role in the monitoring of, collection of information on and reporting on State practice in the implementation of the new legal regime. It will also have a significant role to play in reporting on activities of States and relevant international organizations in marine affairs and on major trends and developments. This information will be of great assistance to States in the acceptance and ratification of the Convention, as well as its early entry into force and implementation.

A number of new duties falls upon the Secretary-General of the United Nations. These include the depositing of charts and coordinates showing the maritime limits of coastal States and servicing of the Commission on the Limits of the Continental Shelf. The Secretary-General is also called upon to convene meetings of States Parties to elect the members of the International Tribunal for the Law of the Sea and to adopt its budget. Meetings of States Parties may also be called for a Review Conference dealing with the provisions on deep seabed mining or for amending the Convention.

The United Nations will continue to strengthen the cooperation that has developed over the last two decades among the organizations in the United Nations system involved in marine affairs. Such close cooperation would be of great benefit to States, since it would avoid duplication and overlapping of activities. It would also help to coordinate multidisciplinary activities related to the management of marine affairs.

With the passage of time, United Nations involvement with the law of the sea is expected to expand as awareness increases that not only ocean problems but also global problems as a whole are interrelated.

LOST Would Be a Loser for the U.S.*

By James Carafano
The Washington Examiner, June 12, 2011

In 1823, President James Monroe had a simple message to the great states of Europe: Hands off.

"The American continents, by the free and independent condition which they have assumed and maintain, are henceforth not to be considered as subjects for future colonization by any European powers," he wrote in his annual message to Congress.

European reaction to the "Monroe Doctrine" proved all too predictable. The Marquis de Lafayette, pretty much America's lone cheerleader in the Old World, called the declaration "the best little piece of paper that God had ever permitted any man to give the World."

It was a minority view. Austrian Prince Klemens von Metternich, Europe's most hard-boiled diplomat, pronounced it "an indecent declaration." Russia's Tsarist government informed its representative in Washington that "the document in question . . . merits only the most profound contempt."

Though the great powers grumbled, the doctrine stood its ground—but not because they respected the "little piece of paper." No, they feared the British navy. Britain had no interest in letting other European powers establish bases in the New World.

Such a toehold might help them challenge British mastery of the seas. No other power could risk launching a new colonial venture in the Americas, lest it draw the ire and fire of the world's most powerful fleet.

The Monroe Doctrine worked because of the force behind the paper—even though the force was not Monroe's. No foreign policy doctrine is worth the paper it is written on unless it is backed with sufficient power to uphold it.

It is not clear that this White House understands this truism. Indeed, the president often appears to believe that a treaty (i.e., an agreement on paper) can substitute for the capacity to protect and defend a nation's interest.

* Copyright © The Washington Examiner. All rights reserved. Reprinted with permission. www.washingtonexaminer.com

Hence we get the New START nuclear agreement. This treaty bound the U.S. to draw down its nuclear arsenal to the level of Russia, while ceding Moscow an overwhelming advantage in tactical nuclear weapons. Still, the president concluded because we had a signed piece of paper—we are safer. Neither the New START math nor Mr. Obama's strategy add up.

Now, the president is at again. The White House is signaling that it wants the Senate to take up the Law of the Sea Treaty, a pact with a most apt acronym: "LOST."

LOST was hammered out in 1982. That fact alone ought to raise eyebrows. If joining the treaty were really in the interest of the United States, one would have thought the Senate would have ratified it long ago.

There are two parts to the treaty. The "navigation" provisions basically list the rules of the road of using the sea. There is nothing wrong with them. They codify the custom of freedom of the seas.

And since the U.S. Navy is committed to defending the principle of freedom of the seas—the system works fine. Maintaining a powerful navy—not this piece of paper—ensures the U.S. can enjoy freedom of the seas. Approving these provisions, then, gets us nothing.

Signing on to LOST, however, could cost us a lot, due to its "non-navigation" provisions. Among them is a provision that would require the U.S. to pay royalties to an unaccountable international bureaucracy for the right to exploit oil and gas resources on the U.S. continental shelf. We already have the right to those resources. Why pay an international bureaucracy for what's already ours?

Perhaps, the most serious concern is that the president will just use LOST as another excuse to gut the armed forces. After all, why maintain a powerful navy when we have a treaty to ensure freedom of the seas? If START can replace America's nuclear deterrent, why couldn't LOST substitute for carriers and submarines?

Here's hoping the Senate is smarter than that and won't lose its way on LOST, a little piece of paper that gets us nothing.

Examiner *Columnist* **JAMES JAY CARAFANO** *is a senior research fellow for national security at the Heritage Foundation.*

Editorial[*]

A Treaty Whose Time Has Come

The New York Times, August 25, 2007

A solemn international treaty known as the Law of the Sea Convention will celebrate its 25th anniversary this December, and for 25 years the mere mention of its name has been enough to induce deep slumber. Yet for all kinds of reasons—not least growing fears about the availability of energy resources—people are finally paying attention. That includes the Senate, where right-wing scare tactics and official inertia have long blocked the treaty's ratification, leaving America as the only major power standing on the sidelines.

That could change this fall, when the treaty will again be presented for Senate approval. One reason for optimism is that President Bush has added his voice to a diverse pro-treaty coalition that includes the environmental community, fishing interests, the oil and gas industry, the shipping industry, the State Department and the Navy.

But the main reason is this: unless the United States joins up, it could very well lose out in what is shaping up as a mad scramble to lay claim to what are believed to be immense deposits of oil, gas and other resources under the Arctic ice—deposits that are becoming more and more accessible as the earth warms and the ice melts.

The Law of the Sea will provide the forum for determining who gets what. The law gives each nation control over its own coastal waters—an "exclusive economic zone" extending 200 miles offshore. The rest is regarded as international waters, subject to agreed-upon rules governing fishing, protection of the marine environment, navigation and mining on the ocean floor. A country can claim territory and mineral deposits beyond the 200-mile limit, but only if it can prove that the seabed is a physical extension of its continental shelf. Claims and disputes will be resolved by arbitration panels established by the treaty.

* From *The New York Times*, August 25, 2007. Copyright © 2011 The New York Times. All rights reserved. Used by permission and protected by the Copyright Laws of the United States. The printing, copying, redistribution, or retransmission of the Material without express written permission is prohibited.

The Russians, the Canadians and the Danes are all busily staking claims to thousands of square miles of the Arctic seabed beyond their 200-mile zones; the Russians have already planted a flag 15,000 feet under the North Pole. And two weeks ago, a U.S. Coast Guard cutter, Healy, embarked on the third in a series of polar mapping expeditions to help strengthen the United States' territorial claims to the seabed off Alaska.

But the United States will have a hard time pressing those claims unless it ratifies the treaty and gets a seat at the negotiating table. One of the main right-wing arguments over the years is that the treaty would threaten American sovereignty by impeding unfettered exploitation of the ocean's resources—a "giant giveaway of American wealth," in the words of one critic. The facts suggest just the reverse. By not signing, we could easily find ourselves out of the hunt altogether.

LOST Ratification Would Sacrifice Sovereignty, Weaken Military*

Exclusive Interview

By Chris Carter
The U.S. Report, June 23, 2010

For nearly 30 years, the United Nations has sought US ratification of the onerous Law of the Sea Treaty (LOST). Although numerous presidents have supported LOST—formally known as the U.N. Convention on the Law of the Sea—fortunately, the Senate has never managed to ratify the treaty.

What is LOST and why should it concern the American voter?

We ask Cliff Kincaid, editor of the Accuracy in Media Report and president of America's Survival, Inc. Kincaid has led a national education campaign about LOST.

Chris Carter: How does LOST threaten American sovereignty?

Cliff Kincaid: This treaty is the biggest giveaway of American sovereignty and resources since the Panama Canal Treaty. It gives the United Nations bureaucracy control over the oceans of the world—seven-tenths of the world's surface. It sets up an International Seabed Authority to decide who gets access to oil, gas and minerals in international waters. The companies that get those rights to harvest those resources have to pay a global tax to the International Seabed Authority.

Carter: You wrote that the passage of LOST "could be the final nail in the coffin of U.S. Naval superiority." How so?

KINCAID: It would cement in place a procedure to use the treaty, rather than Navy ships, to safeguard U.S. interests. That would cause a further decline in the number of Navy ships, on the ground that we don't need them.

Carter: If LOST weakens our military, why do you think the Joint Chiefs support the treaty?

* Article by Chris Carter originally published in *The U.S. Report*, June 23, 2010. Permission granted by author. All rights reserved.

KINCAID: Several reasons. One, the influence of international lawyers in the Judge Advocate General (JAG) offices; and two, the dramatic decline in the number of Navy ships. We have gone from 594 under President Reagan to only 276 today. Susan Biniaz, Assistant Legal Adviser, Oceans, International Environmental and Scientific Affairs, U.S. Department of State, speaking July 17, 2007, at the American Enterprise Institute, said, "I think someone said how few ships there are compared to how many there used to be. We don't have the capacity to be challenging every maritime claim throughout the world solely through the use of naval power. And [we] certainly can't use the Navy to meet all the economic interests." This was her justification for ratifying the treaty.

Carter: While previous presidents have endorsed—or expressed support of—LOST, the treaty has never been ratified. What provisions kept the U.S. from ratifying LOST, and have those provisions since been addressed?

KINCAID: [Pres.] Bill Clinton claimed he had solved some of the problems with the treaty in a 1994 side agreement. But [Pres. Ronald] Reagan's people have said that it was not fixed. Some of the supporters of the treaty say Reagan only objected to the provisions on deep-sea mining. But the fact is that his chief negotiator to the Law of the Sea convention, a man named James L. Malone, gave testimony in 1995 saying that President Reagan rejected this treaty as a whole—that it was flawed in concept and in detail. Reagan's diaries have now come out and one of those diary entries quotes the former president as saying he rejected this treaty not just because of the deep-sea mining provisions; his objections were far broader than that. Reagan rejected the whole concept of the treaty.

Carter: What kind of timeline are we looking at for a possible ratification of LOST, and what can the American people do to stop it?

KINCAID: I am not aware of any action on the treaty being planned at this time. What we should be focused on instead is the fact that China is building what could be the largest navy in the world by 2020. Our response should be to deep-six the treaty and build more American Navy ships, striving for the 600-ship Navy envisioned by Reagan.

Carter: While LOST isn't headed for immediate ratification, numerous government officials and reports have endorsed the treaty. Pres. Barack Obama, Vice-Pres. Joe Biden, Sec. of State Hillary Clinton, and the military's Joint Chiefs of Staff have endorsed LOST. The National Security Strategy and the Quadrennial Defense Review both call for its passage.

But do we want to subject ourselves to an international law that prohibits submarines from traveling underwater, prohibits aircraft operations, prohibits training with weapons, and even limits our ability to board ships—even when there is a possibility that the ship is carrying weapons of mass destruction? The Constitution states that once a treaty is ratified, it becomes the supreme law of the land. And the U.S. would be only one vote among 155 that historically have proven to vote against U.S. interests.

LOST grants us no rights that we do not already have. We have everything to lose and nothing to gain.

The US armed forces are the sole reason that American liberty and security has endured for over 200 years. If our nation is to survive for another 200, we must continue to rely on "peace through strength" and not corrupt international lawyers and bureaucrats.

Sea Treaty Has Broad Support, But Little Chance of Ratification*

By Andrew Jensen
Alaska Journal of Commerce, May 7, 2010

The Law of the Sea Treaty has bipartisan support as well the endorsement of the military, energy industry and environmental groups. Still, it has almost no chance of being ratified this year.

On the table in revised form since a 1994 agreement eliminated its most objectionable provisions, ratification of LOST requires 67 votes in the United States Senate and is being pushed hard by Alaska's delegation of Republican Sen. Lisa Murkowski and Democrat Sen. Mark Begich.

Originally put forward by the United Nations in 1982, LOST sets up an international structure governing the use of the high seas for transportation, military and mineral extraction purposes. It allows for the extension of a nation's sovereign rights beyond the current 200-mile limit to include the reach of the continental shelf extending from its shoreline. The United States is a signatory to the treaty and follows most of its provisions, but has not ratified the treaty.

For the U.S., ratifying LOST would allow it to potentially lay claim to an additional area of outer continental shelf as large as California in the Arctic Ocean. As Arctic ice melts, more areas become open to transportation and exploration, with estimates of as much as 22 percent of the world's remaining oil and gas reserves lying beneath the seafloor.

For Begich and Murkowski, the benefits to Alaska of ratifying LOST are clear.

"We benefit from any coastal development," Begich said. "There will be more Coast Guard facilities in Alaska to manage the traffic flow. There would be a huge economic short-term and long-term impact. It's critical that we lay claim to what we have as our right."

Murkowski said her "palms start to sweat" in anticipation of what increased traffic through the Arctic would mean for Alaska, drawing a parallel between the

* Courtesy of the *Alaska Journal of Commerce*. Reprinted with permission.

Panama Canal and the transit route created by ice melt that could save shipping companies billions in transport costs.

"It can either be the Panama Canal and open up the world, or it can become like the Straight [sic] of Hormuz, where from a national security perspective you are in this tight little window," she said, referring to the chokepoint of the world's oil supply at the mouth of the Persian Gulf. "Are we good with that risk?"

Among those challenges are coordinating search and rescue responsibilities and transit routes among Arctic nations, of which the U.S. is the only country not to ratify LOST.

"It will allow for us as a nation, I believe, to be a better participant not only in the rules of the road when it comes to commerce and environmental issues, but how we deal with an increased level of activity up north," Murkowski said.

STAKING CLAIMS

In August 2007, Russia symbolically planted its flag more than 13,000 feet under the Arctic ice cap claiming an area that extends more than 1,100 miles from its coast, asserting its rights under LOST that the Lomonosov Ridge extending from Siberia as part of its territory.

Canada and the U.S. both scoffed at the claim's merits, but only Canada can take its dispute to the international arbitration panels set up under the treaty.

LOST opponents largely cite infringements on national sovereignty by ratification that would bind the U.S. to a dispute resolution process and the Senate has a well-established history of resisting treaties that even hint at subjugating the country's interests to international bodies.

While President Bill Clinton signed on to the Kyoto Protocol global warming agreement and the International Criminal Court, he sent neither to the Senate for ratification with both facing certain defeat.

The Senate recorded a 95-0 vote in opposition to Kyoto and President George W. Bush withdrew the U.S. signature to the ICC in 2002.

However, neither the ICC nor Kyoto offered the economic benefits to the U.S. while expanding resource claims, as LOST would. And that fact turns the usual sovereignty argument on its head, Begich said.

"Right now our sovereignty is being decided by other countries," he said.

President Ronald Reagan's initial rejection of LOST was based on its onerous requirements to transfer mining royalties, claims and technology to "geographically disadvantaged" countries through the International Seabed Authority.

The ISA's authority and funding through developed nations was all but neutered as part of the 1994 agreement, along with the elimination of technology transfers. However, restrictions on military activity in territorial waters such as requiring submarines to surface and fly the flag remain.

Murkowski said the U.S. could exempt itself from aspects of LOST it finds disagreeable when it ratifies the treaty. At a Senate Armed Forces Committee hearing,

U.S. Northern Commander Gen. Victor Renuart Jr. told Begich he didn't believe LOST would impact U.S. sovereignty and endorsed ratification.

STRANGE BEDFELLOWS

The confluence of the energy industry and environmental groups supporting ratification of LOST is a particularly interesting one given their traditional conflicts. Ratification opposition from influential conservative think tanks like the Heritage Foundation point to the environmental impact regulations of LOST as yet another tool environmental groups will use to challenge offshore drilling.

Clinton signed LOST after the 1994 agreement amending the original 1982 language but it was never sent to the Senate for ratification. Nonetheless, the Natural Resources Defense Council cited the U.S. status as a signatory to LOST when it successfully fought the Navy's sonar testing off the coast of California.

Groups like the NRDC support the treaty but oppose drilling in the Arctic National Wildlife Refuge and anywhere offshore, which makes them unlikely to support any exploitation of mineral resources in the Arctic Ocean.

Begich, who generally bucks his party by supporting increased OCS development in Alaska, sidestepped as a hypothetical the potential for environmental groups to use LOST to fight mineral extraction.

"We can't have that discussion because we're not a part of the treaty," he said.

Murkowski was more blunt in her assessment, but echoed Begich on the need to have a seat at the table.

"I have no, no, no, optimism the environmental groups that have opposed development onshore or offshore are going to change that opposition," she said. "When it comes to our ability to claim additional area under the Law of the Sea based on the continental shelf, we can't do anything until we ratify that and are a participant."

NRDC spokesperson Lisa Speer said Republican resistance to LOST has always been the largest hurdle to ratification.

"We have nothing but praise for Alaska's senators trying to push this ahead," Speer said. "Periodically we make a big push and just run into a wall of Republican opposition. The United States is the only major participant that has not ratified. It sends a negative signal to the rest of the world about the seriousness with which we see Arctic issues."

Overcoming Republican opposition led by David Vitter of Louisiana and Jim DeMint of South Carolina—who helped kill ratification efforts introduced in 2004 and 2007 by the Bush Administration—is tougher than ever with the political well on the Potomac poisoned by the rancorous health care debate of the last 14 months and looming battles over financial reform, immigration reform and cap-and-trade climate legislation figuring to suck whatever oxygen is left out of the atmosphere in Washington with less than 45 days remaining before the August recess and the 2010 midterm elections approaching.

"It's a very unusual grouping that is supportive of this," Speer said. "One would think that is enough. But it's not enough to garner the votes on the Republican side that we really need."

The Obama Administration favors LOST ratification, but blocking out a week of floor time to debate the measure will be virtually impossible, especially as the White House seems more inclined to push for consideration of its recent nuclear pact updating the Strategic Arms Reduction Treaty with Russia, which likely will face an uphill climb in the Senate as well.

2

Lines in the Water:
Territorial Disputes in the Arctic and Beyond

Courtesy of Patrick Kelley

The Canadian Coast Guard ship *Louis S. St-Laurent* makes an approach to the U.S. Coast Guard vessel *Healy* while on joint maneuvers in the Arctic Ocean, on September 5, 2009. The thawing of the Arctic has created a number of potential territorial disputes among nations in the region.

Courtesy of the Library of Congress

This map shows the territory Bolivia ceded to Chile following its defeat in the War of the Pacific. Though the war ended over 125 years ago, to many in Bolivia, including President Evo Morales, the wounds are still fresh.

Editor's Introduction

In September 2007, for the first time since scientists began keeping records in 1978, the Northwest Passage was declared "fully navigable" by the European Space Agency. The much-mythologized waterway has historically been frozen throughout the year, but as a result of climate change, dreams of shipping goods between Europe and Asia via Canada's Arctic territory—the most direct route between the two continents—have become a reality. While that's good news for businessmen, the thawing Arctic could dampen the spirits of lawmakers in the eight countries with territorial claims to the ocean. Although the Arctic Council—comprising representatives from the United States, Denmark, Canada, Finland, Norway, Iceland, Sweden, and Russia—has served since 1996 as a non-binding authority over the region, some experts insist new treaties will be necessary to ensure peace in the future.

Territorial disputes aren't unique to the Arctic Ocean. India and China are competing for economic and military control of the Indian Ocean, which has grown in strategic importance in recent years. The world's third-largest body of water connects the Far East with the Islamic world and plays a key role in everything from global trade to the U.S. War on Terror. Meanwhile, in South America, Evo Morales, the leftist president of landlocked Bolivia, has been demanding access to the Pacific Ocean through Chile. The two countries have been at loggerheads over the issue for decades, and while Chile is prepared to grant Bolivia a route to the sea, it won't offer sovereign rights over the land.

The articles in this chapter explore territorial issues in the Arctic, Indian, and Pacific oceans. In the first piece, "From Sea to Shining Sea to Arctic Ocean: Sovereignty Issues and Energy Opportunities Can No Longer Be Ignored," former NATO supreme allied commander General Joe Ralston shares with *Washington Times* readers his opinions on why the United States needs to take a more active role in the Arctic. Ralston praises Hillary Rodham Clinton for being the first U.S. secretary of state to attend a meeting of the Arctic Council and credits her with "bringing the United States to the table at the right time to protect our sovereignty, national energy and economic security and to add wisdom and diplomacy to policies being forged."

With "As Ice Melts and Technology Improves, Interest in Arctic Grows," the subsequent entry, Jarondakie Patrick and Erika Bolstad take a closer look at the nations angling for control at the top of the world. In 2007, Russia planted a flag on the ocean floor beneath the North Pole, while China—a nation not part of the Arctic Council—has also shown interest in the region. As quoted by Patrick and Bolstad, Senator Lisa Murkowski of Alaska cites Clinton as one of the few politicians that recognizes the importance of the Arctic, and pushes for ratification of the United Nations (UN)'s Law of the Sea Treaty (LOST).

Next up, in "As the Far North Melts, Calls Grow for Arctic Treaty," a piece for *Yale Environment 360*, Ed Struzik provides a history of international relations in the Arctic and considers the "hard-law" and "soft-law" approaches to dealing with future conflicts. Advocates of the former, such as Timo Koivurova, director of the University of Lapland's Northern Institute for Environmental and Minority Law at the Arctic Centre, would like to see the region's major players establish new treaties and governing bodies with the authority to enforce laws. Others, such as University of California at Santa Barbara scholar Oran Young, believe existing treaties, such as LOST, are sufficient. "While it is important to consider the possibility of worst-case scenarios unfolding in the Arctic, I think this idea of a Wild West-like land rush is far-fetched," Young tells Struzik. Young believes that LOST, coupled with a "somewhat messy patchwork" of agreements between nations, would solve any problems that might arise.

In the following piece, "Bolivia-Chile Dispute Could Turn Ugly," *Miami Herald* writer Andres Oppenheimer accuses Morales of using the Pacific Ocean debate to distract from his country's economic woes. Other Bolivian leaders have tried similar strategies in the past, Oppenheimer reports, but none have gone so far as to brand the country's army "socialist" and "anti-imperialist," as Morales has done, giving the conflict an ideological edge. Oppenheimer fears Morales will pick a fight with Chile in order to help his chances of winning reelection—a tactic he contends "would have been unthinkable in recent times, but not in today's Bolivia."

The chapter concludes with "Center-Stage for the Twenty-First Century," Robert D. Kaplan's in-depth *Foreign Affairs* article on the Indian Ocean. "[M]ore than just a geographic feature," Kaplan writes, "the Indian Ocean is also an idea." He examines the ways in which divergent cultures have coexisted—or failed to coexist—over time and looks ahead at how the power struggle between China and India could affect global politics in the 21st century. China is seeking to exert its influence over the region by enacting a "string of pearls" strategy and building naval bases and commercial ports in such locations as Pakistan, Sri Lanka, and Myanmar. India has done likewise, ramping up its navy, which now stands at 155 ships, and establishing economic ties with Iran, Pakistan, and Myanmar. Kaplan calls on the United States to "serve as a stabilizing power in this newly complex area." "Rather than ensure its dominance," he writes, "the U.S. Navy simply needs to make itself continually useful."

From Sea to Shining Sea to Arctic Ocean[*]

Sovereignty Issues and Energy Opportunities Can No Longer Be Ignored

By General Joe Ralston
The Washington Times, May 16, 2011

Old-school thinking sees America as a nation bounded by two great oceans. Yet the world has changed. The Arctic Ocean is no longer optional. In fact, it has become our nation's third great ocean border—and the opportunity of a lifetime.

Secretary of State Hillary Rodham Clinton's recent visit to Greenland on May 12 confirmed that realization. She became the first U.S. secretary of state to attend the Arctic Council.

A neighborhood meeting of eight Arctic nations, the Arctic Council is also no longer optional. Mrs. Clinton's attendance underscores how, onshore and offshore, the Arctic is of strategic importance to national security, global commerce and climate, and in meeting the world's energy needs.

Cooperation in the neighborhood now can prevent conflicts later over sovereignty, shipping, the environment, energy and national security.

Scientists predict that within two decades, the Arctic Ocean will have open waters for a full month each year. With open waters, unresolved border issues can no longer be ignored.

For example, the U.S.-Canadian Arctic maritime border is not yet agreed to as the firm line you may see on a map.

The U.S.-Russia border through the Bering Sea, Chukchi Sea and Arctic Ocean remains unratified by Russia's Duma. Norway, Russia, Denmark and Canada are advancing their negotiations to resolve already-active border disputes.

The Arctic nations are preparing claims to take control of extended continental shelves that could carve up the Arctic Ocean floor—almost to the North Pole.

[*] Copyright © 2011 The Washington Times, LLC. Reprinted by permission.

Shipping is expanding exponentially. Russia's northern-route shipping volume is predicted to increase 500 percent this year over last, and Russia is granting permits for foreign vessels to transit its northern route.

Eager to show its interest, China is allocating more to polar research, even going so far as to send an icebreaker north of Alaska last summer and north of Iceland this summer to do reconnaissance on shipping routes. Other nations, such as South Korea, also are gearing up because the northern routes can save billions of dollars in time, fuel and piracy problems.

How will search-and-rescue operations be undertaken if there are no prior agreements? Does the United States have assets in place in Alaska to protect our 1,000 miles of Arctic coastline in the event a ship founders?

The first-ever Arctic Council binding instrument was signed May 12—a search-and-rescue pact that puts border issues aside and establishes areas of responsibility to make sure ships and people in trouble are rescued. It would help if the United States would follow up with a plan to replace its ailing Polar Class icebreakers that were commissioned during the Nixon administration.

In addition to sovereignty and shipping, energy is a looming global problem, and the Arctic provides solutions. The U.S. Geological Survey estimates that 13 percent of the world's undiscovered oil and 23 percent of the world's undiscovered gas will be found in the Arctic.

Major offshore energy projects are in the works in northern Canada, Russia, Greenland, Norway and even Iceland. America lags in Arctic energy exploration as federal permits are endlessly delayed.

The world needs the energy the Arctic is beginning to produce. With eight nations bordering the Arctic Ocean and many others eyeing its potential, the leadership and cooperation of the United States is needed now.

Finally, there is the matter of our nation's own interconnected energy and national security. The oil and gas potential of Arctic Alaska can help us build a bridge to the future, when non-petroleum-based technologies become commercially viable over the next several decades.

We already have a pipeline from Prudhoe Bay; the infrastructure is in place, and the exploration companies are willing. With responsible development, Alaska's Arctic can guarantee decades more supply of both oil and gas to keep America strong.

As the Arctic Ocean becomes more accessible, our nation's 1,000-mile northern coast is suddenly strategic and our vital national interests have a new frontier.

Mrs. Clinton is bringing the United States to the table at the right time to protect our sovereignty, national energy and economic security and to add wisdom and diplomacy to policies being forged. We're watching history being made.

Gen. JOE RALSTON is former supreme allied commander of NATO in Europe and former vice chairman of the Joint Chiefs of Staff. He is vice chairman of the Cohen Group.

As Ice Melts and Technology Improves, Interest in Arctic Grows[*]

By Jarondakie Patrick and Erika Bolstad
McClatchy Newspapers, May 24, 2011

WASHINGTON—As declining sea ice and better mapping and technology make the Arctic more accessible, nations with interests there—including the United States—are beginning to stake their claims on the resource-rich region.

Russia planted a flag on the seafloor below the North Pole in 2007. Denmark announced this week that it would ask the United Nations to recognize the North Pole as an extension of Greenland, its territory. The U.S. sent a secretary of state to a meeting of eight Arctic nations earlier this month for the first time, a sign that Americans also have their eye on the region's potential resources.

"This region matters greatly to us," Secretary of State Hillary Clinton said after the conference in Nuuk, Greenland.

The U.S. is committed to the Arctic Council's mission as well as the challenges the Arctic faces, Clinton said, including possible resource development.

Although numerous logistical challenges to oil and gas exploration in the region remain, the U.S. Geological Survey estimates that as much of a third of the world's undiscovered gas and 13 percent of its undiscovered oil may be in the offshore Arctic, in relatively shallow water.

"The melting of sea ice, for example, will result in more shipping, fishing and tourism, and the possibility to develop newly accessible oil and gas reserves," Clinton said. "We seek to pursue these opportunities in a smart, sustainable way that preserves the Arctic environment and ecosystem."

The U.S. has been slow to recognize not just the importance of the Arctic but also the implications of the melting ice and what it means for commercial and economic interests, said John Bellinger III, who was a senior adviser to Condoleezza Rice when she was the secretary of state in the George W. Bush administration. Other nations have been far more focused on the region while the U.S. has been distracted by other events.

* Copyright © McClatchy-Tribune Information Services. All Rights Reserved. Reprinted with permission.

"Secretary Clinton attending a summit of Arctic Council members at a time when so many other things are going on in the world does demonstrate that the U.S. understands the importance of the Arctic," Bellinger said.

Clinton took with her to Greenland Interior Secretary Ken Salazar and Sen. Lisa Murkowski, R-Alaska, who's long worked to remind other officeholders that the U.S. is an Arctic nation and its foreign policy should reflect that. Murkowski's presence was also the first time that anyone from Congress had attended such a gathering.

"It's been frustrating getting anyone's attention on Arctic issues, but Hillary Clinton is one who I could engage on this topic," Murkowski said.

Murkowski said she first got Clinton's attention on Arctic matters long before the former first lady was the secretary of state. Several senators, including Clinton, visited Alaska one summer a few years ago, and Murkowski and her husband hosted them at a salmon barbecue.

It was obvious that Clinton's trip to some of Alaska's Arctic regions had inspired her, Murkowski said. Clinton got it, Murkowski said, including the region's strategic importance to the U.S. Since then, the two women have had regular policy discussions about the region.

In Greenland, the eight countries—the United States, Russia, Canada, Denmark, Norway, Iceland, Sweden and Finland—signed several accords, including a pact to cooperate on search and rescue missions in a region that has minimal resources for such expeditions. The agreement is recognition that more people will be in the area, whether they're on cruise ships, cargo planes or oil rigs.

They also laid the groundwork for a multi-nation task force to address oil and gas development in the Arctic. Since last year's oil spill in the Gulf of Mexico, many nations have re-evaluated the safety of offshore drilling, and the U.S. is considering how to proceed in the Arctic Ocean off Alaska's northern coast.

Environmental groups such as Oceana have been keeping close tabs on potential oil and gas development in the region, and they think it's crucial for the U.S. to take the lead in Arctic matters. The Arctic is changing rapidly and is more sensitive to the impacts of climate change than other regions are, said Chris Krenz, the lead Arctic project manager for Oceana's office in Juneau, Alaska.

"The Arctic is a very spectacular place," Krenz said. "It really captures the imagination of people."

Many of those who attended the council meeting, including Clinton, called for the U.S. to ratify the Law of the Sea treaty. The treaty, which governs worldwide navigation rights and resources such as fisheries, also provides a framework for settling territorial claims in the Arctic. Although the United States participated in the negotiations that resulted in the treaty, conservatives, led by Sen. James Inhofe, R-Okla., have blocked Senate ratification since 1994.

The U.S. and Canada, which are cooperating on research to develop better maps of the Arctic, have their own disputes over boundaries, Murkowski said. And there are differences between the countries about navigational access through the Northwest Passage, the sea route through the Arctic Ocean along the northern coast of North America.

Even non-Arctic nations have an eye on the potentially resource-rich prize. Some non-Arctic nations—such as China—have been exploring the region. No one is quite certain what the Chinese want, Murkowski said.

"That concerns me," she said. "If we don't (sign the treaty) . . . we have no right to lay claim or to make a case for it."

As the Far North Melts, Calls Grow for Arctic Treaty[*]

By Ed Struzik
Yale Environment 360, June 14, 2010

Few people around the world have more closely watched the unfolding Gulf of Mexico oil spill disaster than those concerned about the environmental impact of oil and gas development on a swiftly thawing Arctic Ocean. A similar-sized offshore spill would likely have even more profound consequences in the Arctic, a pristine environment that is home to a wide variety of seabirds, marine mammals, and fish. And cleanup efforts would be hamstrung for parts of the year by sea ice and the lack of the well-developed spill-response infrastructure that exists along the Gulf of Mexico.

With numerous nations and oil companies preparing for the day when wide-spread oil exploration will be possible in the Arctic Ocean, the Gulf spill has crystallized the fears of conservationists and native people in the Far North. And the prospect of such a disaster in the Arctic has brought to the fore a question that regional experts have debated for decades: Should the Arctic be protected by the same sort of international treaty that has safeguarded Antarctica for nearly half a century?

In late April, in the wake of the spill, the conservation group WWF released three lengthy reports calling for the establishment of an "Arctic Ocean Framework Convention" that would lead to formal regulation of fisheries, shipping, and oil and gas development in the Arctic Ocean.

"The melting of the Arctic ice is opening a new ocean, bringing new possibilities for commercial activities in a part of the world that has previously been inaccessible," said Lasse Gustavsson, incoming executive conservation director for WWF-International.

Until recently, the Arctic Ocean—locked in ice year-round, which prevents maritime passage through the region and inhibits most resource exploitation—has not needed a strict regime of protection. Regional issues have been resolved by the

[*] Article by Ed Struzik from *Yale Environment 360*. (www.e360.yale.edu). Reprinted with permission of the author.

intergovernmental Arctic Council, which has had non-binding authority to handle disputes among the eight Arctic states.

But WWF and a sizeable number of politicians, scientists, and academics are calling for a new form of governance in the Arctic Ocean, which could be ice-free in summer within two decades, opening up the region to an unprecedented surge of shipping, fishing, and hydrocarbon development.

"Few—if any—seriously question any longer that the Arctic Ocean meltdown has now become irreversible," said one of the WWF reports. "The governance and regulatory regime that currently exists in the Arctic may have been adequate for a hostile environment that allows very little human activity for most of the year. But when the Arctic Ocean becomes increasingly similar to regional seas in other parts of the world for longer and longer parts of the year, adequacy cannot be assumed and reform of the regime is indispensable."

Yet as sorely needed as an international agreement on managing the Arctic may be, there is no consensus on what an Arctic treaty would look like or whether a treaty or charter is the best way to manage and protect economic, environmental, cultural, and security interests in the region. The debate has broken down into two camps, those—such as WWF—that prefer a "hard-law" approach of new treaties and protocols, and those who advocate a "soft-law" approach of regional coop-eration and management under existing regulations, such as the United Nations Convention on the Law of the Sea. Most everyone agrees, however, that failure to cooperate in a more meaningful way will result in a series of chaotic scenarios that could result in environmental disaster and heightened tensions among Arctic states.

The idea of drafting a treaty to deal with Arctic issues is nothing new. University of Toronto political scientist Franklyn Griffiths came up with a proposal in 1979 that would have set up a demilitarized zone in the Arctic in which polar nations would cooperate in areas of pollution control and scientific study. Lincoln Bloom-field, the former director of Global Issues for the National Security Council in the United States, expanded on that idea with a much broader proposal two years later. The Soviet Union's Mikhail Gorbachev gave the concept international credibility in 1987 when he called for a treaty on cooperation in the Arctic.

While the concept has evolved, it has never been able to cut through the com-plexity of the issues in the Arctic. The Antarctic Treaty, which went into effect in 1961, covered an uninhabited continent (save for scientific bases) that was almost entirely covered in ice. The Antarctic Treaty and ensuing protocols, signed by na-tions representing 80 percent of the world's population, set aside the southernmost continent as a scientific preserve. The treaty also bans military activities and pro-hibits resource exploitation. Few international agreements have worked as well.

Unlike Antarctica, there are people living in the Arctic. Nearly 2 million people in Russia, 130,000 in Canada, and a little more than a million total in Greenland, Iceland, the Scandinavian countries, and the Faeroe Islands reside above the Arc-tic Circle. The cultural and economic interests of these people would have to be accounted for in any future treaty. And many of them, including the Inuit of the

Canadian Arctic and Alaska, won a certain degree of self-governing powers when they became landowners through various claims processes.

Maritime territorial boundaries in the Arctic, including the status of the Northwest Passage through Canada, have also not been resolved. Canada maintains that the passage, which for the past two summers has been navigable for the first time in recorded history, is part of its territorial waters. The United States and the European Union claim that it is an international strait. And although all of the lands and islands of the Arctic are under the control of Arctic states, the core of the Arctic Ocean remains part of the high seas.

For this reason, WWF and other advocates of the hard-law approach say that a comprehensive international treaty is needed to protect the Arctic Ocean. WWF's proposed Arctic convention would apply only to the marine environment of the Arctic. Building on the Arctic Council and the Law of the Sea Convention, WWF calls for a legally-binding framework that would seek to establish "ecosystem-based ocean management" both in territorial and international waters. It would create protocols for shipping and resource development, create a network of marine protected areas throughout the Arctic Ocean, ensure that commercial activity followed approved environmental practices, and require polluters to pay for cleanup efforts.

"This is a region that is undergoing dramatic change," said Timo Koivurova, director of the Northern Institute for Environmental and Minority Law at the Arctic Centre, University of Lapland, who co-wrote the WWF reports. "We know that economic activities are going to enter the region. There is no evidence to suggest that the soft-law approach that we have now will be effective in regulating these activities in the future. What is required is the establishment of regional institutions with legal powers to regulate."

Rob Huebert, associate director of the Centre for Military and Strategic Studies at the University of Calgary in Canada, thinks soft-law proponents are underestimating the scope of the problems bearing down on the Arctic. "The soft approach, which relies largely on voluntary cooperation, is insufficient to deal with the challenges that climate change, energy development, and increased shipping will bring to the Arctic," he said in an interview. "Without a stronger framework for cooperative management, the living resources of the Arctic are likely to suffer, essential habitat will be degraded, and the traditional subsistence way of life of many Arctic communities will be endangered."

Yet as rich as the Arctic's resources are, not everyone agrees that there is a race to exploit them. Nor do they see crises looming.

Oran Young, for example, is perhaps the leading scholar on the subject of Arctic governance. Based at the University of California, Santa Barbara, he is also director of the Institute of Arctic Studies at the University of Tromsø in Norway. No one has been on top of this subject longer than he has been.

Young believes that fears of an Arctic resource rush, expressed in media reports in recent years, are substantially exaggerated. He and others see no need for an overarching treaty when the future is so uncertain.

"While it is important to consider the possibility of worst-case scenarios unfolding in the Arctic, I think this idea of a Wild West-like land rush is far-fetched," he said in an interview. "The development of oil and gas reserves located beneath the continental shelves of the Arctic, beyond the limits of the existing exclusive economic zones, is highly unlikely during the foreseeable future."

Young believes that issues pertaining to territorial claims and future shipping practices can be dealt with adequately by the UN Convention on the Law of the Sea, which the Obama administration recently pledged to sign.

Nevertheless, Young says there is good reason to reassess current governance arrangements in the Arctic in light of what is going on. The solution is not a treaty, he adds, but what he describes as a "somewhat messy patchwork made up of disparate pieces"—a soft-law approach that can be quickly adapted to rapidly changing circumstances. Arctic nations could agree, for example, to manage walrus, beluga, and cod or halibut fishing in mutually beneficial ways.

Such soft laws could be administered by the Arctic Council, which currently promotes cooperation among Arctic governments on a number of key issues, such as trans-boundary pollution, overfishing, and oil and gas development. Although member states—which include Canada, Denmark (including Greenland and the Faroe Islands), Finland, Iceland, Norway, Sweden, Russia, and the United States—make the final decisions, the council provides a forum in which indigenous people living in the North have a say in the decision-making process, which they would not be able to exercise in more formal treaty negotiations.

"Even if it were feasible, would we want to have a formal, legally binding treaty for the Arctic?" Young wonders. "There is a tendency to think of formal arrangements like the Antarctic Treaty system, but there are also advantages to having a soft approach in addressing Arctic issues. Unlike treaties that are rigid and take tremendous time and effort, informal agreements can be made more quickly. They can have more substance and they can provide for greater adaptability."

Canada and Greenland, for example, recently signed an agreement to deal with the increasingly unsustainable hunting of polar bears in Baffin Bay. The two countries are collaborating to determine how many bears can be hunted on each side of the maritime border. It will be left to each country, not a legally binding treaty, to honor the agreement.

In recent months, the United States, the European Union, Russia, and Canada have distanced themselves from the idea of an overarching treaty. And so far, the Arctic Council has shown no appetite for such a treaty.

Critics see this as a sign that the council believes it is currently doing a good job. Koivurova, co-author of the WWF reports, says that one possible first step is to forge a framework treaty that formalizes the current membership of the Arctic Council and adds certain guiding principles related to environmental protection.

"The Arctic Council may not like it," he concedes. "But if it continues without a legal mandate, there is great danger of it becoming a façade under which unilateral and uncoordinated development-oriented parties of the Arctic states can proceed."

Bolivia-Chile Dispute Could Turn Ugly[*]

By Andres Oppenheimer
The Miami Herald, April 30, 2011

Leftist populist President Evo Morales—until recently one of Latin America's most popular presidents—is playing a dangerous card to improve his falling support at home: reviving a 132-year-old territorial conflict with neighboring Chile.

During a three-day visit here [Santa Cruz, Bolivia] last week, I was surprised to find out that Morales had declared April 29 as national Day of Sea Reclamation, only a few weeks after the country had celebrated its traditional Day of the Sea on March 23.

The new national observance, just like the old one, was marked by government-organized rallies throughout the country to demand that this landlocked country be given an outlet to the Pacific Ocean through what today is Chilean territory.

Morales announced recently that Bolivia will go to international tribunals "to demand free and sovereign access to the sea." Since then, in addition to creating the new "Sea Reclamation" day, he has vowed to demand that Chile pay Bolivia for its use of the Silala River on the two countries' border.

Chile claims that it is willing to continue ongoing negotiations that could provide Bolivia with a passage to the Pacific Ocean through Chile, but without giving Bolivia sovereign rights over that territory.

The two countries broke diplomatic ties in 1978 over the issue, but had been negotiating a solution to the conflict in recent years.

What's going on?, I asked several Bolivian politicians and journalists. Virtually all responded that Morales, who won a second term in 2009 with a massive 64 percent of the vote, has been in a political free fall since December, and is propping up the fight with Chile for domestic political reasons.

Morales' poll numbers fell abruptly in December, when he announced a 70 percent increase in gasoline prices.

* Copyright © The Miami Herald. All Rights Reserved. Reprinted with permission.

Facing massive street protests, including from many leftist unions and indigenous groups that had been his allies, he backed down, but he has yet to recover from the political blow.

Morales' popularity has fallen to 32 percent in most polls, his lowest number since he took office five years ago.

"The government is rapidly losing popular support, and this fight with Chile is a consequence of that," says Samuel Doria Medina, a business tycoon and opposition leader who is currently facing several government suits for alleged economic crimes. "Morales is trying to divert public attention from our economic problems."

Santa Cruz governor Ruben Costas, one of the few Bolivian opposition governors who remain in their jobs after the government forced most of his colleagues out of office through lawsuits or intimidation, told me that he expects a "continued and irreversible deterioration" of the Morales government.

Despite record world prices for Bolivia's mineral exports, which increased the country's income by a whopping 160 percent since Morales took office five years ago, the economy is in a mess.

Silver prices soared from $7 an ounce years ago to $45 nowadays, and tin prices rose from $2 to $14 over the same period.

And yet, Morales' massive cash handouts, disastrous government takeovers of major companies and mounting debts with Venezuela and other countries have left the government broke.

To make things worse, there are virtually no investments, because nationalizations have scared away national and foreign investors. While the government has changed the way it measures inflation to report lower figures, real inflation is at about 15 percent, and rising.

"I'm afraid that inflation is going to soar, and the government will become even more radical," Costas said. "They will try to generate even greater confrontations, to create a climate that will allow them to maintain this populist project."

My opinion: It is not unusual for Bolivian presidents to revive their country's territorial dispute with Chile whenever their poll numbers are low. I can remember several of Morales' predecessors, centrists and rightists, who did the same thing when in trouble at home.

The difference this time is that Morales has added an ideological element that didn't exist before—the political partisanship of his country's armed forces. Last year, at the request of Morales, the Bolivian army declared itself "socialist," "anti-imperialist" and "anti-capitalist."

While Bolivia's army is no match to Chile's, by a long stretch, one could not rule out its willingness to create a border skirmish with Chile in an effort to help Morales draw support at home and win the 2014 elections. That would have been unthinkable in recent times, but not in today's Bolivia.

Center-Stage for the Twenty-First Century[*]

By Robert D. Kaplan
Foreign Affairs, March/April 2009

For better or worse, phrases such "the Cold War" and "the clash of civilizations" matter. In a similar way, so do maps. The right map can stimulate foresight by providing a spatial view of critical trends in world politics. Understanding the map of Europe was essential to understanding the twentieth century. Although recent technological advances and economic integration have encouraged global thinking, some places continue to count more than others. And in some of those, such as Iraq and Pakistan, two countries with inherently artificial contours, politics is still at the mercy of geography.

So in what quarter of the earth today can one best glimpse the future? Because of their own geographic circumstances, Americans, in particular, continue to concentrate on the Atlantic and Pacific Oceans. World War II and the Cold War shaped this outlook: Nazi Germany, imperial Japan, the Soviet Union, and communist China were all oriented toward one of these two oceans. The bias is even embedded in mapping conventions: Mercator projections tend to place the Western Hemisphere in the middle of the map, splitting the Indian Ocean at its far edges. And yet, as the pirate activity off the coast of Somalia and the terrorist carnage in Mumbai last fall suggest, the Indian Ocean—the world's third-largest body of water—already forms center stage for the challenges of the twenty-first century.

The greater Indian Ocean region encompasses the entire arc of Islam, from the Sahara Desert to the Indonesian archipelago. Although the Arabs and the Persians are known to Westerners primarily as desert peoples, they have also been great seafarers. In the Middle Ages, they sailed from Arabia to China; proselytizing along the way, they spread their faith through sea-based commerce. Today, the western reaches of the Indian Ocean include the tinderboxes of Somalia, Yemen, Iran, and Pakistan—constituting a network of dynamic trade as well as a network of global terrorism, piracy, and drug smuggling. Hundreds of millions of Muslims—the

[*] Reprinted by permission of *Foreign Affairs*, March/April 2009. Copyright 2009 by the Council on Foreign Relations, Inc. www.ForeignAffairs.org.

legacy of those medieval conversions—live along the Indian Ocean's eastern edges, in India and Bangladesh, Malaysia and Indonesia.

The Indian Ocean is dominated by two immense bays, the Arabian Sea and the Bay of Bengal, near the top of which are two of the least stable countries in the world: Pakistan and Myanmar (also known as Burma). State collapse or regime change in Pakistan would affect its neighbors by empowering Baluchi and Sindhi separatists seeking closer links to India and Iran. Likewise, the collapse of the junta in Myanmar—where competition over energy and natural resources between China and India looms—would threaten economies nearby and require a massive seaborne humanitarian intervention. On the other hand, the advent of a more liberal regime in Myanmar would undermine China's dominant position there, boost Indian influence, and quicken regional economic integration.

In other words, more than just a geographic feature, the Indian Ocean is also an idea. It combines the centrality of Islam with global energy politics and the rise of India and China to reveal a multilayered, multipolar world. The dramatic economic growth of India and China has been duly noted, but the equally dramatic military ramifications of this development have not. India's and China's great-power aspirations, as well as their quests for energy security, have compelled the two countries "to redirect their gazes from land to the seas," according to James Holmes and Toshi Yoshihara, associate professors of strategy at the U.S. Naval War College. And the very fact that they are focusing on their sea power indicates how much more self-confident they feel on land. And so a map of the Indian Ocean exposes the contours of power politics in the twenty-first century.

Yet this is still an environment in which the United States will have to keep the peace and help guard the global commons—interdicting terrorists, pirates, and smugglers; providing humanitarian assistance; managing the competition between India and China. It will have to do so not, as in Afghanistan and Iraq, as a land-based, in-your-face meddler, leaning on far-flung army divisions at risk of getting caught up in sectarian conflict, but as a sea-based balancer lurking just over the horizon. Sea power has always been less threatening than land power: as the cliché goes, navies make port visits, and armies invade. Ships take a long time to get to a war zone, allowing diplomacy to work its magic. And as the U.S. response to the 2004 tsunami in the Indian Ocean showed, with most sailors and marines returning to their ships each night, navies can exert great influence on shore while leaving a small footprint. The more the United States becomes a maritime hegemon, as opposed to a land-based one, the less threatening it will seem to others.

Moreover, precisely because India and China are emphasizing their sea power, the job of managing their peaceful rise will fall on the U.S. Navy to a significant extent. There will surely be tensions between the three navies, especially as the gaps in their relative strength begin to close. But even if the comparative size of the U.S. Navy decreases in the decades ahead, the United States will remain the one great power from outside the Indian Ocean region with a major presence there—a unique position that will give it the leverage to act as a broker between India and

China in their own backyard. To understand this dynamic, one must look at the region from a maritime perspective.

SEA CHANGES

Thanks to the predictability of the monsoon winds, the countries on the Indian Ocean were connected well before the age of steam power. Trade in frankincense, spices, precious stones, and textiles brought together the peoples flung along its long shoreline during the Middle Ages. Throughout history, sea routes have mattered more than land routes, writes the historian Felipe Fernández-Armesto, because they carry more goods more economically. "Whoever is lord of Malacca has his hand on the throat of Venice," went one saying during the late fifteenth century, alluding to the city's extensive commerce with Asia; if the world were an egg, Hormuz would be its yolk, went another. Even today, in the jet and information age, 90 percent of global commerce and about 65 percent of all oil travel by sea. Globalization has been made possible by the cheap and easy shipping of containers on tankers, and the Indian Ocean accounts for fully half the world's container traffic. Moreover, 70 percent of the total traffic of petroleum products passes through the Indian Ocean, on its way from the Middle East to the Pacific. As these goods travel that route, they pass through the world's principal oil shipping lanes, including the Gulfs of Aden and Oman—as well as some of world commerce's main chokepoints: Bab el Mandeb and the Straits of Hormuz and Malacca. Forty percent of world trade passes through the Strait of Malacca; 40 percent of all traded crude oil passes through the Strait of Hormuz.

Already the world's preeminent energy and trade interstate seaway, the Indian Ocean will matter even more in the future. Global energy needs are expected to rise by 45 percent between 2006 and 2030, and almost half of the growth in demand will come from India and China. China's demand for crude oil doubled between 1995 and 2005 and will double again in the coming 15 years or so; by 2020, China is expected to import 7.3 million barrels of crude per day—half of Saudi Arabia's planned output. More than 85 percent of the oil and oil products bound for China cross the Indian Ocean and pass through the Strait of Malacca.

India—soon to become the world's fourth-largest energy consumer, after the United States, China, and Japan—is dependent on oil for roughly 33 percent of its energy needs, 65 percent of which it imports. And 90 percent of its oil imports could soon come from the Persian Gulf. India must satisfy a population that will, by 2030, be the largest of any country in the world. Its coal imports from far-off Mozambique are set to increase substantially, adding to the coal that India already imports from other Indian Ocean countries, such as South Africa, Indonesia, and Australia. In the future, India-bound ships will also be carrying increasingly large quantities of liquefied natural gas (LNG) across the seas from southern Africa, even as it continues importing LNG from Qatar, Malaysia, and Indonesia.

As the whole Indian Ocean seaboard, including Africa's eastern shores, becomes a vast web of energy trade, India is seeking to increase its influence from the Plateau of Iran to the Gulf of Thailand—an expansion west and east meant to span the zone of influence of the Raj's viceroys. India's trade with the Arab countries of the Persian Gulf and Iran, with which India has long enjoyed close economic and cultural ties, is booming. Approximately 3.5 million Indians work in the six Arab states of the Gulf Cooperation Council and send home $4 billion in remittances annually. As India's economy continues to grow, so will its trade with Iran and, once the country recovers, Iraq. Iran, like Afghanistan, has become a strategic rear base for India against Pakistan, and it is poised to become an important energy partner. In 2005, India and Iran signed a multibillion-dollar deal under which Iran will supply India with 7.5 million tons of LNG annually for 25 years, beginning in 2009. There has been talk of building a gas pipeline from Iran to India through Pakistan, a project that would join the Middle East and South Asia at the hip (and in the process could go a long way toward stabilizing Indian-Pakistani relations). In another sign that Indian-Iranian relations are growing more intimate, India has been helping Iran develop the port of Chah Bahar, on the Gulf of Oman, which will also serve as a forward base for the Iranian navy.

India has also been expanding its military and economic ties with Myanmar, to the east. Democratic India does not have the luxury of spurning Myanmar's junta because Myanmar is rich in natural resources—oil, natural gas, coal, zinc, copper, uranium, timber, and hydropower—resources in which the Chinese are also heavily invested. India hopes that a network of east-west roads and energy pipelines will eventually allow it to be connected to Iran, Pakistan, and Myanmar.

India is enlarging its navy in the same spirit. With its 155 warships, the Indian navy is already one of the world's largest, and it expects to add three nuclear-powered submarines and three aircraft carriers to its arsenal by 2015. One major impetus for the buildup was the humiliating inability of its navy to evacuate Indian citizens from Iraq and Kuwait during the 1990–91 Persian Gulf War. Another is what Mohan Malik, a scholar at the Asia-Pacific Center for Security Studies, in Hawaii, has called India's "Hormuz dilemma," its dependence on imports passing through the strait, close to the shores of Pakistan's Makran coast, where the Chinese are helping the Pakistanis develop deep-water ports.

Indeed, as India extends its influence east and west, on land and at sea, it is bumping into China, which, also concerned about protecting its interests throughout the region, is expanding its reach southward. Chinese President Hu Jintao has bemoaned China's "Malacca dilemma." The Chinese government hopes to eventually be able to partly bypass that strait by transporting oil and other energy products via roads and pipelines from ports on the Indian Ocean into the heart of China. One reason that Beijing wants desperately to integrate Taiwan into its dominion is so that it can redirect its naval energies away from the Taiwan Strait and toward the Indian Ocean.

The Chinese government has already adopted a "string of pearls" strategy for the Indian Ocean, which consists of setting up a series of ports in friendly countries along the ocean's northern seaboard. It is building a large naval base and listening post in Gwadar, Pakistan (from which it may already be monitoring ship traffic through the Strait of Hormuz); a port in Pasni, Pakistan, 75 miles east of Gwadar, which is to be joined to the Gwadar facility by a new highway; a fueling station on the southern coast of Sri Lanka; and a container facility with extensive naval and commercial access in Chittagong, Bangladesh. Beijing operates surveillance facilities on islands deep in the Bay of Bengal. In Myanmar, whose junta gets billions of dollars in military assistance from Beijing, the Chinese are constructing (or upgrading) commercial and naval bases and building roads, waterways, and pipelines in order to link the Bay of Bengal to the southern Chinese province of Yunnan. Some of these facilities are closer to cities in central and western China than those cities are to Beijing and Shanghai, and so building road and rail links from these facilities into China will help spur the economies of China's landlocked provinces. The Chinese government is also envisioning a canal across the Isthmus of Kra, in Thailand, to link the Indian Ocean to China's Pacific coast—a project on the scale of the Panama Canal and one that could further tip Asia's balance of power in China's favor by giving China's burgeoning navy and commercial maritime fleet easy access to a vast oceanic continuum stretching all the way from East Africa to Japan and the Korean Peninsula.

All of these activities are unnerving the Indian government. With China building deep-water ports to its west and east and a preponderance of Chinese arms sales going to Indian Ocean states, India fears being encircled by China unless it expands its own sphere of influence. The two countries' overlapping commercial and political interests are fostering competition, and even more so in the naval realm than on land. Zhao Nanqi, former director of the General Logistics Department of the People's Liberation Army, proclaimed in 1993, "We can no longer accept the Indian Ocean as an ocean only of the Indians." India has responded to China's building of a naval base in Gwadar by further developing one of its own, that in Karwar, India, south of Goa. Meanwhile, Zhang Ming, a Chinese naval analyst, has warned that the 244 islands that form India's Andaman and Nicobar archipelago could be used like a "metal chain" to block the western entrance to the Strait of Malacca, on which China so desperately depends. "India is perhaps China's most realistic strategic adversary," Zhang has written. "Once India commands the Indian Ocean, it will not be satisfied with its position and will continuously seek to extend its influence, and its eastward strategy will have a particular impact on China." These may sound like the words of a professional worrier from China's own theory class, but these worries are revealing: Beijing already considers New Delhi to be a major sea power.

As the competition between India and China suggests, the Indian Ocean is where global struggles will play out in the twenty-first century. The old borders of the Cold War map are crumbling fast, and Asia is becoming a more integrated unit, from the Middle East to the Pacific. South Asia has been an indivisible part of the greater Islamic Middle East since the Middle Ages: it was the Muslim Ghaznavids of eastern Afghanistan who launched raids on India's northwestern coast in the early eleventh century; Indian civilization itself is a fusion of the indigenous Hindu culture and the cultural imprint left by these invasions. Although it took the seaborne terrorist attacks in Mumbai last November for most Westerners to locate India inside the greater Middle East, the Indian Ocean's entire coast has always constituted one vast interconnected expanse.

What is different now is the extent of these connections. On a maritime-centric map of southern Eurasia, artificial land divisions disappear; even landlocked Central Asia is related to the Indian Ocean. Natural gas from Turkmenistan may one day flow through Afghanistan, for example, en route to Pakistani and Indian cities and ports, one of several possible energy links between Central Asia and the Indian subcontinent. Both the Chinese port in Gwadar, Pakistan, and the Indian port in Chah Bahar, Iran, may eventually be connected to oil- and natural-gas-rich Azerbaijan, Kazakhstan, Turkmenistan, and other former Soviet republics. S. Frederick Starr, a Central Asia expert at the Johns Hopkins School of Advanced International Studies, said at a conference in Washington last year that access to the Indian Ocean "will help define Central Asian politics in the future." Others have called ports in India and Pakistan "evacuation points" for Caspian Sea oil. The destinies of countries even 1,200 miles from the Indian Ocean are connected with it.

ELEGANT DECLINE

The United States faces three related geopolitical challenges in Asia: the strategic nightmare of the greater Middle East, the struggle for influence over the southern tier of the former Soviet Union, and the growing presence of India and China in the Indian Ocean. The last seems to be the most benign of the three. China is not an enemy of the United States, like Iran, but a legitimate peer competitor, and India is a budding ally. And the rise of the Indian navy, soon to be the third largest in the world after those of the United States and China, will function as an antidote to Chinese military expansion.

The task of the U.S. Navy will therefore be to quietly leverage the sea power of its closest allies—India in the Indian Ocean and Japan in the western Pacific—to set limits on China's expansion. But it will have to do so at the same time as it seizes every opportunity to incorporate China's navy into international alliances; a U.S.-Chinese understanding at sea is crucial for the stabilization of world politics in the twenty-first century. After all, the Indian Ocean is a seaway for both energy and hashish and is in drastic need of policing. To manage it effectively, U.S. military planners will have to invoke challenges such as terrorism, piracy, and smuggling to bring together India, China, and other states in joint sea patrols. The goal of the United States must be to forge a global maritime system that can minimize the risks of interstate conflict while lessening the burden of policing for the U.S. Navy.

Keeping the peace in the Indian Ocean will be even more crucial once the seas and the coasts from the Gulf of Aden to the Sea of Japan are connected. Shipping options between the Indian Ocean and the Pacific Ocean will increase substantially in the future. The port operator Dubai Ports World is conducting a feasibility study on constructing a land bridge near the canal that the Chinese hope will be dug across the Isthmus of Kra, with ports on either side of the isthmus connected by rails and highways. The Malaysian government is interested in a pipeline network that would link up ports in the Bay of Bengal with those in the South China Sea. To be sure, as sea power grows in importance, the crowded hub around Malaysia, Singapore, and Indonesia will form the maritime heart of Asia: in the coming decades, it will be as strategically significant as the Fulda Gap, a possible invasion route for Soviet tanks into West Germany during the Cold War. The protective oversight of the U.S. Navy there will be especially important. As the only truly substantial blue-water force without territorial ambitions on the Asian mainland, the U.S. Navy may in the future be able to work with individual Asian countries, such as India and China, better than they can with one another. Rather than ensure its dominance, the U.S. Navy simply needs to make itself continually useful.

It has already begun to make the necessary shifts. Owing to the debilitating U.S.-led wars in Afghanistan and Iraq, headlines in recent years have been dominated by discussions about land forces and counterinsurgency. But with 75 percent of the earth's population living within 200 miles of the sea, the world's military future may well be dominated by naval (and air) forces operating over vast regions. And to a greater extent than the other armed services, navies exist to protect economic interests and the system in which these interests operate. Aware of how much the international economy depends on sea traffic, U.S. admirals are thinking beyond the fighting and winning of wars to responsibilities such as policing a global trading arrangement. They are also attuned to the effects that a U.S. military strike against Iran would have on maritime commerce and the price of oil. With such concerns in mind, the U.S. Navy has for decades been helping to secure vital chokepoints in the Indian Ocean, often operating from a base on the British atoll of Diego Garcia, a thousand miles south of India and close to major sea-lanes. And in October 2007, it implied that it was seeking a sustained forward presence in the Indian Ocean and the western Pacific but no longer in the Atlantic—a momentous shift in overall U.S. maritime strategy. The document Marine Corps Vision and Strategy 2025 also concluded that the Indian Ocean and its adjacent waters will be a central theater of global conflict and competition this century.

Yet as the challenges for the United States on the high seas multiply, it is unclear how much longer U.S. naval dominance will last. At the end of the Cold War, the U.S. Navy boasted about 600 warships; it is now down to 279. That number might rise to 313 in the coming years with the addition of the new "littoral combat ships," but it could also drop to the low 200s given cost overruns of 34 percent and the slow pace of shipbuilding. Although the revolution in precision-guided weapons means that existing ships pack better firepower than those of the Cold War fleet did, since a ship cannot be in two places at once, the fewer the vessels, the riskier every decision to deploy them. There comes a point at which insufficient quantity hurts quality.

Meanwhile, by sometime in the next decade, China's navy will have more warships than the United States'. China is producing and acquiring submarines five times as fast as is the United States. In addition to submarines, the Chinese have wisely focused on buying naval mines, ballistic missiles that can hit moving targets at sea, and technology that blocks signals from GPS satellites, on which the U.S. Navy depends. (They also have plans to acquire at least one aircraft carrier; not having one hindered their attempts to help with the tsunami relief effort in 2004–5.) The goal of the Chinese is "sea denial," or dissuading U.S. carrier strike groups from closing in on the Asian mainland wherever and whenever Washington would like. The Chinese are also more aggressive than U.S. military planners. Whereas the prospect of ethnic warfare has scared away U.S. admirals from considering a base in Sri Lanka, which is strategically located at the confluence of the Arabian Sea and the Bay of Bengal, the Chinese are constructing a refueling station for their warships there.

There is nothing illegitimate about the rise of China's navy. As the country's economic interests expand dramatically, so must China expand its military, and particularly its navy, to guard these interests. The United Kingdom did just that in the nineteenth century, and so did the United States when it emerged as a great power between the American Civil War and World War I. In 1890, the American military theorist Alfred Thayer Mahan published *The Influence of Sea Power Upon History, 1660–1783*, which argued that the power to protect merchant fleets had been the determining factor in world history. Both Chinese and Indian naval strategists read him avidly nowadays. China's quest for a major presence in the Indian Ocean was also evinced in 2005 by the beginning of an extensive commemoration of Zheng He, the Ming dynasty explorer and admiral who plied the seas between China and Indonesia, Sri Lanka, the Persian Gulf, and the Horn of Africa in the early decades of the fifteenth century—a celebration that signals China's belief that these seas have always been part of its zone of influence.

Just as at the end of the nineteenth century the British Royal Navy began to reduce its presence worldwide by leveraging the growing sea power of its naval allies (Japan and the United States), at the beginning of the twenty-first century, the United States is beginning an elegant decline by leveraging the growing sea power of allies such as India and Japan to balance against China. What better way to scale back than to give more responsibilities to like-minded states, especially allies that, unlike those in Europe, still cherish military power?

India, for one, is more than willing to help. "India has never waited for American permission to balance [against] China," the Indian strategist C. Raja Mohan wrote in 2006, adding that India has been balancing against China since the day the Chinese invaded Tibet. Threatened by China's rise, India has expanded its naval presence from as far west as the Mozambique Channel to as far east as the South China Sea. It has been establishing naval staging posts and listening stations on the island nations of Madagascar, Mauritius, and the Seychelles, as well as military relationships with them, precisely in order to counter China's own very active military cooperation with these states. With a Chinese-Pakistani alliance taking shape, most visibly in the construction of the Gwadar port, near the Strait of Hormuz, and an Indian naval buildup on the Andaman and Nicobar Islands, near the Strait of Malacca, the Indian-Chinese rivalry is taking on the dimensions of a maritime Great Game. This is a reason for the United States to quietly encourage India to balance against China, even as the United States seeks greater cooperation with China. During the Cold War, the Pacific and Indian oceans were veritable U.S. lakes. But such hegemony will not last and the United States must seek to replace it with a subtle balance-of-power arrangement.

COALITION BUILDER SUPREME

So how exactly does the United States play the role of a constructive, distant, and slowly declining hegemon and keep peace on the high seas in what Fareed Zakaria, the editor of *Newsweek International*, has called "the post-American world"? Several years ago, Admiral Michael Mullen, then the chief of naval operations (and now chairman of the Joint Chiefs of Staff), said the answer was a "thousand-ship navy . . . comprised of all freedom-loving nations—standing watch over the seas, standing watch with each other." The term "thousand-ship navy" has since been dropped for sounding too domineering, but the idea behind it remains: rather than going it alone, the U.S. Navy should be a coalition builder supreme, working with any navy that agrees to patrol the seas and share information with it.

Already, Combined Task Force 150 (CTF-150), a naval force based in Djibouti and comprising roughly 15 vessels from the United States, four European countries, Canada, and Pakistan, conducts antipiracy patrols around the troubled Gulf of Aden. In 2008, about a hundred ships were attacked by pirates in the region, and over 35 vessels, with billions of dollars worth of cargo, were seized. (As of the end of 2008, more than a dozen, including oil tankers, cargo vessels, and other ships, along with over 300 crew members, were still being held.) Ransom demands routinely exceed $1 million per ship, and in the recent case of one Saudi oil tanker, pirates demanded $25 million. Last fall, after the capture of a Ukrainian vessel carrying tanks and other military equipment, warships from the United States, Kenya, and Malaysia steamed toward the Gulf of Aden to assist CTF-150, followed by two Chinese warships a few weeks later. The force, which is to be beefed up and rechristened CTF-151, is likely to become a permanent fixture: piracy is the maritime ripple effect of land-based anarchy, and for as long as Somalia is in the throes of chaos, pirates operating at the behest of warlords will infest the waters far down Africa's eastern coast.

The task-force model could also be applied to the Strait of Malacca and other waters surrounding the Indonesian archipelago. With help from the U.S. Navy, the navies and coast guards of Malaysia, Singapore, and Indonesia have already combined forces to reduce piracy in that area in recent years. And with the U.S. Navy functioning as both a mediator and an enforcer of standard procedures, coalitions of this kind could bring together rival countries, such as India and Pakistan or

India and China, under a single umbrella: these states' governments would have no difficulty justifying to their publics participating in task forces aimed at transnational threats over which they have no disagreements. Piracy has the potential to unite rival states along the Indian Ocean coastline.

Packed with states with weak governments and tottering infrastructure, the shores of the Indian Ocean make it necessary for the United States and other countries to transform their militaries. This area represents an unconventional world, a world in which the U.S. military, for one, will have to respond, expeditionary style, to a range of crises: not just piracy but also terrorist attacks, ethnic conflicts, cyclones, and floods. For even as the United States' armed forces, and particularly its navy, are in relative decline, they remain the most powerful conventional military on earth, and they will be expected to lead such emergency responses. With population growth in climatically and seismically fragile zones today placing more human beings in danger's way than at almost any other time in history, one deployment will quickly follow another.

It is the variety and recurrence of these challenges that make the map of the Indian Ocean in the twenty-first century vastly different from the map of the North Atlantic in the twentieth century. The latter illustrated both a singular threat and a singular concept: the Soviet Union. And it gave the United States a simple focus: to defend Western Europe against the Red Army and keep the Soviet navy bottled up near the polar icecap. Because the threat was straightforward, and the United States' power was paramount, the U.S.-led North Atlantic Treaty Organization arguably became history's most successful alliance.

One might envision a "NATO of the seas" for the Indian Ocean, composed of South Africa, Oman, Pakistan, India, Singapore, and Australia, with Pakistan and India bickering inside the alliance much as Greece and Turkey have inside NATO. But that idea fails to capture what the Indian Ocean is all about. Owing to the peripatetic movements of medieval Arab and Persian sailors and the legacies of Portuguese, Dutch, and British imperialists, the Indian Ocean forms a historical and cultural unit. Yet in strategic terms, it, like the world at large today, has no single focal point. The Gulf of Aden, the Persian Gulf, the Bay of Bengal—all these areas are burdened by different threats with different players. Just as today NATO is a looser alliance, less singularly focused than it was during the Cold War, any coalition centered on the Indian Ocean should be adapted to the times. Given the ocean's size—it stretches across seven time zones and almost half of the world's latitudes—and the comparative slowness at which ships move, it would be a challenge for any one multinational navy to get to a crisis zone in time. The United States was able to lead the relief effort off the coast of Indonesia after the 2004 tsunami only because the carrier strike group the USS *Abraham Lincoln* happened to be in the vicinity and not in the Korean Peninsula, where it was headed.

A better approach would be to rely on multiple regional and ideological alliances in different parts of the Indian Ocean. Some such efforts have already begun. The navies of Thailand, Singapore, and Indonesia have banded together to deter piracy in the Strait of Malacca; those of the United States, India, Singapore, and Australia have exercised together off India's southwestern coast—an implicit rebuke to China's designs in the region. According to Vice Admiral John Morgan, former deputy chief of U.S. naval operations, the Indian Ocean strategic system should be like the New York City taxi system: driven by market forces and with no central dispatcher. Coalitions will naturally form in areas where shipping lanes need to be protected, much as taxis gather in the theater district before and after performances. For one Australian commodore, the model should be a network of artificial sea bases supplied by the U.S. Navy, which would allow for different permutations of alliances: frigates and destroyers from various states could "plug and play" into these sea bases as necessary and spread out from East Africa to the Indonesian archipelago.

Like a microcosm of the world at large, the greater Indian Ocean region is developing into an area of both ferociously guarded sovereignty (with fast-growing economies and militaries) and astonishing interdependence (with its pipelines and land and sea routes). And for the first time since the Portuguese onslaught in the region in the early sixteenth century, the West's power there is in decline, however subtly and relatively. The Indians and the Chinese will enter into a dynamic great-power rivalry in these waters, with their shared economic interests as major trading partners locking them in an uncomfortable embrace. The United States, meanwhile, will serve as a stabilizing power in this newly complex area. Indispensability, rather than dominance, must be its goal.

ROBERT D. KAPLAN, *a National Correspondent for* The Atlantic *and a Senior Fellow at the Center for a New American Security, in Washington, D.C., is writing a book on the Indian Ocean. He recently was the Class of 1960 Distinguished Visiting Professor in National Security at the U.S. Naval Academy.*

3

Trouble in the Gulf: The BP Oil Spill

Courtesy of the U.S. Coast Guard

Fire boat response crews battle the blazing remnants of the offshore oil rig *Deepwater Horizon* on April 21, 2011. A Coast Guard MH-65C Dolphin helicopter and crew document the fire while searching for survivors. Multiple Coast Guard helicopters, planes, and cutters responded to rescue the *Deepwater Horizon*'s 126-person crew.

Courtesy of the U.S. Air Force

A C-130 Hercules drops an oil-dispersing chemical into the Gulf of Mexico on May 5, 2010, as part of the *Deepwater Horizon* response effort.

Editor's Introduction

On April 20, 2010, methane gas shot up through the drill column of the *Deep-water Horizon*, a BP oil rig floating in the Gulf of Mexico some 50 miles off the coast of Louisiana. The surge sparked a massive explosion, killing 11 workers and ultimately sinking the 32,000-ton structure. The blast also damaged a well-head 5,000 feet below the surface, unleashing a torrent of oil into the water. At first, government officials claimed the flow rate to be 5,000 barrels per day, but as weeks dragged on and scientists struggled to cap the gusher, the projections crept higher. By September, when the well was finally declared dead, 4.9 million barrels of oil had seeped into the Gulf, making *Deepwater* the largest accidental oil spill in history.

As might be expected with a disaster of such magnitude, the political fallout from *Deepwater* was immense. The articles in this chapter look back on the finger pointing that followed the spill and consider some of the major policy questions lawmakers must face in its aftermath. In the opening piece, "The Oil Spill's Surprise Endings," *Newsweek* marks the one-year anniversary of *Deepwater* by checking in with some of the major players. While things look grim for fish, fishermen, and oil workers, the magazine reports, President Barack Obama seems to have emerged unscathed, despite predictions that *Deepwater* would be to his administration what Hurricane Katrina was to George W. Bush's.

Rolling Stone political muckraker Tim Dickinson isn't ready to let Obama off the hook, however. In "The Spill, The Scandal and the President," the subsequent piece, Dickinson compares the BP fiasco to the 9/11 terror attacks, insisting that the government had prior warning and failed to act accordingly. In particular, Dickinson takes Obama to task for leaving the Interior Department's Minerals Management Service (MMS) in the hands of, in his view, corrupt bureaucrats beholden to corporate interests. Had the MMS done its job, Dickinson writes, BP wouldn't have been allowed to cut corners and ignore the safety regulations that might have prevented the mishap.

In "Oil and Water," the next entry, *Texas Monthly* writer Paul Burka explains why he believes the reorganization of the MMS—done in response to the Gulf spill—is unlikely to prevent future disasters. In Burka's estimation, federal regulators are too corrupt and ineffective to protect the public from Big Business. While he salutes angry voters for holding lawmakers accountable, he suggests the public direct its rage at the real enemies: "the oil companies, the insurance companies, all the repositories of wealth and power that have created the messes we are in—and not just in the Gulf of Mexico."

In "BP Oil Spill: Forgotten But Not Gone," an op-ed for the *Los Angeles Times*, Charles Wohlforth laments how quickly the public forgot about *Deepwater* and lost interest in environmental issues. "The rate at which environmental disasters recede in our collective rearview mirror marks how fast the culture is moving," he writes. Whereas past disasters galvanized environmentalists and led to genuine policy change, Wohlforth adds, the BP spill has brought us no closer to climate-change legislation or a much-needed "national discussion about our energy sources." Wohlforth finds some hope at the local level, where concerned citizens have managed to enact meaningful environmental protections. "The key," he insists, "is giving those who live in an ecosystem the power to care for it."

Ruth Conniff doesn't pull any rhetorical punches in her piece, "America's Chernobyl," vividly comparing the *Deepwater Horizon* tragedy to the infamous 1986 nuclear disaster in the former Soviet Union. She lays the blame for the BP debacle on our insatiable appetite for fossil fuels and calls for transforming our energy infrastructure, declaring "We can't afford to wait for another oil spill—and another poisoned sea."

The Oil Spill's Surprise Endings*

Newsweek, April 17, 2011

One year after the Deepwater Horizon disaster sent 200 million gallons of oil into the Gulf of Mexico, the region is still struggling. Who's recovering, and who's stuck in the muck?

TONY HAYWARD: MAY FINALLY PAY

The BP chief executive, once America's most-hated man, whined "I want my life back"—and seemed to get it. But now it looks like the feds are eyeing Hayward for possible manslaughter charges related to the 11 deaths caused by the Deepwater Horizon explosion. Still, the gaffe-prone Brit might skate by. Lately, Hayward's been reported to be in talks to create an investment fund with financier Nathaniel Rothschild.

OIL WORKERS: NEW HEADACHES

The moratorium on deepwater drilling was lifted in October, but for the oil-men who need the work, the return has been too little and too late. A Louisiana State University economist says the local oil business has shed 13,000 jobs. But the White House says oil workers have their bosses to blame for their being out of work; it recently released a report claiming that two thirds of the Gulf of Mexico's oil and gas leases are sitting idle. More oil rigs are pumping nationwide than were running during the Bush years.

* From *Newsweek*, April 17, 2011. Copyright © 2011 Newsweek, Inc. All rights reserved. Used by permission and protected by the Copyright Law of the United States. The printing, copying, redistribution, or retransmission of the Material without express written permission is prohibited.

FISH: STILL BELLY-UP

It's shrimp season again in the gulf, and the FDA says people should have no fear of grabbing a po' boy or sitting down to a bowl of gumbo. But nearly 85 percent of oyster reefs were lost. Catches of grouper and red snapper remain small. Government scientists have tracked three spikes in dolphin deaths since the gusher. On average, more than one dolphin a day has washed up on the shores of the gulf in 2011. Whale and dolphin deaths could be 50 times the number of carcasses actually discovered, researchers say.

FISHERMEN: WORSE THAN EVER

Oceanographers worry that the spill has harmed marine life's ability to reproduce, endangering the livelihood of generations of fishermen on the Gulf Coast. Many fishermen believe BP has been negligent in paying restitution. Some claim that Bourbon Street strippers, New Orleans cabdrivers, and Hooters girls are getting restitution from BP while seafarers are being stiffed. In addition to the $20 billion pledged to the region, BP has promised $500 million for research and to boost local fishing.

REPUBLICAN GOVERNORS: SEIZED THE DAY

Unlike Hurricane Katrina, which was a disaster for Louisiana politicians, the oil spill gave the gulf's leaders a chance to shine. Mississippi Gov. Haley Barbour played his "aw shucks" part to the hilt. "Come on down here and play golf," he beckoned. Louisiana Gov. Bobby Jindal, always a comer, took a more alarmist tone, giving constant and detailed updates on his state's distress. Florida's Charlie Crist didn't fare so well: after losing his Senate race, he fled the GOP and is now out of office.

BARACK OBAMA: GETS OUT UNSCATHED

Remember when the spill was going to be Obama's Katrina? Back then, Peggy Noonan said, "I don't see how you politically survive this." But the spill proved just a small detour, and now it barely ranks on the list of issues threatening his approval ratings. With skyrocketing oil prices, a looming battle over the debt ceiling, and turmoil in the Middle East, the spill is the least of Obama's headaches.

The Spill, The Scandal and the President[*]

By Tim Dickinson
Rolling Stone, June 24, 2010

On May 27th, more than a month into the worst environmental disaster in U.S. history, Barack Obama strode to the podium in the East Room of the White House. For weeks, the administration had been insisting that BP alone was to blame for the catastrophic oil spill in the Gulf—and the ongoing failure to stop the massive leak. "They have the technical expertise to plug the hole," White House spokesman Robert Gibbs had said only six days earlier. "It is their responsibility." The president, Gibbs added, lacked the authority to play anything more than a supervisory role—a curious line of argument from an administration that has reserved the right to assassinate American citizens abroad and has nationalized much of the auto industry. "If BP is not accomplishing the task, can you just federalize it?" a reporter asked. "No," Gibbs replied.

Now, however, the president was suddenly standing up to take command of the cleanup effort. "In case you were wondering who's responsible," Obama told the nation, "I take responsibility." Sounding chastened, he acknowledged that his administration had failed to adequately reform the Minerals Management Service, the scandal-ridden federal agency that for years had essentially allowed the oil industry to self-regulate. "There wasn't sufficient urgency," the president said. "Absolutely I take responsibility for that." He also admitted that he had been too credulous of the oil giants: "I was wrong in my belief that the oil companies had their act together when it came to worst-case scenarios." He unveiled a presidential commission to investigate the disaster, discussed the resignation of the head of MMS, and extended a moratorium on new deepwater drilling. "The buck," he reiterated the next day on the sullied Louisiana coastline, "stops with me."

What didn't stop was the gusher. Hours before the president's press conference, an ominous plume of oil six miles wide and 22 miles long was discovered snaking its way toward Mobile Bay from BP's wellhead next to the wreckage of its Deepwater Horizon rig. Admiral Thad Allen, the U.S. commander overseeing the cleanup,

[*] Copyright © Rolling Stone LLC. All rights reserved.

framed the spill explicitly as an invasion: "The enemy is coming ashore," he said. Louisiana beaches were assaulted by blobs of oil that began to seep beneath the sand; acres of marshland at the "Bird's Foot," where the Mississippi meets the Gulf, were befouled by s**t-brown crude—a death sentence for wetlands that serve as the cradle for much of the region's vital marine life. By the time Obama spoke, it was increasingly evident that this was not merely an ecological disaster. It was the most devastating assault on American soil since 9/11.

Like the attacks by Al Qaeda, the disaster in the Gulf was preceded by ample warnings—yet the administration had ignored them. Instead of cracking down on MMS, as he had vowed to do even before taking office, Obama left in place many of the top officials who oversaw the agency's culture of corruption. He permitted it to rubber-stamp dangerous drilling operations by BP—a firm with the worst safety record of any oil company—with virtually no environmental safeguards, using industry-friendly regulations drafted during the Bush years. He calibrated his response to the Gulf spill based on flawed and misleading estimates from BP—and then deployed his top aides to lowball the flow rate at a laughable 5,000 barrels a day, long after the best science made clear this catastrophe would eclipse the *Exxon Valdez*.

Even after the president's press conference, *Rolling Stone* has learned, the administration knew the spill could be far worse than its "best estimate" acknowledged. That same day, the president's Flow Rate Technical Group—a team of scientists charged with establishing the gusher's output—announced a new estimate of 12,000 to 25,000 barrels, based on calculations from video of the plume. In fact, according to interviews with team members and scientists familiar with its work, that figure represents the plume group's minimum estimate. The upper range was not included in their report because scientists analyzing the flow were unable to reach a consensus on how bad it could be. "The upper bound from the plume group, if it had come out, is very high," says Timothy Crone, a marine geophysicist at Columbia University who has consulted with the government's team. "That's why they had resistance internally. We're talking 100,000 barrels a day."

The median figure for Crone's independent calculations is 55,000 barrels a day—the equivalent of an *Exxon Valdez* every five days. "That's what the plume team's numbers show too," Crone says. A source privy to internal discussions at one of the world's top oil companies confirms that the industry privately agrees with such estimates. "The industry definitely believes the higher-end values," the source says. "That's accurate—if not more than that." The reason, he adds, is that BP appears to have unleashed one of the 10 most productive wells in the Gulf. "BP screwed up a really big, big find," the source says. "And if they can't cap this, it's not going to blow itself out anytime soon."

Even worse, the "moratorium" on drilling announced by the president does little to prevent future disasters. The ban halts exploratory drilling at only 33 deepwater operations, shutting down less than one percent of the total wells in the Gulf. Interior Secretary Ken Salazar, the Cabinet-level official appointed by Obama to rein in the oil industry, boasts that "the moratorium is not a moratorium that will affect production"—which continues at 5,106 wells in the Gulf, including 591 in deep water.

Most troubling of all, the government has allowed BP to continue deep-sea production at its Atlantis rig—one of the world's largest oil platforms. Capable of drawing 200,000 barrels a day from the seafloor, Atlantis is located only 150 miles off the coast of Louisiana, in waters nearly 2,000 feet deeper than BP drilled at Deepwater Horizon. According to congressional documents, the platform lacks required engineering certification for as much as 90 percent of its subsea components—a flaw that internal BP documents reveal could lead to "catastrophic" errors. In a May 19th letter to Salazar, 26 congressmen called for the rig to be shut down immediately. "We are very concerned," they wrote, "that the tragedy at Deepwater Horizon could foreshadow an accident at BP Atlantis."

The administration's response to the looming threat? According to an e-mail to a congressional aide from a staff member at MMS, the agency has had "zero contact" with Atlantis about its safety risks since the Deepwater rig went down.

It's tempting to believe that the Gulf spill, like so many disasters inherited by Obama, was the fault of the Texas oilman who preceded him in office. But, though George W. Bush paved the way for the catastrophe, it was Obama who gave BP the green light to drill. "Bush owns eight years of the mess," says Rep. Darrell Issa, a Republican from California. "But after more than a year on the job, Salazar owns it too."

During the Bush years, the Minerals Management Service, the agency in the Interior Department charged with safeguarding the environment from the ravages of drilling, descended into rank criminality. According to reports by Interior's inspector general, MMS staffers were both literally and figuratively in bed with the oil industry. When agency staffers weren't joining industry employees for coke parties or trips to corporate ski chalets, they were having sex with oil-company officials. But it was American taxpayers and the environment that were getting screwed. MMS managers were awarded cash bonuses for pushing through risky offshore leases, auditors were ordered not to investigate shady deals, and safety staffers routinely accepted gifts from the industry, allegedly even allowing oil companies to fill in their own inspection reports in pencil before tracing over them in pen.

"The oil companies were running MMS during those years," Bobby Maxwell, a former top auditor with the agency, told *Rolling Stone* last year. "Whatever they wanted, they got. Nothing was being enforced across the board at MMS."

Salazar himself has worked hard to foster the impression that the "prior administration" is to blame for the catastrophe. In reality, though, the Obama administration was fully aware from the outset of the need to correct the lapses at MMS that led directly to the disaster in the Gulf. In fact, Obama specifically nominated Salazar—his "great" and "dear" friend—to force the department to "clean up its act." For too long, Obama declared, Interior has been "seen as an appendage of commercial interests" rather than serving the people. "That's going to change under Ken Salazar."

Salazar took over Interior in January 2009, vowing to restore the department's "respect for scientific integrity." He immediately traveled to MMS headquarters outside Denver and delivered a beat-down to staffers for their "blatant and criminal conflicts of interest and self-dealing" that had "set one of the worst examples of corruption and abuse in government." Promising to "set the standard for reform," Salazar declared, "The American people will know the Minerals Management Service as a defender of the taxpayer. You are the ones who will make special interests play by the rules." Dressed in his trademark Stetson and bolo tie, Salazar boldly proclaimed, "There's a new sheriff in town."

Salazar's early moves certainly created the impression that he meant what he said. Within days of taking office, he jettisoned the Bush administration's plan to open 300 million acres—in Alaska, the Gulf, and up and down both coasts—to offshore drilling. The proposal had been published in the Federal Register literally at midnight on the day that Bush left the White House. Salazar denounced the plan as "a headlong rush of the worst kind," saying it would have put in place "a process rigged to force hurried decisions based on bad information." Speaking to *Rolling Stone* in March 2009, the secretary underscored his commitment to reform. "We have embarked on an ambitious agenda to clean up the mess," he insisted. "We have the inspector general involved with us in a preventive mode so that the department doesn't commit the same mistakes of the past." The crackdown, he added, "goes beyond just codes of ethics."

Except that it didn't. Salazar did little to tamp down on the lawlessness at MMS, beyond referring a few employees for criminal prosecution and ending a Bush-era program that allowed oil companies to make their "royalty" payments—the amount they owe taxpayers for extracting a scarce public resource—not in cash but in crude. And instead of putting the brakes on new offshore drilling, Salazar immediately throttled it up to record levels. Even though he had scrapped the Bush plan, Salazar put 53 million offshore acres up for lease in the Gulf in his first year alone—an all-time high. The aggressive leasing came as no surprise, given Salazar's track record. "This guy has a long, long history of promoting offshore oil drilling—that's his thing," says Kierán Suckling, executive director of the Center for Biological Diversity. "He's got a highly specific soft spot for offshore oil drilling." As a senator, Salazar not only steered passage of the Gulf of Mexico Energy Security Act, which opened 8 million acres in the Gulf to drilling, he even criticized President Bush for not forcing oil companies to develop existing leases faster.

Salazar was far less aggressive, however, when it came to making good on his promise to fix MMS. Though he criticized the actions of "a few rotten apples" at the agency, he left long-serving lackeys of the oil industry in charge. "The people that are ethically challenged are the career managers, the people who come up through the ranks," says a marine biologist who left the agency over the way science was tampered with by top officials. "In order to get promoted at MMS, you better get invested in this pro-development oil culture." One of the Bush-era managers whom Salazar left in place was John Goll, the agency's director for Alaska. Shortly after, the Interior secretary announced a reorganization of MMS in the wake of the Gulf disaster, Goll called a staff meeting and served cake decorated with the words "Drill, baby, drill."

Salazar also failed to remove Chris Oynes, a top MMS official who had been a central figure in a multibillion-dollar scandal that Interior's inspector general called "a jaw-dropping example of bureaucratic bungling." In the 1990s, industry lobbyists secured a sweetheart subsidy from Congress: Drillers would pay no royalties on oil extracted in deep water until prices rose above $28 a barrel. But this trip-wire was conveniently omitted in Gulf leases overseen by Oynes—a mistake that will let the oil giants pocket as much as $53 billion. Instead of being fired for this [foul-up], however, Oynes was promoted by Bush to become associate director for offshore drilling—a position he kept under Salazar until the Gulf disaster hit.

"Employees describe being in Interior—not just MMS, but the other agencies—as the third Bush term," says Jeff Ruch, executive director of Public Employees for Environmental Responsibility, which represents federal whistle-blowers. "They're working for the same managers who are implementing the same policies. Why would you expect a different result?"

The tale of the Deepwater Horizon disaster is, at its core, the tale of two blow-out preventers: one mechanical, one regulatory. The regulatory blowout preventer failed long before BP ever started to drill—precisely because Salazar kept in place the crooked environmental guidelines the Bush administration implemented to favor the oil industry.

MMS has fully understood the worst-case scenarios for deep-sea oil blowouts for more than a decade. In May 2000, an environmental assessment for deepwater drilling in the Gulf presciently warned that "spill responses may be complicated by the potential for very large magnitude spills (because of the high production rates associated with deepwater wells)." The report noted that the oil industry "has estimated worst-case spill volumes ranging from 5,000 to 116,000 barrels a day for 120 days," and it even anticipated the underwater plumes of oil that are currently haunting the Gulf: "Oil released subsea (e.g., subsea blowout or pipeline leak) in these deepwater environments could remain submerged for some period of time and travel away from the spill site." The report ominously concluded, "There are few practical spill-response options for dealing with submerged oil."

That same month, an MMS research document developed with deepwater drillers—including the company then known as BP Amoco—warned that such a spill could spell the end for offshore operations. The industry could "ill afford a deepwater blowout," the document cautions, adding that "no single company has the solution" to such a catastrophe. "The real test will come if a deepwater blowout occurs."

Enter the Bush administration. Rather than heeding such warnings, MMS simply assumed that a big spill couldn't happen. "There was a complete failure to even contemplate the possibility of a disaster like the one in the Gulf," says Holly Doremus, an environmental-law expert at the University of California. "In their thinking, a big spill would be something like 5,000 barrels, and the oil wouldn't even reach the shoreline." In fact, Bush's five-year plan for offshore drilling described a "large oil spill" as no more than 1,500 barrels. In April 2007, an environmental assessment covering the area where BP would drill concluded that blowouts were "low probability and low risk," even though a test funded by MMS had found that blowout preventers failed 28 percent of the time. And an environmental assessment for BP's lease block concluded that offshore spills "are not expected to damage significantly any wetlands along the Gulf Coast."

In reality, MMS had little way to assess the risk to wildlife, since a new policy instituted under Bush scrapped environmental analysis and fast-tracked permits. Declaring that oil companies themselves were "in the best position to determine the environmental effects" of drilling, the new rules pre-qualified deep-sea drillers to receive a "categorical exclusion"—an exemption from environmental review that was originally intended to prevent minor projects, like outhouses on hiking trails, from being tied up in red tape. "There's no analytical component to a cat-ex," says a former MMS scientist. "You have technicians, not scientists, that are simply checking boxes to make sure all the T's are crossed. They just cut and paste from previous approvals."

Nowhere was the absurdity of the policy more evident than in the application that BP submitted for its Deepwater Horizon well only two months after Obama took office. BP claims that a spill is "unlikely" and states that it anticipates "no adverse impacts" to endangered wildlife or fisheries. Should a spill occur, it says, "no significant adverse impacts are expected" for the region's beaches, wetlands and coastal nesting birds. The company, noting that such elements are "not required" as part of the application, contains no scenario for a potential blowout, and no site-specific plan to respond to a spill. Instead, it cites an Oil Spill Response Plan that it had prepared for the entire Gulf region. Among the sensitive species BP anticipates protecting in the semitropical Gulf? "Walruses" and other cold-water mammals, including sea otters and sea lions. The mistake appears to be the result of a sloppy cut-and-paste job from BP's drilling plans for the Arctic. Even worse: Among the "primary equipment providers" for "rapid deployment of spill response resources," BP inexplicably provides the Web address of a Japanese home-shopping network. Such glaring errors expose the 582-page response "plan" as nothing more than a paperwork exercise. "It was clear that nobody read it," says Ruch, who represents government scientists.

"This response plan is not worth the paper it is written on," said Rick Steiner, a retired professor of marine science at the University of Alaska who helped lead the scientific response to the *Valdez* disaster. "Incredibly, this voluminous document never once discusses how to stop a deepwater blowout."

Scientists like Steiner had urgently tried to alert Obama to the depth of the rot at MMS. "I talked to the transition team," Steiner says. "I told them that MMS was a disaster and needed to be seriously reformed." A top-to-bottom restructuring of MMS didn't require anything more than Ken Salazar's will: The agency only exists by order of the Interior secretary. "He had full authority to change anything he wanted," says Rep. Issa, a longtime critic of MMS. "He didn't use it." Even though Salazar knew that the environmental risks of offshore drilling had been covered up under Bush, he failed to order new assessments. "They could have said, 'We cannot conclude there won't be significant impacts from drilling until we redo those reviews,'" says Brendan Cummings, senior counsel for the Center for Biological Diversity. "But the oil industry would have cried foul. And what we've seen with Salazar is that when the oil industry squeaks, he retreats."

Under Salazar, MMS continued to issue categorical exclusions to companies like BP, even when they lacked the necessary permits to protect endangered species. A preliminary review of the BP disaster conducted by scientists with the independent Deepwater Horizon Study Group concludes that MMS failed to enforce a host of environmental laws, including the Clean Water Act. "MMS and Interior are equally responsible for the failures here," says the former agency scientist. "They weren't willing to take the regulatory steps that could have prevented this incident."

Had MMS been following the law, it would never have granted BP a categorical exclusion—which are applicable only to activities that have "no significant effect on the human environment." At a recent hearing, Sen. Sheldon Whitehouse grilled Salazar about Interior's own handbook on categorical exclusions, which bars their issuance for offshore projects in "relatively untested deep water" or "utilizing new or unusual technology"—standards that Whitehouse called "plainly pertinent" for BP's rig. "It's hard for me to see that that's a determination that could have been made in good faith," Whitehouse said, noting that the monstrously complex task of drilling for oil a mile beneath the surface of the ocean appeared to have been given less oversight than is required of average Americans rewiring their homes. "Who was watching?"

Not the Interior secretary. Salazar did not even ensure that MMS had a written manual—required under Interior's own rules—for complying with environmental laws. According to an investigation in March by the Government Accountability Office, MMS managers relied instead on informal "institutional knowledge"—passed down from the Bush administration. The sole written guidance appeared on a website that only provided, according to the report, "one paragraph about assessing environmental impacts of oil and gas activities, not detailed instructions that could lead an analyst through the process of drafting an environmental assessment or environmental impact statement."

"People are being really circumspect, not pointing the finger at Salazar and Obama," says Rep. Raul Grijalva, who oversees the Interior Department as chair of the House subcommittee on public lands. "But the troublesome point is, the administration knew that it had this rot in the middle of the process on offshore drilling—yet it empowered an already discredited, disgraced agency to essentially be in charge."

On April 6th of last year, less than a month after BP submitted its application, MMS gave the oil giant the go-ahead to drill in the Gulf without a comprehensive environmental review. The one-page approval put no restrictions on BP, issuing only a mild suggestion that would prove prescient: "Exercise caution while drilling due to indications of shallow gas."

BP is the last oil company on Earth that Salazar and MMS should have allowed to regulate itself. The firm is implicated in each of the worst oil disasters in American history, dating back to the *Exxon Valdez* in 1989. At the time, BP directed the industry consortium that bungled the cleanup response to *Valdez* during the fateful early hours of the spill, when the worst of the damage occurred. Vital equipment was buried under snow, no cleanup ship was standing by and no containment barge was available to collect skimmed oil. Exxon, quickly recognizing what still seems to elude the Obama administration, quickly shunted BP aside and took control of the spill.

In March 2006, BP was responsible for an Alaska pipeline rupture that spilled more than 250,000 gallons of crude into Prudhoe Bay—at the time, a spill second in size only to the *Valdez* disaster. Investigators found that BP had repeatedly ignored internal warnings about corrosion brought about by "draconian" cost cutting. The company got off cheap in the spill: While the EPA recommended slapping the firm with as much as $672 million in fines, the Bush administration allowed it to settle for just $20 million.

BP has also cut corners at the expense of its own workers. In 2005, 15 workers were killed and 170 injured after a tower filled with gasoline exploded at a BP refinery in Texas. Investigators found that the company had flouted its own safety procedures and illegally shut off a warning system before the blast. An internal cost-benefit analysis conducted by BP—explicitly based on the children's tale *The Three Little Pigs*—revealed that the oil giant had considered making buildings at the refinery blast-resistant to protect its workers (the pigs) from an explosion (the wolf). BP knew lives were on the line: "If the wolf blows down the house, the piggy is gobbled." But the company determined it would be cheaper to simply pay off the families of dead pigs.

After the blast, BP pleaded guilty to a felony, paying $50 million to settle a criminal investigation and another $21 million for violating federal safety laws. But the fines failed to force BP to change its ways. In October, Labor Secretary Hilda Solis hit the company with a proposed $87 million in new fines—the highest in history—for continued safety violations at the same facility. Since 2007, according to analysis by the Center for Public Integrity, BP has received 760 citations for "egregious and willful" safety violations—those "committed with plain indifference to or intentional disregard for employee safety and health." The rest of the oil industry combined has received a total of one.

The company applied the same deadly cost-cutting mentality to its oil rig in the Gulf. BP, it is important to note, is less an oil company than a bank that finances oil exploration; unlike ExxonMobil, which owns most of the equipment it uses to drill, BP contracts out almost everything. That includes the Deepwater Horizon rig that it leased from a firm called Transocean. BP shaved $500,000 off its overhead by deploying a blowout preventer without a remote-control trigger—a failsafe measure required in many countries but not mandated by MMS, thanks to intense industry lobbying. It opted to use cheap, single-walled piping for the well, and installed only six of the 21 cement spacers recommended by its contractor,

Halliburton—decisions that significantly increased the risk of a severe explosion. It also skimped on critical testing that could have shown whether explosive gas was getting into the system as it was being cemented, and began removing mud that protected the well before it was sealed with cement plugs.

As BP was cutting corners aboard the rig, the Obama administration was plotting the greatest expansion of offshore drilling in half a century. In 2008, as prices at the pump neared $5 a gallon, President Bush had lifted an executive moratorium on offshore drilling outside the Gulf that had been implemented by his father following the *Exxon Valdez*. On the campaign trail, Obama had stressed that offshore drilling "will not make a real dent in current gas prices or meet the long-term challenge of energy independence." But once in office, he bowed to the politics of "drill, baby, drill." Hoping to use oil as a bargaining chip to win votes for climate legislation in Congress, Obama unveiled an aggressive push for new offshore drilling in the Arctic, the Southeastern seaboard and new waters in the Gulf, closer to Florida than ever before. In doing so, he ignored his administration's top experts on ocean science, who warned that the offshore plan dramatically understated the risks of an oil spill and petitioned Salazar to exempt the Arctic from drilling until more scientific studies could be conducted.

Undeterred, Obama and Salazar appeared together at Andrews Air Force Base on March 31st to introduce the plan. The stagecraft was pure Rove in its technicolor militaristic patriotism. The president's podium was set up in front of the cockpit of an F-18, flanked by a massive American flag. "We are not here to do what is easy," Salazar declared. "We are here to do what is right." He insisted that his reforms at MMS were working: "We are making decisions based on sound information and sound science." The president, for his part, praised Salazar as "one of the finest secretaries of Interior we've ever had" and stressed that his administration had studied the drilling plan for more than a year. "This is not a decision that I've made lightly," he said. Two days later, he issued an even more sweeping assurance. "It turns out, by the way, that oil rigs today generally don't cause spills," the president said. "They are technologically very advanced."

Eighteen days later, on the eve of the 40th anniversary of Earth Day, the Deepwater Horizon rig went off like a bomb.

From the start of its operation in the Gulf, BP had found itself struggling against powerful "kicks" from gas buildup, just as MMS had warned. Now, on April 20th, the pent-up methane exploded in a fireball that incinerated 11 workers. Like a scene out of a real-life Jerry Bruckheimer film, the half-billion-dollar rig—32,000 tons and 30 stories tall—listed over and sank to the bottom two days later, taking a mile of pipe down with it.

Within hours, the government assembled a response team at the "war room" of the National Oceanographic and Atmospheric Administration in Seattle. The scene, captured by a NOAA cameraman and briefly posted on the agency's website, provides remarkable insight into the government's engagement during the earliest hours of the catastrophe, and, more troubling, the role of top administration figures in downplaying its horrific scope.

At a conference table, nearly a dozen scientists gather around a map of the Gulf. Joshua Slater, a commissioned NOAA officer dressed in his uniform, runs the show. "So far we've created a trajectory [of the slick] that was passed up the chain of command to the Coast Guard and eventually to the president showing where the oil might go," he tells the assembled team. BP's remote operated sub, he adds, "was unsuccessful in activating the blowout preventers, so we're gearing up right now."

An NOAA expert on oil disasters jumps in: "I think we need to be prepared for it to be the spill of the decade."

Written on a whiteboard at the front of the room is the government's initial, worst-case estimate of the size of the spill. While the figure is dramatically higher than any official estimate issued by BP or the government, it is in line with the high-end calculations by scientists who have monitored the spill.

"Estm: 64k–110k bbls/Day." The equivalent of up to three *Exxon Valdez* spills gushing into the Gulf of Mexico every week.

Damningly, the whiteboard also documents the disconnect between what the government suspected to be the magnitude of the disaster and the far lower estimates it was feeding to the public. Written below the federal estimate are the words, "300,000 gal/day reported on CNN." Appearing on the network that same day on a video feed from the Gulf, Coast Guard Rear Adm. Mary Landry insisted that the government had no figure. "We do not have an estimate of the amount of crude emanating from the wellhead," she said.

Later in the video, a voice on speakerphone with a heavy Southern accent reveals that government scientists were concerned from the very beginning about underwater plumes of oil—a reality that NOAA administrator Jane Lubchenco and BP executives are still seeking to downplay. "They weren't sure how that oil was going to react once it was spilled," the voice says. "Whether it was going to rise, or form layers and start twisting around." The government, in short, knew from the start that surface measurements of the oil slick—on which it would premise its absurdly low estimate of 5,000 barrels a day—were likely to be unreliable.

By that evening, the White House was gearing up for an urgent response. The president convened an emergency meeting in the Oval Office with Adm. Thad Allen, Homeland Security Secretary Janet Napolitano, Interior Secretary Ken Salazar and top White House deputies Rahm Emanuel, Carol Browner and Larry Summers. Obama forcefully instructed his team that the response to the oil spill should be treated as a "number-one priority."

But then the fog of war set in. The following day, the Coast Guard—relying on assurances from BP—declared that the spill appeared to be limited to oil that was stored aboard the sunken rig. With a worst-case crisis seemingly averted, Obama checked out, heading off for a long weekend in Asheville, North Carolina, where he and the first lady would stop for ribs at a barbecue joint called 12 Bones Smokehouse before checking into the Grove Park Inn, a golf resort and spa. Asked whether the spill would hamper the president's offshore drilling agenda, spokesman Gibbs made light of the disaster. "I don't honestly think it opens up a whole new series of questions," he said. "I doubt this is the first accident that has happened, and I doubt it will be the last."

The next day, April 24th, Landry told reporters that leaks had been discovered in the riser pipe and estimated the flow at 1,000 barrels a day. "This is a very serious spill," she said. Over the next five days, the administration took significant steps to deal with the spill, but the effort fell far short of what was needed to tackle a crisis that BP was already privately estimating could be as catastrophic as 14,000 barrels a day. A Joint Information Center—a strange partnership involving BP, the Coast Guard and MMS—was set up in Louisiana. Senior officials met with BP CEO Tony Hayward to "receive briefings on the company efforts to stop the flow." The Navy opened a base in Florida as a staging area for BP's cleanup work. Salazar ordered inspections for rigs throughout the Gulf and visited BP's command center in Houston. Napolitano began an investigation into the disaster.

The president himself was occupied elsewhere. After returning from his vacation, Obama spent Monday, April 26th palling around with Derek Jeter and the New York Yankees, congratulating them on their World Series victory. He later took time to chat with the president of Honduras. When he put in a call to Gov. Haley Barbour of Mississippi, it was to talk about tornadoes that had caused damage in that state, with only a brief mention of the oil spill. On Tuesday the 27th, Obama visited a wind-turbine plant in Iowa. Wednesday the 28th, he toured a biofuels refinery in Missouri and talked up financial reform in Quincy, Illinois. He didn't mention the oil spill or the Gulf.

That evening, administration officials received news that—to judge from their subsequent response—scared the s**t out of them. "The following is not public," a confidential NOAA advisory stressed. "Two additional release points were found today in the tangled riser. If the riser pipe deteriorates further, the flow could become unchecked, resulting in a release volume an order of magnitude higher than previously thought. There is no official change in the volume released but the [Coast Guard] is no longer stating that the release rate is 1,000 barrels a day. Instead they are saying that they are preparing for a worst-case release and bringing all assets to bear."

Standing before the cameras, a visibly shaken Landry bumbled through the reading of a press release. Although BP continued to believe its estimate of 1,000 barrels a day, she said, "NOAA experts believe the output could be as much as 5,000 barrels." The remarks established, for the first time, a figure that both BP and the government would stick to long past its sell-by date.

After he was briefed that evening, Obama told his deputies to contact the Pentagon. The following day, Napolitano declared the BP disaster, which was now approaching the size of Puerto Rico, an "Oil Spill of National Significance"—the designation required to draw on regional resources and to appoint an incident commander to coordinate a federal response. It had taken a full week after Deepwater Horizon exploded for the government to become fully engaged—a critical lapse that allowed the crisis to spiral out of control.

The White House press office organized a show of overwhelming force, with Gibbs convening Browner, Napolitano, Deputy Interior Secretary David Hayes, EPA chief Lisa Jackson and Coast Guard Rear Adm. Sally Brice-O'Hara for a single press conference on April 29th. Though clearly meant to signal engagement, the all-star crew didn't have their message straight. When Brice-O'Hara praised "the professionalism of our partner, BP," Napolitano quickly barked, "They are not our partner! They are not our partner!" For her part, Napolitano revealed that she didn't know whether the Defense Department possessed any assets that could help contain the spill, and referred vaguely to "whatever methodologies" BP was using to seal the well.

Instead of seizing the reins, the Obama administration cast itself in a supporting role, insisting that BP was responsible for cleaning up the mess. "When you say the company is responsible and the government has oversight," a reporter asked Gibbs on May 3rd, "does that mean that the government is ultimately in charge of the cleanup?" Gibbs was blunt: "No," he insisted, "the responsible party is BP." In fact, the National Oil and Hazardous Substances Pollution Contingency Plan— the federal regulations that lay out the command-and-control responsibilities for cleaning up an oil spill—makes clear that an oil company like BP cannot be left in charge of such a serious disaster. The plan plainly states that the government must "direct all federal, state or private actions" to clean up a spill "where a discharge or threat of discharge poses a substantial threat to the public health or welfare of the United States."

"The government is in a situation where it's required to be in charge," says William Funk, a professor of environmental and administrative law at Lewis and Clark College who previously worked as a staff attorney in the Justice Department.

What's more, the administration failed to ensure that BP was prepared to respond to the mess on the surface, where a lack of ships and equipment has left more than 100 miles of the coast—including vast stretches of fragile marshlands— covered in crude. According to MMS regulations, the agency is supposed to "inspect the stockpiles of industry's equipment for the containment and cleanup of oil spills." In BP's case, the agency should have made sure the company was prepared to clean up a spill of 250,000 barrels a day. But when *Rolling Stone* asked MMS whether BP had the required containment equipment on hand, the agency's head of public affairs in the Gulf replied, "I am not clear if MMS has the info that you are requesting."

The effect of leaving BP in charge of capping the well, says a scientist involved in the government side of the effort, has been "like a drunk driver getting into a car wreck and then helping the police with the accident investigation." Indeed, the administration has seemed oddly untroubled about leaving the Gulf's fate in the hands of a repeat criminal offender, and uncurious about the crimes that may have been committed leading up to the initial sinking of the rig. The Obama Justice Department took more than 40 days after the initial blast killed 11 workers to announce it was opening a criminal probe.

From the start, the administration has seemed intent on allowing BP to operate in near-total secrecy. Much of what the public knows about the crisis it owes to Rep. Ed Markey, who chairs the House Subcommittee on Energy and the Environment. Under pressure from Markey, BP was forced to release footage of the gusher, admit that its early estimates put the leak as high as 14,000 barrels a day and post a live feed of its undersea operations on the Internet—video that administration officials had possessed from the earliest days of the disaster. "We cannot trust BP," Markey said. "It's clear they have been hiding the actual consequences of this spill."

But rather than applying such skepticism to BP's math, the Obama administration has instead attacked scientists who released independent estimates of the spill. When one scientist funded by NOAA released a figure much higher than the government's estimate, he found himself being pressured to retract it by officials at the agency. "Are you sure you want to keep saying this?" they badgered him. Lubchenco, the head of NOAA, even denounced as "misleading" and "premature" reports that scientists aboard the research vessel *Pelican* had discovered a massive subsea oil plume. Speaking to PBS, she offered a bizarre denial of the obvious. "It's clear that there is something at depth," she said, "but we don't even know that it's oil yet."

Scientists were stunned that NOAA, an agency widely respected for its scientific integrity, appeared to have been co-opted by the White House spin machine. "NOAA has actively pushed back on every fact that has ever come out," says one ocean scientist who works with the agency. "They're denying until the facts are so overwhelming, they finally come out and issue an admittance." Others are furious at the agency for criticizing the work of scientists studying the oil plumes rather than *leading* them. "Why they didn't have vessels there right then and start to gather the scientific data on oil and what the impacts are to different organisms is incxcusable," says a former government marine biologist. "They should have been right on top of that." Only six weeks into the disaster did the agency finally deploy its own research vessel to investigate the plumes.

The failure of the Obama administration to crack down on BP—and to tackle the crisis with the full force of the federal government—is likely to haunt the Gulf Coast for decades to come. Oil continues to lap up onshore in Louisiana, Alabama, Mississippi and Florida. Pelican rookeries are fouled, their eggs and nests soaked in oil. The region's fisheries—some of the richest in the world—are imperiled; anglers and shrimpers have been barred from more than a third of the Gulf's waters, which may never fully recover from the toxic stew of crude and chemical dispersant now twisting in its depths. The region's beaches are empty, and tourist towns are dying. Administration officials now admit that the oil may continue to gush into the Gulf until August, when relief wells are finally in place.

Both the government and BP have reasons to downplay the extent of the spill. For BP, the motive is financial: Under the Clean Water Act, the company could owe fines of as much as $4,300 for every barrel spilled, in addition to royalties for the oil it is squandering. For the Obama administration, the disaster threatens to derail the president's plan to expand offshore drilling. "It's crystal clear what the federal response to the tragedy ought to be," said Sen. Frank Lautenberg, who chairs the Senate subcommittee on environmental health. "Bring a dangerous off-shore drilling pursuit to an end."

The administration, however, has made clear that it has no intention of reversing its plan to expand offshore drilling. Four weeks into the BP disaster, when Salazar was questioned in a Senate hearing about the future of the president's plan, he was happy to stand up for the industry's desire to drill at any cost. "Isn't it true," asked Sen. Lamar Alexander, a Republican from Tennessee, "that as terrible as the tragedy is, that unless we want $14, $16, $18, $20-a-gallon gasoline, that it's not realistic to think that we would actually stop drilling for oil in the Gulf?" Unbowed by the catastrophe that was still unfolding on his watch, Salazar heartily agreed, testifying that the president had directed him to "move forward" on offshore drilling.

That may help explain why the administration has gone to unusual lengths to contain the spill's political fallout. On May 14th, two days after the first video of the gusher was released, the government allowed BP to apply a toxic dispersant that is banned in England at the source of the leak—an unprecedented practice in the deep ocean. "The effort should be in *recovering* the oil, not making it more difficult to recover by dispersing it," says Sylvia Earle, a famed oceanographer and former NOAA chief scientist who helped the agency confront the world's worst-ever oil spill in the Persian Gulf after the first Iraq War. The chemical assault appeared geared, she says, "to improving the appearance of the problem rather than solving the problem."

Critics of the administration's drilling plans fear that the president's decision to postpone drilling in the Arctic and appoint a commission to investigate the BP spill are merely stalling tactics, designed to blunt public anger about the disaster. "The way the PR is spinning is once that spill is plugged, then people declare victory," says Rep. Grijalva. "The commission stalls it long enough where the memory of the American people starts to fade a little bit on the issue. After that, we're back to where we were."

President Obama pushed to expand offshore drilling, in part, to win votes for climate legislation, which remains blocked in the Senate. The political calculus is understandable—the risk of an oil spill weighed against the far greater threat posed by global warming—but in the end, he may have succeeded only in compounding one environmental catastrophe with another. Even if the climate bill is eventually approved, the disaster in the Gulf will serve as a lasting and ugly reminder of the price we paid for our addiction to oil. "It was a bargain with the devil," says Steiner, the marine scientist who helped lead the response to the *Valdez* disaster. "And now the devil is gloating."

Oil and Water[*]

By Paul Burka
Texas Monthly, July 2010

The ability of nature to frustrate the will of man was already on full display in the Gulf of Mexico following the deadly explosion of the Deepwater Horizon rig when the ability of man to frustrate and embarrass himself came into focus as well. Apparently, the Minerals Management Service, the federal agency charged with regulating oil and gas operations on the outer continental shelf, believed that despite the catastrophic environmental disaster unfolding before it, the time was still right to drill, baby, drill. Even as oil gushed from the ocean floor, the MMS issued seventeen new permits and nineteen environmental waivers for offshore operations. This action was so tone-deaf that MMS director Elizabeth Birnbaum was forced to resign, and she was soon followed by associate director Chris Oynes. The house has been cleaned. Unfortunately, the Gulf of Mexico hasn't.

In a strange political season that has given rise to the tea party movement and energized a wave of conservative voters, the calamity in the Gulf raises one of the most volatile issues in American politics: What kind of government do we want? A government, as Rick Perry is fond of saying, that secures the border and delivers the mail and then gets out of the way? Or a government that recognizes that powerful interest groups have the ability to undermine the public interest to their own benefit and enters the fray to level the playing field? Big government or small? The argument goes back to the respective visions of America—an industrial and commercial powerhouse or a nation of yeoman farmers—as seen by Alexander Hamilton and Thomas Jefferson in the late eighteenth century. These competing visions continue to dominate American politics more than two hundred years later.

The massive spill has revealed a problem that reaches beyond the Gulf Coast. It is one more instance in which regulatory agencies like the MMS have failed to protect the public. One does not have to have a long memory: the lack of stringent enforcement of safety laws by the Mine Safety and Health Administration before the deadly explosion at the Upper Big Branch Mine, in West Virginia; the ability of

[*] Reprinted with permission from the July 2010 issue of TEXAS MONTHLY.

Toyota to persuade regulators to limit or avoid safety recalls and rules concerning uncontrolled acceleration; the warning by the Government Accountability Office that the Food and Drug Administration was not doing enough to protect the national food supply; the failure of the FDA to ensure the quality of children's medications made by Johnson & Johnson; and, of course, the ineptness of financial regulators who didn't foresee and couldn't mitigate the subprime mortgage crisis and the resulting economic meltdown.

An increasing number of people have lost faith in the government's ability to solve problems, and the continuing saga of the BP oil spill has emerged as a metaphor for the times. The Deepwater Horizon disaster is not, as Perry so rashly said, an act of God. It is incontrovertibly an act of man—of ineffectual regulators and corner-cutting oil companies. Both were charged with the duty of making certain that oil production in an ecologically sensitive area could proceed without harm to the environment. Both failed miserably. BP, for example, claimed in its permitting process that it was capable of containing a spill ten times as large as the current one. As for the MMS, it uses a lot of high-sounding words on its website, stating that its "oversight and regulatory framework ensure production and drilling are done in an environmentally responsible manner, and done safely." A more accurate statement would be "MMS oversight ensures that oil companies can do whatever they want to do without fear of consequences."

The BP debacle could have profound political implications in an election year. Barack Obama's critics have already charged that the oil spill is his Hurricane Katrina. There are a number of apt comparisons with that terrible storm: It is another disaster afflicting our neighbors in Louisiana; it is another indication that government is incapable of responding to a crisis; and it is another occasion to doubt the judgment of a president. Obama, like George W. Bush in 2005, was slow to appreciate the seriousness of the crisis and the political damage it could inflict on his presidency. But there is a significant difference between the Katrina and Deepwater Horizon disasters. Getting food and water to New Orleans after Katrina was the responsibility of the Federal Emergency Management Agency. The responsibility for responding to an oil spill belongs to the industry, thanks to a law passed after the *Exxon Valdez* spill, in 1989. The federal government has neither the legal standing nor the equipment nor the know-how to repair a damaged well. Unfortunately, BP, which has the legal standing and the equipment, doesn't seem to possess the know-how.

In addition to its failure to stop the oil from spewing out of the well, BP must depend on twenty-year-old technology like booms, skimmers, and dispersants to clean up the water and protect the coast. BP is using a dispersant called Corexit, which some marine toxicologists have warned will kill shrimp eggs and larvae. It may also be lethal to the microbes that naturally break down oil. Local fishermen who are unable to ply their trade have been hired by BP to clean up the oil, but toxicity levels in South Louisiana are already so high that workers have reported suffering from headaches and nausea. The fishermen told the *Los Angeles Times* that the company did not provide protective gear. BP is in control of the cleanup, but the government can still use its powers of persuasion.

So what has the government done? The same thing it did after 9/11: reorganize itself. Secretary of the Interior Ken Salazar announced in May a plan to break up the MMS into three divisions, one to supervise the leasing of federal lands for oil and gas operations, another to oversee safety and environmental protection, and a third to collect and audit royalty payments. But I doubt that any of this will make a difference. The problems involved in government regulation are so ingrained that it will take more than restructuring to overcome them. Foremost among them is the tendency for the regulators to become captives of the industry that they regulate. Government investigators charged in 2008 that the MMS suffered from "a culture of ethical failure." And how. Agency employees, their report said, had accepted gratuities such as meals and tickets to sporting events; some had even used drugs and had sex with energy company officials. As if that weren't bad enough, a recent investigation found that MMS regulators allowed industry representatives to fill in their inspection reports in pencil, after which the regulators traced over them in ink before turning them in to their superiors.

Even when the MMS tried to carry out its duty of protecting the safety of drilling operations, it was no match for Big Oil. At one point, the MMS proposed a rule establishing "Safety and Environmental Management Systems [SEMS] for Outer Continental Shelf Oil and Gas Operations" and invited comment from the industry. The response was uniformly negative. "The U.S. offshore industry has an excellent safety record; we strive for continuous improvement voluntarily, and thus this rulemaking is not justified," wrote a company called Wild Well Control, adding, "We strongly disagree that a mandated program as proposed is needed." ExxonMobil weighed in to urge that the MMS "allow operators and contractors with existing SEMS-equivalent programs [to] use their management systems in lieu of the proposed rule." Translation: Leave us alone.

If the oversight agencies don't have the power to rein in the companies they monitor, the last resort is the courts. Litigation is a long and slow process—the Supreme Court made its final ruling in the *Exxon Valdez* case in June 2008, nearly twenty years after the spill—but it does have the virtue, if successful, of hitting negligent companies in the one place that hurts them most: their bottom line. Attorney General Eric Holder has already announced that the federal government will pursue both criminal and civil investigations against BP. Criminalizing negligent drilling operations will hold guilty parties responsible; civil remedies such as canceling the leases of oil companies that despoil the environment will provide another deterrent. The president should ask Congress to lift the cap on damages, which in certain circumstances protects companies from large verdicts.

Among the casualties of the explosion could be U.S. energy policy. Major oil spills resulting from drilling operations are terrible environmental hazards, but fortunately they are rare. It would be self-defeating to permanently shut down operations on the outer continental shelf. The MMS estimates that the shelf contains 60 percent of the nation's remaining oil and 40 percent of its natural gas. America needs that energy. Risky though it may be, offshore oil and gas production must go on safely.

Ultimately the only thing that can improve the performance of government is public pressure. This election cycle happens to be one in which the public is engaged—or, if you prefer, enraged. I believe that the anger being expressed in the tea parties is a healthy development. Politics is always better when people are paying attention. But their anger is directed primarily at politicians, and that's the wrong target. It needs to be harnessed and redirected at the bad guys: the banks, the oil companies, the insurance companies, all the repositories of wealth and power that have created the messes we are in—and not just in the Gulf of Mexico.

BP Oil Spill[*]

Forgotten But Not Gone

By Charles Wohlforth
Los Angeles Times, April 20, 2011

From April into midsummer last year, Americans watched BP's oil spew from the seafloor into the Gulf of Mexico with outrage and guilt that came to feel like a chronic stomachache.

Then, on July 15, it stopped. And within a couple of weeks the bad feelings for a lot of us stopped too. There were reports that the surface oil was quickly disappearing. There was a government study that hopeful journalists misinterpreted to mean that most of the oil was gone.

But the oil wasn't gone, and it still isn't. Tar balls are washing around the gulf. Marshes are dying. Scientists say it's still too early to know the greatest share of the spill's environmental damage.

"The media left, so everyone assumed that meant the oil was gone too," said Aaron Viles of the Gulf Restoration Network in New Orleans.

The nation flits from one spectacle to the next with ever-accelerating speed, but the processes of nature unfold at their same, deliberate pace. Quick, superficial information alienates us from the ecosystems that sustain life, and that's made it more difficult to solve environmental problems.

The rate at which environmental disasters recede in our collective rearview mirror marks how fast the culture is moving. The Exxon Valdez oil spill in 1989 stuck in our consciousness much longer than BP's spill. Alaska's disaster happened in March; in August it was still major national news when Exxon tried to back off on needed cleanup efforts—the spotlight forced the company to promise more work. Public attention on the Alaska mess kept Congress focused until historic oil spill legislation passed, a year and a half after the accident.

[*] Article by Charles Wohlforth from the *Los Angeles Times*, originally published on April 20, 2011. All rights reserved. Reprinted with permission of the author.

Going back to an even slower time, historians credit the Santa Barbara blowout and oil spill of 1969 as starting the modern environmental movement. Images of oiled animals stuck around long enough to mobilize the public and power legislation and policy for years. Results included the Clean Water Act (1972), a beefed-up Clean Air Act (1970), the National Environmental Policy Act (1970) and the first Earth Day (1970).

Now, the anniversary of the BP spill comes with a feeling of "Whatever happened to . . . ?" Legislative efforts have stalled, and they're not particularly ambitious anyway. The BP spill spawned a commission, but its recommendations to Congress have been ignored.

Viles calls the situation "this national ADD about environmental issues." The attention deficit has many causes. Scholars have documented reduced interest in environmental issues when the economy is down. Storytelling biases also play a role. The story "Oil is still there" doesn't thrill like a starlet's fresh scandal or the predicament of the Chilean miners, which in August 2010 pulled the spotlight away from underwater oil plumes and potential gulf dead zones.

Compared with 1969 and 1989, the news cycle is on fast-forward, and our information sources are fractured. "Now it is so much easier to turn the page or click the channel and not have to deal with this stuff," said Anthony Leiserowitz of the Yale School of Forestry and Environmental Studies, "because we're creating these self-reflective mirrored halls where we don't have to see anything we don't want to think about."

Our disintegrating attention span matches our disintegrating common will to act on shared problems, at least at the national level. The country has needed federal policy on energy and climate change for decades, but that seems further away than ever. And even the largest oil spill in history, shown live on TV, couldn't spawn a national discussion about our energy sources.

But we do still act at the local level, where people still share knowledge and sustained interest. The newspapers of the Gulf Coast have stayed with the oil spill story, in all its complexity. Viles' Restoration Network has brought together 46 concerned groups to guide response and prevention efforts.

On climate change, as well, action has happened locally, in communities, cities, states and public-spirited businesses. University of Colorado policy scientist Ronald D. Brunner maintains that that's how it has to work: Social change must always precede dramatic political change.

Brunner has studied how communities that are empowered to deal with environmental threats tend to make the right decisions. Examples are diverse, including preparing for floods in the Midwest and dealing with melting permafrost in the Arctic. The key is giving those who live in an ecosystem the power to care for it.

That's an idea that has worked in Alaska, where post-spill legislation set up a well-funded local advisory council that has monitored oil handling in Prince William Sound and fought for improvements—like powerful tugboats to escort tankers all the way to open ocean—that have demonstrably prevented another accident.

We can't count on the federal government to stop disasters, because we can't count on the media or ourselves to pay attention to all the risks that face us as a nation. But community by community, we can watch over our own land and water. And we can demand that the nation respect our decisions.

CHARLES WOHLFORTH *is author of "The Fate of Nature: Rediscovering Our Ability to Rescue the Earth" (www.FateOfNature.com).*

America's Chernobyl[*]

By Ruth Conniff
The Progressive, July 2010

It is the worst environmental disaster our country has ever seen. Since the Deepwater Horizon oil rig blew up on April 20, killing eleven workers, tens of millions of gallons of oil have gushed into the ocean, poisoning birds and fish, destroying marine habitats, and devastating communities along the Gulf.

So much for "Drill, baby, drill."

Residents, local officials, and fishermen in Louisiana, Mississippi, Alabama, and Florida are stunned and grief-stricken as they watch the oil wash over beaches and oyster beds, coating birds with a sickening black film, destroying livelihoods, and altering, forever, the beautiful, fragile ecosystem of the Gulf.

The oil spill is "America's Chernobyl," Louie Miller of the Sierra Club in Gulfport, Mississippi, told local reporters. People who once thought offshore drilling was necessary now see it as "unacceptable," he adds. "I think that debate is over as a result of this. This is going to destroy the Mississippi and the Gulf Coast as we know it."

The disaster has had a powerful impact on the whole country's psyche. Energy exploration and environmental protection have reversed themselves as public priorities in the wake of the spill, according to a May 24–25 *USA Today*/Gallup poll. In March, 50 percent of Americans polled said it was more important to develop U.S. energy supplies than to protect the environment, as compared to 43 percent who took the opposite view. In the latest poll, 55 percent favored environmental protection while 39 percent chose energy development.

The fiasco in the Gulf made it painfully clear how our government left the oil companies in charge of deciding how to protect the environment, with devastating results.

The Minerals Management Service follows a 2005 policy that states: "The lessee or operator is in the best position to determine the environmental effects of its proposed activity."

* This piece was originally written for *The Progressive* magazine, 409 E Main St, Madison, WI 53703. www.progressive.org.

President Obama subsequently denounced the "cozy and corrupt" relationship between regulators and drillers, and he let the head of the minerals agency go. But only weeks before the spill, he had announced a plan—now on hold—to vastly expand offshore drilling and declared that it was not risky.

During Congressional hearings in May, Representative Henry Waxman, Democrat of California, cited BP documents that showed the company knew its blowout preventer on the Deepwater platform had failed a negative pressure test right before the disaster. A government engineer testified at the hearings that he never asked for proof that the blowout preventer worked. And a BP whistleblower told the *Huffington Post* that the company routinely falsified blowout preventer tests in Alaska.

The workers who lost their lives on the Deepwater rig knew before the explosion that something was terribly wrong. Survivors testified that their superiors told them to keep drilling even after problems had begun cropping up—right up until the explosion cost many of them their lives.

"It was hardly the first thing to go wrong," survivor Stephen Stone told Waxman's committee. Stone was a roustabout for Transocean, the company that owned the rig and leased it to BP. "We had to stop pumping four times in twenty days because of pumping problems," he testified.

After the explosion, when his lifeboat failed to descend, "I was pretty certain I was going to die," Stone testified. After he escaped, Transocean held him for twenty-eight hours, refusing to let him call his wife and tell her he was alive until he had taken a drug test and filed a written report. Transocean also asked him to sign a form releasing the company from liability for his injuries, he said.

"When these companies put their savings over our safety, they are gambling with our lives," he said. "You cannot allow BP and Transocean to conduct business this way."

For years, Transocean, BP, and other companies have been cutting corners on safety, causing massive environmental damage, and getting away with it.

It would be tragic if the Deepwater oil spill did not change that. Yet some members of Congress argue against lifting a liability cap of $75 million on the companies for disasters like the one in the Gulf.

On June 1, President Obama and Attorney General Eric Holder announced that the Administration had begun a criminal investigation into the causes of the spill. But the government's dependence on BP to clean up the spill complicates the matter. The "cozy and corrupt" relationship is not easy to unravel.

What we need now is a far more aggressive stance by the government.

BP has a long criminal record, including:

—A massive explosion in Texas in 2005 that killed fifteen workers and injured 170. The company pleaded guilty to felony charges and was fined more than $50 million.

—A leak in Prudhoe Bay that caused 4,800 barrels of oil to spill into Alaskan waters. Congress found company negligence and cost-cutting that led to safety violations.

Skimping on worker and environmental safety helped make BP the most profitable oil company in the world.

Abrahm Lustgarten, who has been reporting on BP's crimes for years, points out that the EPA could ban BP from receiving government contracts or drilling in federally controlled oil fields, through a process called "discretionary debarment."

This "could also lead to the cancellation of BP's existing federal leases, worth billions of dollars," Lustgarten says.

On behalf of the dead and injured workers and their families, the Justice Department should also file criminal suits.

"The worker safety issue has been completely lost in this story," says Tom O'Connor, executive director of the National Council for Occupational Safety and Health.

This is particularly important because not only rig workers but also the oil-spill cleanup crews say BP isn't giving them the protective equipment they need to work with oil and dispersants. And some workers are claiming that BP is hiding evidence of workers who have become ill as a result.

Bringing BP to justice is just the beginning. We need more visionary leadership. Senator Bernie Sanders of Vermont has introduced legislation that completely prohibits offshore drilling and exploration on the Atlantic and Pacific coasts and in much of the Gulf.

"[Obama] wants a moratorium for six months. We want a permanent ban," Sanders says.

Instead of offshore drilling, Sanders proposes an increase in fuel-mileage standards for automobiles to fifty miles per gallon by 2030.

Obama has spoken movingly about the need to end our addiction to fossil fuel. But he supports the Kerry-Lieberman American Power Act, a bill in the Senate that calls for a carbon cap, but also expands America's use of nuclear power and offshore drilling.

Environmental and public interest groups, including Friends of the Earth and Public Citizen, call the Kerry-Lieberman plan a gift to industrial polluters. The bill's supporters include BP.

For thirty years, we have known that we can't sustain our oil addiction forever. The spill in the Gulf should snap us out of our bender. We must finally transform our energy infrastructure. The Sierra Club proposes that America could get off fossil fuel entirely within twenty years if we begin seriously investing in renewables and clean energy technology.

We can't afford to wait for another oil spill—and another poisoned sea.

4

Pollution and the Island of Trash

Courtesy of the National Oceanic and Atmospheric Administration (NOAA)

Piles of marine refuse litter a beach in Hawaii.

Courtesy of the U.S. Navy

Sailors and Pacific Missile Range Facility personnel pick up trash during a beach clean up on June 24, 2011, in Barking Sand, Hawaii, in support of World Oceans Day, which was officially observed on June 8.

Editor's Introduction

In 1997, after competing in the Transpac boat race from Los Angeles to Hawaii, sailor, environmentalist, and oceanographer Charles J. Moore spent a week traversing the North Pacific Gyre. Located roughly 800 miles west of San Francisco, this "convergence zone" is home to high-pressure weather systems that cause ocean currents to spiral into each other and collect debris. As Moore looked into the water, he was shocked by the prevalence of plastic junk—"bottles, bottle caps, wrappers, fragments," as he wrote in an essay for *Natural History*. The experience led Moore to investigate the large-scale pooling of plastic pollutants and co-write the study "A Comparison of Plastic and Plankton in the North Pacific Central Gyre," in which he claimed to have found seven times more plastic per square kilometer than any researcher before him.

Moore's paper stoked fears of a "Great Pacific Garbage Patch," a floating trash heap often described as twice the size of Texas. In 2009, Oprah Winfrey called it "the most shocking thing I've ever seen," and in 2010, British musician Damon Albarn used the image as the conceptual centerpiece of *Plastic Beach*, his environmentally themed third album with the cartoon rock band Gorillaz.

In fact, there is no massive island of trash—at least not one that can be seen from a ship, much less walked across. Rather, research has shown the North Pacific is brimming with microscopic plastic particles, and in a 2008 follow-up study, Moore and his Algalita Marine Research Foundation noted a concentration of .004 grams per meter squared—the equivalent of a grain of rice in a bathtub of water. While the notion of a "Garbage Patch" may be gross exaggeration, scientists say the threat posed by plastic is very real. As tiny Myctophids, or "lantern fish," ingest the broken-down particles, they could send harmful chemicals up the food chain, endangering larger fish and the humans who eat them.

In "Wasted Waves: Surveying the Plastic Adrift in the World's Oceans," the piece that opens this chapter on water pollution, Anna Cummins describes the Earth's oceans as carrying "a thin veneer of hardened petroleum, synthesized into long carbon chains that are indigestible, mimic food, absorb oil-loving toxins, and are finding their way into the fish we harvest to feed the world." Rather than skim the water for plastic—a task she likens to "vacuuming America's highways for bubblegum wrappers"—Cummins suggests we resolve to keep new plastic out of our oceans and clean whatever flotsam and jetsam washes up on our shores.

The section continues with "Trashing the Island: Why the 'Garbage Patch' in the Mid-Pacific Is Not Nearly the Disaster It's Been Made Out to Be," in which Charlie Gillis reveals the phenomena to be more a "highly diffuse soup" of microscopic plastic shards. While oceanographer Curtis Ebbesmeyer, the man who first compared the supposed trash heap to Texas, admits that "descriptions have, perhaps, gotten out of hand," he reaffirms the severity of the plastic problem and hypothesizes that increased media attention has had a positive effect. "So it's not an island you can walk on," Ebbesmeyer says. "But it's a really horrific issue."

Up next, in "Out of Sight, Out of Mine: Ocean Dumping of Mine Wastes," a trio of *World Watch* writers discusses submarine tailings disposal (STD), a process by which mine waste materials are dumped underwater—supposedly far enough away from shore and below the surface as to not harm humans or wildlife. As outbreaks of illness in such places as Buyat Bay, Indonesia, suggest, however, STD isn't always safe. Unfortunately, the authors claim, mining companies have a tendency to put profits ahead of public safety and hire pro-business environmental consultants likely to uphold their practices.

In the subsequent piece, "Japanese Tsunami Aftermath Floating Alaska's Way," Doug O'Harra reports that, within three years, wreckage from the March 2011 disaster could begin washing up on the western coast of the United States. According to projections, litter that doesn't reach the shore will likely swirl through the North Pacific Gyre, where it will be broken down into harmful "micro-plastics." "If you put a major city through a trash grinder and sprinkle it on the water, that's what you're dealing with," Ebbesmeyer tells the Associated Press.

In the final piece, Bettina Wassener uses an unusual discovery in the South China Sea—the upper half of a pair of dentures—as a segueway into a discussion of how our plastic refuse is ending up in the oceans in greater and greater quantities and potentially causing far-reaching environmental damage. She also charts possible solutions to the growing problem, while noting that there are no quick fixes.

Wasted Waves[*]

Surveying the Plastic Adrift in the World's Oceans

By Anna Cummins
Waste Age, January 2011

"Looks like we found another ocean of plastic soup," said one of the crew.

Standing on the bow of the 72-foot Sea Dragon, thousands of miles from land in all directions, our crew of 13 sailors, scientists, filmmakers and citizens gazed silently across an endless azure horizon as a blue plastic hard hat and a disposable razor floated by. We began to take stock: A yellow plastic crate. An orange plastic buoy. A bottle cap. A barnacle-encrusted water bottle. Within an hour, 12 identifiable objects floated by, amid a field of smaller fragments. In the middle of nowhere, between Brazil and South Africa, we were witnessing a similar scenario to the North Pacific Gyre, better known as the infamous, though poorly named, "Great Pacific Garbage Patch." This, however, was the South Atlantic.

Many have by now heard about plastic accumulating in the North Pacific Gyre, a massive, slowly spinning oceanic system between California and Japan formed by opposing currents, winds and the earth's rotation. Plastic trash from land—the water bottles, bags, toys, cups and other disposable objects we use and lose daily—make their way down streets and streams to the sea. Swept up into the currents of the gyre, these durable petroleum products can travel thousands of miles, breaking into increasingly smaller fragments, but never fully disappearing, swirling endlessly on. The North Pacific Gyre is only one of five subtropical gyres dominating the world's oceans.

Though virtually unknown to the general public until recently, sailors have observed this phenomenon for decades, navigating through open seascapes dotted with plastic waste. One sailor, Captain Charles Moore, was so disturbed by the sight of this "trashed Pacific," that in 1997 he directed his organization, the Algalita Marine Research Foundation (AMRF), to focus on plastic pollution. Just

[*] Penton Media, Copyright © January 2011. Reprinted with permission. All rights reserved.

how much was out there? What impact was it having on marine ecosystems? And are there any solutions in sight?

In 2008, I joined Captain Moore, Dr. Marcus Eriksen and three others on AMRF's eighth expedition across the North Pacific Gyre, a life-changing voyage. Over the course of a month, covering some 4,000 miles, we skimmed the ocean's surface with a fine-meshed plankton net to collect samples for analysis. From what I had read and heard, I expected to see an "island" of garbage, a tangible mass that I might photograph as proof for naysayers on land. Instead, I was surprised to see endless, pristine blue, marred by a diffuse scattering of consumer products: buckets, toothbrushes, crates, suitcases and countless indistinct plastic fragments.

The samples we sieved from the ocean's surface told a different story. Every last one contained a rainbow of plastic confetti—small, broken-down fragments sharing space with zooplankton and small fish. The quantities were relatively small, averaging .004 grams per meter squared of ocean (akin to a rice grain sized plastic pellet in a bathtub full of water), but they were consistent. Sample after sample contained at least a handful or more of plastic fragments. And the nearest landmass was some 2,000 miles away.

Perhaps of even greater interest to the public, we collected 671 small, foraging fish to bring to the AMRF lab in Redondo Beach, Calif. These Myctophids, or "lantern fish," make up roughly 60 percent of the ocean's fish biomass, and are food for larger species that we eat: tuna, mahimahi and squid. Upon examining their stomach contents, 35 percent of these fish had ingested plastic particles.

The 2008 voyage sparked new questions, projects and a desire to find solutions. Seeing plastic in the stomachs of fish triggered concerns about potential human health risks. Scientists know that plastic particles can absorb pollutants such as Polychlorinated Biphenyls (PCBs), Dichlorodiphenyltrichloroethane (DDT), and other hydrophobic contaminants. Plastics also contain chemical additives: Phthalates and Bisphenol-A (BPA). Are these chemicals getting into the tissues of fish that eat plastic? And if so, are they working their way up the food chain, onto our dinner plate and into our tissues?

We also began to wonder about the other oceanic gyres, the North and South Atlantic, the South Pacific, and the Indian Ocean. Are the other oceans turning into plastic soups as well?

So we formed a new organization, the 5 Gyres Institute, to continue exploring these questions on a global scale. Our goal was to research all five subtropical gyres, bringing this issue to a wider audience, and seeking a diverse range of solutions. We began with voyage to the North Atlantic Gyre, a 3,000-mile expedition from St. Thomas to Bermuda to the Azores. Despite turbulent winter seas and hurricanes, we found plastic in every one of our 35 surface samples. And we saw more evidence of plastic interacting with marine life, including a fish living inside a plastic bucket, grown too large to escape—perhaps a dark metaphor for our own path.

Upon our return, we were invited to cross the Indian Ocean from Perth, Australia, to Mauritius, exploring our first gyre in the southern hemisphere.

We skirted the edge of the Indian Ocean Gyre and documented concentrations of plastic waste similar to the two northern hemisphere gyres. More recently, our expedition across the South Atlantic Gyre gathered the same plethora of plastic waste in varying states of degradation. Civilization has plasticized our seas in less than half a century. Two thirds of the Earth's surface carries a thin veneer of hardened petroleum, synthesized into long carbon chains that are indigestible, mimic food, absorb oil-loving toxins, and are finding their way into the fish we harvest to feed the world. Where do we go from here?

The knee-jerk response from nearly everyone that hears of this problem is, "Well, just go clean it up." This fanciful notion is analogous to sieving the Sahara desert for cigarette butts, or vacuuming America's highways for bubblegum wrappers. Not an impossible task, just impractical. What we have found is that the pace of plastic production, consumption and loss to the sea is not matched by increased accumulation in the gyres. Scientists in the North Atlantic and North Pacific have conducted 20- and 10-year longitudinal studies, respectively, and found no great trend in plastic accumulation. So where does it go?

If we stop the input of plastic, the ocean will regurgitate its waste. Islands in the gyres, like Hawaii and Bermuda, are natural nets for floating debris. Pacific islanders have relied on this activity for years to bring them giant logs from mainland forests. Gyres also wobble east and west, so a plastic bottle cap spinning in the North Pacific for a decade may find its way to the coast of Japan or California as the edges of gyre currents brush the mainland. If we stop adding more, we'll only have to clean our shores. Beach cleanup is gyre cleanup.

The challenge we face today is minimizing loss and maximizing recovery of the plastic we consume. This requires working far upstream, beyond our beaches and rivers, beyond storm drains, to the products we create. Design for Recyclability, Extended Producer Responsibility, and Product Stewardship, are a few strategies that work within the economic models of plastic producers. Legislative efforts to reduce the production and consumption of the most wasteful culprits, like plastic bags and foamed polystyrene, are working around the world. What we can all agree on is that our oceans are vital to our quality of life. Keeping that as our ultimate objective, we can surely solve this problem.

ANNA CUMMINS *and her husband, Dr. Marcus Eriksen, are the co-founders of The 5 Gyres Institute, researching and communicating the issue of plastic marine pollution in the world's oceans. The two have studied plastic waste in the North Pacific, North and South Atlantic, and Indian Ocean Gyres, and will cross the South Pacific Gyre in March 2011.*

Trashing the Island*

Why the 'Garbage Patch' in the Mid-Pacific Is Not Nearly the Disaster It's Been Made Out to Be

By Charlie Gillis
Maclean's, January 31, 2011

The sea, as any poet will tell you, invites metaphor, and scientists are as susceptible to its powers as those who deal in tropes. Having surveyed the stew of shattered plastic, discarded tires and floating refrigerators gathering in the mid-Pacific, the oceanographer Curtis Ebbesmeyer raised a worldwide alarm a decade ago about a burgeoning "garbage patch"—the result of centripetal ocean currents and convergent weather patterns in a vast, subtropical swirl known as the North Pacific Gyre. To say the least, this label captured the public imagination. The Great Pacific Garbage Patch shot up the hierarchy of environmental causes, garnering the sort of attention reserved for clear-cut logging, or global warming.

But it wasn't enough to sate today's multi-platform media monster. By 2005, the fervid accounts of eco-bloggers and mainstream journalists were elevating the patch to an "island"—as if you could step from the deck of a boat and walk across it. Oprah Winfrey's website described it as "the world's largest trash dump" and "the most shocking thing" the TV host had "ever seen." "Estimated to be twice the size of Texas, it swirls across the Pacific from California to Japan," the site proclaimed, notwithstanding the fact Oprah had never seen it first-hand. "In some places, it's 300 feet deep and has killed millions of sea birds and marine mammals."

Er, not quite, says Angelicque White, an oceanographer who has actually visited the gyre. Based on water samples and data gathered during a research voyage in 2008, the Oregon State University scientist last week issued an analysis letting a lot of air out of the Great Pacific Garbage Patch, describing it not so much as an island or even a patch, but as a highly diffuse soup, in which tiny shards of plastic float metres, if not kilometres apart. "Imagine 1,000 one-litre bottles sitting in front [of] you, all full of water from this area," she says from her office in Corval-

* Copyright © 2011 by *Maclean's*. Permission granted by author. All rights reserved.

lis, Ore. "Three to five of those bottles would have one piece of plastic the size of a pencil eraser. It's not twice the size of Texas. You can't see it from space. It's not even something you can see from the deck of a ship."

That's not to say the plastic is a non-issue. White was part of a scientific cruise to the region researching microbial activity springing up around the flotsam, some of which is broken down into microscopic particles. The capacity of plastic to alter life at the bottom of the food chain is regarded in scientific circles as its true threat—in part because researchers know so little about it. White worries that [the] cause will lose steam if the public decides the problem has been overblown. "I don't want people thinking, well, we don't have to conserve resources," she says, "we don't have to recycle or worry about marine pollution because there is no patch that is twice the size of Texas."

How, then, did hyperbole assume the weight of fact? Ebbesmeyer, who is famous for charting surface currents by mapping the locations of recovered flotsam, figures people allowed their imaginations to fill in what they would never see. But he's not sure that's such a bad thing. "The descriptions have, perhaps, gotten out of hand," he says. "But these are large tracts of the planet most people will never view, and I think the media attention has had a benefit. So it's not an island you can walk on. But it's a really horrific issue." As for the comparisons to Texas, he acknowledges they likely came from him. He was referring, he says, to the scale of the North Pacific ocean swirl itself, which has been charted with the use of satellite-tracked buoys. Concentrations may vary, he adds, but it is almost certainly strewn with plastic debris.

Perhaps, but White found a lot less of that junk in the gyre than she was led to expect. Using the standard method of towing a "net" of cheesecloth-like material through the water, she and a team from Hawaii's Center for Microbial Oceanography needed hours to find a handful of small plastic shards, she says. During a separate, more recent trawl in waters between Easter Island and Chile (another area feared to hold vast amounts of sea junk), she found no plastic at all. That's an awkward result to explain, she says, to people imagining a research ship surrounded by flotsam, or satellite photos of a trash flotilla. During a recent radio talk show in Oregon, a dismayed White heard a host demanding to see footage of the hypothetical "island," then derisively adding: "They oughta be selling real estate."

The anticlimactic findings haven't swayed her from her original mission to measure and study the microbial life that is undeniably blooming on and around the man-made crud. "I'd hate for reliable science to get lost in this along the way," she says. But it's a safe bet that she'll temper the language of her final study—lest her own modest observations morph into something she doesn't recognize.

Out of Sight, Out of Mine[*]

Ocean Dumping of Mine Wastes

By Robert Moran, Amada Reichelt-Brushett, and Roy Young
World Watch, March/April 2009

Beginning in 1996 and continuing through at least mid-2004, the Newmont Minahasa Raya gold mine dumped 2,000 tons per day of wastes into the tropical, coral-rich waters of Buyat Bay, off the island of Sulawesi, Indonesia—waters that previously had been the main source of food and income for local families. Soon stories began circulating that the fish were disappearing and that those remaining had deformities. Villagers also complained of strange skin rashes, tumors, and other forms of disease, all of which they claimed started after the waste disposal began. An independent team of scientists was commissioned by the Indonesian government to review the information and concluded that contamination by the mine had occurred. Newmont Mining Corporation, the U.S.-based parent company, commissioned its own studies and continually claimed that the data showed no water contamination—although they neglected to mention that these very studies clearly revealed the polluting of bay sediments by mercury, arsenic, antimony, and other metals and the likely uptake of these pollutants by bottom-dwelling organisms.

Buyat stories appeared everywhere in the media throughout the Pacific and quickly were investigated by the *New York Times*. Soon the Indonesian government arrested the head of Newmont Minahasa Raya and five other employees. A series of lawsuits followed. In 2007, an Indonesian court found both Newmont and its local director not guilty of the alleged crimes, but the state prosecutor subsequently appealed the ruling to the Indonesian Supreme Court. Some villagers were relocated in response to fears about the alleged contamination, but the claims and counterclaims have left the villagers confused and the issue hanging. Meanwhile, Newmont received permission from the Indonesian government to commence operating a copper-gold mine, Batu Hijau, which dumps up to 160,000 tons per day

[*] Copyright © 2009 | Worldwatch Institute | All Rights Reserved. Reprinted with permission. (www.worldwatch.org)

of wastes off the coast of another Indonesian island, Sumbawa—70 to 80 times the volume of waste disposed into Buyat Bay.

TAILINGS TRAIL

This story is a classic example of a common tragedy, usually occurring in the developing world, in which it is largely impossible to render an unbiased verdict because most of the technical data are collected by the interested company or their paid consultants; in which the local environmental oversight and legal systems are incapable of reaching an informed ruling, especially where so much outside money and political influence easily control the processes; and in which all sides therefore mistrust the actions of the officials and the companies.

The tailings (processed wastes) from the Minahasa Raya and Batu Hijau mines were discharged into the oceans via near-shore pipelines at relatively shallow depths: the pipeline from Minahasa Raya into Buyat Bay ran 1.0 kilometer off-shore and terminated at 82 meters depth; the Batu Hijau pipeline discharges about 2.9 kilometers offshore at 108 meters depth. Given all the Buyat Bay troubles, this seems exceptionally shallow, especially as many oceanographers say that truly deep waters begin at about 800 to 1,000 meters depth. Newmont argues that the Batu Hijau tailings migrate toward their final resting place in the Java Trench at depths in excess of 4,000 meters, although what little is known about ocean stratification and current flows reveals remarkable complexity and unpredictability.

In fact, nobody knows where all those tailings might be going. And it matters: more than 50 million tons of waste per year are discharged into the ocean from Batu Hijau alone. Several additional operating mines employ submarine tailings disposal (STD), and international corporations are pushing for many more. The desire for developed-world infrastructure and consumer products worldwide is driving a huge (and notwithstanding the recent economic slump, longterm) in-crease in the demand for metals, especially in cash-strapped countries near Asia that have relatively "flexible" business and environmental practices.

Mine tailings have been dumped into near-shore, shallow marine environments, either directly through pipelines or via rivers, for many decades, possibly for at least the last 100 years. These practices have produced documented impacts to marine life (and alleged impacts to humans) resulting in heated legal disputes in Peru, Chile, Indonesia, and the Philippines among other nations. Modern open-pit metal mines generate much greater volumes of waste than did historical un-derground mining; approximately 99 percent of all rock moved and processed at modern facilities ends as waste. At most mines, these wastes must be stored and managed forever. Hence, there is a great desire to send the wastes somewhere else—preferably out of sight. Traditional near-shore, shallow marine STD is unac-ceptable in modern developed countries, and so industry, often with government assistance, has attempted to justify the argument that disposal of tailings at much greater depths will be free of impacts. Part of the approach has been semantic:

simply changing the process name from submarine tailings disposal to the more benign-sounding deep-sea tailings placement (DSTP). For modern mines located in developing countries, especially those in tropical regions with high rainfall and strong earthquakes, industry has argued that DSTP is the best solution. It is much less expensive for them, and they acknowledge no significant impacts.

Indonesia, the Philippines, Malaysia, Papua New Guinea (PNG), the Solomon Islands, and East Timor have formed a partnership, the Coral Triangle Initiative, to safeguard the region's marine environment and coastal resources. This "triangle" hosts the highest biodiversity of marine life on Earth. Yet mining firms and member governments consider it acceptable to discharge hundreds of thousands of tons of chemical wastes per day into these waters. Would the Europeans allow such madness to occur off the tourist-swarmed southern European coasts, the Costa Brava, Provence, or the Adriatic?

STRANGE BREW

Even though these wastes are discharged into the collective waters of the world's oceans, monitoring of the resources is conducted by the companies and their consultants, and details are often withheld from the public. However, based on data from similar copper-gold operations that dispose of their tailings on land and on partial data from some STD operations, we can get a glimpse into the nature of this chemical soup.

Tailings are composed of crushed, mineralized rock and process chemicals. Rock components include almost every natural element in the periodic table, but common pollutants are arsenic, cadmium, copper, lead, mercury, nickel, selenium, zinc, and uranium. Processing of metal ores typically involves the addition of chemicals such as sodium hydroxide, sulfuric acid, sodium cyanide, copper sulfate, sulfur dioxide, xanthates, diesel oil, amines, polypropylene glycol methyl ether, and dozens more. Most of the chemicals and rock components are known to be individually toxic to marine organisms if present in sufficient concentrations. The synergistic toxic effects of such complicated mixtures of dozens of chemicals are unknown.

Industry knows the toxicity of the individual elements well from the numerous contamination episodes and lawsuits that have resulted worldwide when tailings have been discharged into sensitive areas on land and into shallow marine environments. The U.S. government long ago identified land-based mining as the industry that generates the largest volumes of toxic wastes. These wastes have repeatedly been found toxic to myriad terrestrial and aquatic organisms and are responsible for contaminating thousands of kilometers of rivers and aquifers in countless locations. Disposal of mine tailings into shallow marine environments has contaminated marine waters and forced local populations to restrict their consumption of fish and shellfish in Peru, Chile, Indonesia, the Philippines, and elsewhere. (Local populations have also alleged that these practices harm human health, but usually lack the technical and medical support to win such claims in court.)

Thus the position of some companies has been that dumping these wastes into deep waters is the solution. They argue that such wastes can be carefully placed at the mouths of marine canyons, where they then flow by gravity down to the deepest waters, and that all impacts to either the shallow or deeper organisms are avoided. At these depths, they maintain, chemical reactions proceed at such slow rates that the concentrations of toxic substances released from the tailings will generate insignificant impacts to marine communities. Some industry representatives have even made the disingenuous statement that tailings are inert (non-reactive). In 2005, the CEO of Newmont Mining said at the company's annual shareholders meeting that "once processed [referring to gold tailings], all that remains is sand."

Other experts argue that this is far too simplistic. Australian government scientists have reported the existence of marine currents in northern Papua New Guinea waters that move upward in canyons from the sea floor, carrying materials back toward the coasts. Their studies also show that much of the river sediment discharging into the bays of northern PNG does not enter the marine canyons, but instead is carried off to the northwest and deposited hundreds or thousands of kilometers away.

There are literally hundreds of studies showing the sensitivity of various shallow marine communities to metals and other contaminants in industrial wastes. The research also demonstrates the lethal smothering of shallow communities by tailings sediments. Studies by one of the authors of this article (Reichelt-Brushett) show that the critical life stages of coral reproduction are extremely sensitive to elevated loads of trace metals, particularly copper. Several U.S. oceanographers state that below ordinary SCUBA-diver-depths (about 30 meters) the impacts of pollution and sedimentation on shallow-water ecosystems, including coral reefs, remain largely unexplored. Our understanding of even these shallow reef systems is limited by logistics, accessibility, and funding.

Much less is known about deep marine communities and related contamination below about 800 meters (and for that matter, little is known about the intermediate zone between 100 and 800 meters, either). While it is thought that some deep-sea communities cope with high sedimentation rates, little is understood about the impacts of trace metals and other pollutants (from a variety of sources) on these ecosystems. Few, if any, studies are available that report on the impacts of tailings contaminants on tropical marine or deep-sea organisms, but the few studies that have been done are troubling. For example, from 1986 through 1992 the U.S. government encouraged the disposal of municipal sewage wastes in deep marine waters (2,500 meters) at the "106-mile dumpsite" off the New Jersey coast. This dumping was halted after various studies showed harmful impacts to the plentiful and diverse deep marine communities and to water quality, due to the metals, toxic organic compounds, bacteria, and viruses contained in the sewage sludge.

Most significantly, the natural-resources research arms of the Australian and Canadian governments conducted two reviews of the available literature on DSTP beginning in 2001. The first report was jointly authored by the Australia Commonwealth Scientific and Industrial Research Organization (CSIRO) and the

Canada Centre for Mineral and Energy Technology (CANMET) and completed in September 2004. It was released to an advisory group, but never made available to the general public. The second report, authored by CANMET, has never been made publicly available. When we contacted the CANMET author in August 2008, he was unwilling to provide copies of either report, stating that the studies were originally commissioned by several international mining companies and that these companies controlled the dissemination of the studies.

In fact, most of the studies reviewed in the 2004 report dealt with disposal into relatively shallow marine waters, and almost none evaluated tropical settings. Few relevant studies on truly deep waters existed then, or exist even now. In fact, these two research reviews identified major gaps in the technical knowledge relating to the precise fate and toxicity of these wastes and their impacts on marine communities. The sections on "Recommendations for Further Work" and "Research Needed to Fill Knowledge Gaps" are three pages long. Clearly the authors were saying: we don't adequately understand the complicated impacts.

Evaluating the realistic consequences of marine tailings disposal is impeded by several economic and political realities. It is extremely costly to collect and analyze mining environmental samples at terrestrial and shallow marine sites, and many times more expensive in deep marine waters; so much so that it is essentially beyond the resources of many developing world governments and certainly untouchable by public interest groups. Also, there has been a general trend worldwide to push the national research agencies of developed-world governments to behave more like private industry. That is, they are required to find commercial sources of funding for much of their work and to interact more closely with industry. Without some commercial incentive, these large research groups will generally not undertake such costly and controversial research. Hence most of the research on waters and communities near individual mines is collected and interpreted by the mining companies or their paid consultants. The main goal of such studies is to obtain the necessary operating permits, not raise uncomfortable questions. These projects can continue for decades, providing the consultants' primary source of income. More directly, consultants will never be hired again by any mining corporation if their statements are unacceptable. (As the U.S. writer Upton Sinclair insightfully noted, "It is difficult to get a man to understand something when his salary depends on his not understanding it.") Finally, the national government oversight agencies are in a double bind: they are required to promote mining, which frequently supplies a major source of national revenue, and also enforce the laws. Normally, the government staff lack the technical skills and support to act as a reliable check and balance on industry practices.

Thus the fundamental dilemma is that many of the important issues have not been studied adequately in tropical or truly deep waters by independent and financially disinterested scientists. The available studies have several major flaws: they failed to study communities below about 150 meters' depth; they were conducted or directed by interested parties; and they generally looked only at short-term impacts. To be meaningful, such studies must evaluate conditions over the long term, probably decades. Most DSTP sites lack monitoring locations outside the immediate disposal area and so there is really no way to demonstrate that some tailings fail to harm shallow waters and communities. Moreover, because the interactions of marine physical, biological, chemical, toxicological, engineering, oceanographic, and socioeconomic factors with human activities are extremely complex, the tendency is simply to present study results in isolation rather than to fully integrate them across disciplines; thus the complexities are lost. It's so much easier to say, "That is outside my expertise."

KNOWLEDGE AND POWER

Two of us (Moran and Reichelt-Brushett) got a glimpse into what is driving marine disposal of mine wastes at a European Union-funded conference held in Madang, Papua New Guinea, in early November 2008. The gathering was billed as an opportunity to "assess all existing information on past and present mining operations using deep sea tailings placement . . . in Papua New Guinea . . ." and "provide guidelines for future DSTP marine environmental monitoring in the context of international best practice." The conference was also intended to present the results of recent, independent research efforts on DSTP in Papua New Guinea waters (specifically from near the Misima and Lihir Mines). To this end, the E.U. had contracted with the Scottish Association for Marine Science (SAMS) to review the available literature and conduct sampling activities near the two mines.

Upon our arrival, several strange aspects became immediately apparent. Most of the invited technical speakers represented either industry or government perspectives; almost no general public involvement had been arranged. Ultimately a few representatives of citizens groups did attend, but Madang is far off the beaten path and attending the conference was too expensive for most citizens groups.

None of the industry speakers or their consultants would provide their actual chemical or biological data to the other attendees. When the regional director of Newmont Asia Pacific made a presentation on the impact-free disposal of tailings at the Batu Hijau mine, he was asked to make public the detailed chemical contents of the tailings. He declined: it was not possible at this time, he said, but hopefully in two years; the company wanted to protect the ability of its scientists to publish on these matters. However, this mine had been operating since roughly 2000. Thus, the audience was being told that the chemical details of what was being dumped would not be revealed until more than 10 years after operations commenced.

The E.U. contractor, SAMS, was staffed by clearly competent marine scientists, but had no previous experience with metal mining projects or working in tropical waters. SAMS had little appreciation for the sensitive political and citizens' concerns that normally intrude into such projects. Its work and its scope were actually directed by another E.U. consultant, formerly from the mining industry. SAMS had not actually completed its research and was unable to present most of its conclusions, but it did identify notable changes in the communities of bottom-dwelling organisms from tailings discharges at 100-meter depths. However, the areas studied received wastes from relatively small mines, not large-scale operations as are proposed, so the situations were not really comparable to truly deep disposal scenarios. Nevertheless, on the last day SAMS presented a set of guidelines for future DSTP monitoring, for comment and consideration by the attendees. It is unclear who actually authored these guidelines. Apparently, the organizers had assumed that the attendees would ultimately approve the guidelines before the conference ended, but no such consensus was attained.

The PNG government seemed to want public support for a long-delayed nickel mine, the Ramu project, located not far from Madang (apparently the reason for the remote conference site). The Ramu mine is to be operated largely by a Chinese corporation and it is likely that most of the production would go to China. Thus, the PNG government certainly wanted to demonstrate via the conference that environmental and other impacts from DSTP were acceptable.

Was it the intent of these E.U. representatives to promote deep sea tailings disposal? That is unclear, but one could certainly conclude as much. At minimum, they see their role as one of assisting the PNG and other governments in promoting international investment in mining. Do such governments actually have the ability to competently oversee such complex development projects? It's unlikely without major improvements in the national governance capabilities, as was concluded by the two-year Extractive Industries Review study conducted by an independent team advising the World Bank and released in 2003.

If the E.U. does intend to promote DSTP, it may be only selectively. DSTP is practiced in some regions because many national and international governing bodies have failed to legally forbid, and have largely ignored, such practices. However, submarine disposal of mine wastes has been effectively banned in the waters of the United States, Canada, Australia, and the Philippines, and the European Union's own Marine Directive (June 2008) clearly discourages such practices in the waters of any E.U. member country. The Directive tellingly states, ". . . the Community needs to reduce its impact on marine waters regardless of where their effects occur." One would expect that the United Nations Convention on the Law of the Sea would also forbid tailings disposal, but it has historically been exempted from the Convention.

INSULT TO INJURY?

Read almost any news source and one learns of another assault on the health of marine resources. If it isn't over-fishing and declining catches, it is coastal dead zones in the Gulf of Mexico and many other places, restrictions on the consumption of fish due to mercury content, or the loss of corals and other species due to heat stress. Climate change is causing an increase in the carbon dioxide content of ocean waters, increasing their acidity. Given such extreme pressures on marine ecosystems, it seems foolish to impose additional stresses from disposal of millions of tons of mine wastes—especially when government research scientists say we simply don't understand the risks. And, unlike land disposal, the impacts from deep submarine disposal will be largely irreversible.

Both mining of metals and disposal of mine wastes in the world's oceans clearly involve the ancient concept of the "commons"—resources that are neither public nor private but which are held and used jointly. Disposal of tailings into the oceans at any depth has the potential to degrade a tremendous range of commonly utilized resources, but local publics lack the tools to demonstrate conclusively that such broad consequences may be occurring. At present, only the mining corporations have the financial and political power to have their technical arguments heard. Given the myriad uncertainties noted in the international technical literature, it is all but certain that we and our children will pay for this parochial view on ocean management.

ROBERT MORAN, *Ph.D., is a consulting hydrogeologist and geochemist and a partner in the Golden, Colorado-based consulting firm Michael-Moran Associates.* AMANDA REICHELT-BRUSHETT, *Ph.D., is a marine ecotoxicologist and senior lecturer at Southern Cross University, Lismore, Australia.* ROY YOUNG *is an environmental geologist and advisor to the Global Response network in Boulder, Colorado.*

Japanese Tsunami Aftermath Floating Alaska's Way[*]

By Doug O'Harra
Alaska Dispatch, April 10, 2011

A bobbing mass of wreckage—the shattered flotsam washed to sea after a tsunami swept across 180 square miles of land in northern Japan on March 11—has begun to sweep in slow motion across the Pacific Ocean toward Alaska.

Simulated on a computer model unveiled at an international conference about ocean garbage, this tangled flotilla will begin washing up on beaches in Southeast and other West Coast zones within three years, according to a pair of Hawaiian scientists.

"The plume will reach the US West Coast, dumping debris on Californian beaches and the beaches of British Columbia, Alaska, and Baja California," predicted Nikolai Maximenko and Jan Hafner at the International Pacific Research Center, University of Hawaii at Manoa in this story about their work.

But that's only the beginning.

By the end of 2014, the leading edge will have penetrated Southcentral waters, delivering a high-tide litter that might include tires, household and personal items, toys, shoes, construction fragments, tattered plastic and vinyl scraps, splintered wood, dockage, ropes, floats and the other tragic jetsam of Japan's worst catastrophe since World War II.

What doesn't wash ashore, sink into the abyss or get swallowed by sea creatures will keep circulating, finally roiling into the perpetual deep ocean gyre of human-generated refuse known as the Great Pacific Garbage Patch.

Though some of the stuff will make land in Hawaii within 18 months on its first pass across the ocean, much more will strand over years as the gyre brings the debris around again, and again.

"It moves eastward, just north of Hawaii and moves toward the Pacific garbage patch and stays there and eventually that garbage will escape to our Hawaiian shores," Maximenko told Honolulu's KITV in a story aired in March.

[*] "Japanese Tsunami Aftermath Floating Alaska's Way" by Doug O'Harra. April 10, 2011. (www.alaskadispatch.com). Reprinted with permission of the author.

Within five to six years, a vast mess that originated in a few moments of destruction on Japan will be fouling beaches and reefs of the eastern North Pacific, magnifying the problem of refuse entangling and killing marine life, Maximenko and Hafner later told the Fifth International Marine Debris Conference in Honolulu.

By then, much of it will have been reduced to tiny fragments, what scientists call "micro-plastics," inorganic bits that can be easily ingested by sea life and may end up in the human food chain with unknown health consequences. But Maximenko warned there could be other impacts.

"Who knows, maybe we will see radioactive spews from nuclear reactors," he told KITV. "It is not debris, but it is driven by the same currents so there are many dimensions to this problem."

SPAWNED BY THE EARTH'S FOURTH BIGGEST QUAKE

While most ocean garbage traces to careless practices of industry and spills off ships, this material was launched by what may soon become the most expensive natural tragedy in history.

A 9.0 magnitude Megathrust earthquake struck 45 miles east of the Tōhoku region in northern Japan on March 11, shifting tectonic plates 20 miles beneath the ocean floor in what scientists say is the fourth biggest temblor ever measured.

The quake yanked Japan about eight feet closer to North America and caused the seabed to snap upward about 20 feet along a 110-mile stretch of coast. That sudden lurch generated tsunamis that often rose at least 25 feet (reported in one location as topping 124 feet) when they roared ashore and then rushed up to six miles inland through urban areas and farmland. As they flushed in and then receded, the waves destroyed or damaged more than 140,000 houses and buildings in 28 towns, reducing entire neighborhoods to rubble.

More than four million households lost power, and three nuclear reactors experienced explosions after cooling systems failed, triggering the worst nuclear power plant crisis since the meltdown at Chernobyl 25 years ago. Japanese authorities now believe at least 28,000 people are dead or missing, with searches for bodies still dominating the news almost one month after the disaster.

One aftermath? Uncounted tons of material floated into the ocean on the retreating tsunami waves. Every thing that might float away, the detritus of modern civilization, is now floating toward North America on the currents.

"If you put a major city through a trash grinder and sprinkle it on the water, that's what you're dealing with," is how Curt Ebbesmeyer, a Seattle-based oceanographer and a pioneer in the [of] tracking ocean debris as a way to chart currents, described it to the Associated Press last week.

MAKING THE OCEAN DEBRIS CRISIS EVEN WORSE

The problem of human refuse and floatable trash spreading across the world's seas has grown exponentially worse in recent decades. The items range from mile-long ghost nets that ensnare and strangle marine life to tiny particles that appear almost indistinguishable from plankton, the foundation of the marine food web.

"Even before the tsunami, the World Ocean was a dump for rubbish flowing in from rivers, washed off beaches, and jettisoned from oil and gas platforms and from fishing, tourist, and merchant vessels," the researchers said in this story. "The massive, concentrated debris launched by the devastating tsunami is now magnifying the hazards."

At least 267 species across the world regularly suffer injury from getting snared or eating debris—including most sea turtle species, almost half of all seabirds and 43 percent of marine mammals, according to a United Nations report about the Honolulu conference.

"Marine debris—trash in our oceans—is a symptom of our throw-away society and our approach to how we use our natural resources," said United Nations Environment Programme Executive Director Achim Steiner in a message to conference delegates. "The impact of marine debris today on flora and fauna in the oceans is one that we must now address with greater speed."

Any visitor to the lonely beaches of the Southern Alaska's Gulf Coast, from Prince William Sound to the Kenai Fiords, will find all kinds of plastic and other junk snarled in the driftwood and littering the shore. A recent study found 36,000 pieces of garbage ranging in size from a tiny float to a chest freezer along one stretch of Pacific Northwest coastline, appearing everywhere from deep inside coastal fiords to 90 miles offshore, reported the Vancouver Sun.

"Of that, 49 per cent is Styrofoam or similar polystyrene products, 15 per cent plastic bottles, 10.5 per cent plastic bags and 6.3 per cent fishing gear. The rest of the garbage, slightly less than 20 per cent of the total, includes plastic, cardboard, wrappers, buoys, aluminum cans, and so on."

TRACKING WHERE THE STUFF MIGHT GO

Maximenko is one of a group of oceanographers who has been tracking how this stuff gets carried around the ocean on currents and figuring out where it might land. He has helped pin down the locations of five major regions where human jetsam collects inside immense gyres. Scientists have taken to calling these areas "garbage patches"—one per major ocean basin.

Seattle oceanographer Ebbesmeyer is another. After an Asian ship spilled thousands of Nike sneakers in 1990, he began collecting reports from beachcombers finding unworn (if not soggy) shoes on beaches from California to Alaska. With retired NOAA researcher Jim Ingraham, he adapted a computer program aimed at tracking salmon into tracking spilled cargo.

After 29,000 bath toys washed off a container ship in 1992 in the eastern Pacific, it was Ebbesmeyer and Ingraham who used beachcomber reports and their computer program to track a 17,000-mile itinerary that delivered rubber ducks, blue turtles and green frogs to the beaches of North America, Europe, Australia and South America.

Now Ebbesmeyer and Ingraham plan to use their program to track the tsunami debris as it bears down on the Pacific Coast.

"In two years, there's going to be stuff coming in (from Japan), and probably lots of it," John Anderson, a Forks, Wash., beachcomber, told the Associated Press in a story that appeared in dozens of outlets around the world. "Some of it is bound to come in."

The computer model created by Maximenko and Hafner predicts the Japanese debris will float eastward on the North Pacific Subtropical Gyre for a year before some of it begins washing up on sensitive habitats in the Northwestern Hawaiian Islands Marine National Monument.

With two years, the main Hawaiian Islands will catch some tsunami trash, and by three years, "the plume" will reach the U.S. West Coast, spreading north and south, with tide rips carrying remnants of Japan's nightmare into Alaska's nearshore waters.

"These model projections will help to guide clean-up and tracking operations," the researchers said here. "Tracking will be important in determining what happens to different materials in the tsunami debris, for example, how the composition of the debris plume changes with time, and how the winds and currents separate objects drifting at different speeds."

The Peril of Plastic[*]

By Bettina Wassener
The New York Times, May 22, 2011

For bizarre items floating in the ocean, try topping this: The upper half of a set of false teeth, seen bobbing around in the South China Sea.

"I remember thinking: 'How on earth did it get there?'" said Lindsay Porter, a marine scientist based in the Malaysian city of Kota Kinabalu, who spotted the item from a research vessel about 200 kilometers, or 125 miles, off China in 2009.

The teeth, gripped in their plastic gums, are part of the millions of tons of plastic trash that somehow ends up in oceans around the world every year. Mostly, it is more mundane stuff, the flotsam and jetsam of everyday life: picnic plates, bottles, cigarette lighters, toys, spoons, flip-flops, condoms.

Taken together, the virtually indestructible mass is now so large that it is causing environmentalists, government officials and the plastics industry itself to sit up and take note. Many scientists believe marine plastic pollution is one of the major issues—along with climate change—facing the planet.

The problem is not the plastic itself: Even those who lobby against plastic pollution acknowledge that plastic materials help combat climate change, for example by reducing the weight—and thus fuel consumption—of vehicles, or by helping to insulate buildings.

The problem is the sheer amount of the stuff out there. Low-cost, lightweight and durable, plastic erupted onto the world stage in the 1950s. Annual production of 1.5 million tons back then has swelled to about 250 million tons now, according to the trade association PlasticsEurope .

Half of the plastic produced is used only once before being discarded. Think packaging, shampoo bottles, disposable razors, yogurt cups.

In North America and Western Europe, every single person uses about 100 kilograms of plastic every year. That figure is forecast to rise to 140 kilograms by

* From *The New York Times*, May 22, 2011. Copyright © 2011 The New York Times. All rights reserved. Used by permission and protected by the Copyright Laws of the United States. The printing, copying, redistribution, or retransmission of the Material without express written permission is prohibited.

2015. In fast-growing Asian countries, the current average of about 20 kilograms will nearly double, to 36 kilograms, by 2015, researchers estimate.

Most of that ends up in landfills. Some is recycled. But a significant amount ends up in the sea, swept there via rivers or sewage drains, discarded on beaches or dumped from ships.

Exact figures are hard to come by, but some researchers estimate that 4.7 million tons reaches the sea each year, according to Plastic Oceans, a London-based charity that has enlisted numerous scientists to create a full-length documentary film on the topic.

Bear in mind that this stuff does not just biodegrade like food waste, wood or paper. Scientists believe it takes decades, if not centuries, for most types of plastic to degrade. That means virtually all the plastic material that has ever ended up in the ocean is still out there.

"When a plastic crate or bottle floats around in the ocean, it does not biodegrade. It only breaks into smaller and smaller pieces—which are still plastic," said Peter Kershaw of the British marine science center Cefas, who helps advise the United Nations on marine environmental protection issues.

Some of the debris sinks to the ocean floor. Some washes back onto land, sometimes in remote and once-pristine parts of the world.

But most is gradually swept up by ocean currents, which have assembled the assorted mess into five "gyres," or garbage patches, in the Pacific, Atlantic and Indian oceans.

Do not imagine these to be vast, tangible floating islands of trash that you can walk across. Yes, there are visible chunks of debris—some large enough to trap or choke wildlife. Mostly, however, the plastic soup consists of tiny fragments, some the size of a fingernail, some much smaller, floating on or below the surface across thousands of kilometers.

The gunk cannot be seen via satellite, making it hard for scientists to measure or track the problem. It is, however, clearly visible from up close.

"It's kind of like chunky dust, hovering in the water. You can see the change in the texture of the water," said Ms. Porter, a senior research scientist at the University of St. Andrews in Scotland.

"The samples taken from the sea in the middle of these gyres are a glutinous-looking mess," said Craig Leeson, the Hong Kong-based director of the Plastic Oceans documentary.

Although these tiny fragments do not trap or choke animals the way plastic bags or abandoned nets do, they are increasingly the focus of scientific concern. Microplastics are easily swallowed and prone to absorb chemical pollutants in the sea, like pesticides, research has shown. Some scientists worry that these contaminants could end up in the food chain, the U.N. Environment Program noted in a report in February, calling for intensified research.

On the upside, plastic pollution has at least started to be recognized as a serious issue.

At a conference in Hawaii in March, plastics industry associations from around the world pledged to work with governments and nongovernmental organizations to increase research and promote efforts to recycle and prevent litter.

Still, recycling rates in many countries remain low.

The U.S. Environmental Protection Agency, for example, estimates that only 7 percent of plastics were recycled in the United States in 2009. In many developing nations, where plastics consumption is expected to rise sharply in coming years, awareness, and collection and recycling efforts, are still [in] their infancy.

Fishing out the soupy gunk in the ocean gyres, meanwhile, is not really an option. The costs of traveling hundreds of kilometers out to sea are prohibitive, and most of the fragments are so small they cannot simply be scooped up.

The focus thus has to be on preventing new debris from getting into the oceans in the first place, said Keith Christman of the American Chemistry Council in Washington.

That means more efforts by companies to minimize packaging; more efforts by the authorities to step up collection and public awareness; and more efforts by ordinary people—yes, that is you and me—to avoid throwaway plastic products and to recycle those we do use.

As for the false teeth spotted by Ms. Porter—they will probably continue to travel the oceans for years to come.

5

Scourge of the Seas:
Piracy

Courtesy of the U.S. Navy

The Arleigh Burke-class guided missile destroyer USS *Farragut* (DDG 99) passes by the smoke from a suspected pirate skiff it had just disabled on March 31, 2010. USS *Farragut* is part of Combined Task Force 151, a multinational effort to combat piracy in and around the Gulf of Aden.

Courtesy of the U.S. Navy

Suspected pirates keep their hands in the air as directed by the guided-missile cruiser USS *Vella Gulf* (CG-72) as the visit, board, search, and seizure (VBSS) team prepares to apprehend them on Feburary 11, 2009. *Vella Gulf* is the flagship for Combined Task Force 151, an international force conducting counterpiracy operations in and around the Gulf of Aden, Arabian Gulf, Indian Ocean, and Red Sea.

Editor's Introduction

In the late 2000s, as reports of piracy became widespread along the coast of Somalia, there was a tendency among many to make light of what were actually very serious crimes. It's not surprising, given that pirates—once feared scourges of the sea—have become the stuff of comic books, cartoons, and Johnny Depp movies. When children go trawling for Halloween candy with patches over their eyes and stuffed parrots on their shoulders, spouting lines like "Shiver me timbers," few have any idea they're emulating violent thieves who once wreaked havoc on the world's trade routes.

Today's pirates are nothing like the lovable louts often seen in the children's movies. Dressed in ski masks and armed with machine guns, they hijack merchant and civilian ships, demanding lofty ransoms and sometimes killing their hostages. In "Somalia: Total Cost of Piracy Menace Hits U.S. $12 Billion," the piece that begins this chapter's look at modern-day piracy, Christine Mungai, for the *Business Daily* (Nairobi, Kenya), highlights the staggering financial impact of this type of crime. Between 2005 and 2010, the number of pirate attacks in the Indian Ocean increased from 276 to 445, while the average ransom demand climbed from $150,000 to $5.4 million. In response, shipping companies have been forced to reroute boats and buy extra insurance, while governments have footed the bill for prevention efforts and legal prosecutions. Despite the presence of three international naval task forces in the region, experts say the cost of piracy could hit $15 billion by 2015.

In the subsequent selection, "As Pirate Attacks Grow, Shipowners Take Arms," Reuters writer Peter Apps attends a training session for aspiring security personnel—the type many companies have begun hiring to protect their ships from pirates. As NATO, European Union (EU), and U.S. forces have ramped up efforts in the Gulf of Aden and other "choke-points," Apps reports, pirates have shifted their operations further into the Indian Ocean. While the United Nations (UN)'s International Maritime Organization recommends that sailors not carry weapons, the legality of hiring armed guards is "complicated, to put it mildly," according to Nick Williams, a former British Royal Marine who now co-runs the company Independent Maritime Security Associates. "If you look at the way things are going in the Indian Ocean, it's just getting worse," Williams tells Apps. "The work is there, and there are guys who want to do it."

Somalia isn't the only African nation with a major piracy problem. In the next piece, "Nigeria: The 'Other' Maritime Piracy Hotbed," Donna J. Nincic shifts the focus to Africa's west coast, examining the increasingly violent attacks in the oil-rich Niger Delta region. In addition to targeting oil ships, Nigerian pirates also plunder fishing boats, and in doing so, they've reduced the supply of seafood, thus driving up prices. As Nincic reports, some young men become pirates for political reasons—such as the government's inequitable distribution of oil profits—while others simply lack alternative career prospects. Given Nigeria's rampant unemployment, she concludes, efforts to thwart piracy must ultimately address the nation's longstanding economic problems and focus on putting people back to work.

While not exactly a defense of piracy, Ishaan Tharoor's *Time* story "How Somalia's Fishermen Became Pirates," the subsequent entry in this chapter, explains how the world's exploitation of the East African nation has contributed to the present situation. When the first Somali pirates emerged in the 1990s, Tharoor writes, they were poor fishermen fighting encroachment from better-equipped foreign competitors. Somalia hasn't had a functional government since 1991, and in the absence of proper regulations, the fertile waters off Somalia are a "free for all" of international fishing boats. What's more, foreign companies have a history of dumping toxic materials off Somali shores, further spurring angry citizens to take up arms. Even so, Tharoor concludes, most of today's pirates aren't freedom-fighting fishermen, but rather "poor folk seeking their fortune."

In the final selection, "We're Firing Blanks in the War Against Piracy," Praveen Swami outlines some of the legal challenges associated with combating piracy. In early 2011, British authorities were forced to free 17 Somalis they apparently had no right to prosecute, Swami reports, while the UN Security Council has struggled to establish special courts for pirates. The author stops short of endorsing a return to the anti-piracy methods employed in 1816, when British ships waged war off the coast of Algiers, but he leaves open the possibility of such "punitive action," since "the easier, softer way is leading nowhere."

Somalia[*]

Total Cost of Piracy Menace Hits U.S. $12 Billion

By Christine Mungai
Business Daily (Nairobi, Kenya), May 9, 2011

The total cost of piracy in the Indian Ocean in 2010—almost all of it by Somali pirates—is estimated to be between $7 billion (Sh560 billion) and $12 billion (Sh960 billion), and could top $15 billion by 2015, according to analysts.

This bill includes ransoms, insurance payments, the cost of naval operations, prosecutions and of rerouting ships.

A recent study reported that Somali pirates are earning up to $79,000 a year, 150 times the average annual income in Somalia.

The study by political and economic intelligence consultancy firm, Geopolicity, revealed that the area under the threat of piracy has steadily extended to some 2.5 million square nautical miles off Somalia's coastline, an increase of one million nautical miles from two years ago.

Another study by anti-piracy organisation, Oceans Beyond Piracy, forecasts piracy could cost $15 billion in the next four years, as more pirates sign up and bigger intervention measures are consequently rolled out.

The Indian Ocean accounts for fully half of the world's container traffic, and 70 per cent of total global petroleum traffic passes through it.

The gulfs of Aden and Oman are among the world's major shipping lanes: About 21,000 ships, and 11 per cent of global crude oil traffic, cross the Gulf of Aden every year.

The ports of Mombasa and Dar es Salaam handled a combined cargo of 25 million tonnes in 2008—not just for Kenya and Tanzania respectively, but also for inland countries such as Uganda, the Democratic Republic of the Congo, Southern Sudan, Rwanda and Burundi.

---

* *Business Daily* article copyright © 2011 by Nation Media Group (www.bdafrica.com). All rights reserved. Reprinted with permission.

Together, East Africa's ports account for approximately a fifth of sub-Saharan Africa's container traffic, with an average annual growth of 6 per cent since 1995.

The Indian Ocean is particularly significant for the region in terms of communication: A 17,000 km undersea fibre-optic cable connects South Africa, Tanzania, Kenya, Uganda and Mozambique to Europe and Asia.

Incidents of piracy have soared from 276 in 2005 to 445 in 2010. According to the International Maritime Bureau, there were 142 attacks between January and March 2011—97 off the coast of Somalia—up from 35 in the same period the previous year and an all-time high.

Pirates managed to seize 18 vessels worldwide, capturing more than 340 hostages in attacks in which seven crew members died and 34 were injured.

Over the past five years, Somali pirates' ransom demands have increased a staggering thirty-six fold, from an average of $150,000 in 2005 to $5.4 million in 2010.

The largest known ransom payment was for the South Korean oil tanker Samho Dream, for which a record $9.5 million was paid in November 2010.

Somali pirates' income for 2010 was around $238 million.

Oceans Beyond Piracy estimates that the total excess costs of insurance due to Somali piracy are between $460 million and $3.2 billion per year, which have steadily increased since the Gulf of Aden was classified as a war risk area in May 2008.

The cost of piracy trials and imprisonment in 2010 was around $31 million, and the excess cost of re-routing ships to avoid risk zones is estimated to be between $2.4 billion and $3 billion per year.

This, coupled with the cost of naval forces and protection, puts the total bill at between $7 billion and $12 billion.

The study reports that the continued growth of piracy could see the numbers of pirates, estimated to be at least 1,500, rise by up to 400 every year.

As a result, the costs of piracy could reach more than $15 billion by 2015.

Currently there are three international naval task forces in the region, with numerous national vessels and task forces entering and leaving the region, engaging in counter-piracy operations for various lengths of time.

The primary mission is Combined Task Force 151 (CTF-151), also patrolling are warships from Russia, China and India, among others.

As Pirate Attacks Grow, Shipowners Take Arms[*]

'If You Look at the Way Things Are Going in the Indian Ocean, It's Just Getting Worse'

By Peter Apps
Reuters, May 3, 2011

Poole, England—Upstairs in a public house on the English south coast, 18 men are preparing to take on the pirates of the Indian Ocean.

Around antique polished wooden tables scattered with laminated charts, handouts and smartphones, they sit in attentive silence as teachers in jeans and T-shirts discuss pirate tactics and the hazards of the law. Almost to a man, the students—their haircuts short, their arms muscled and tattooed—have military experience: some on well-paid, dangerous private security contracts in Iraq or Afghanistan.

It almost feels as if history is repeating itself. The Blue Boar pub is in a building that dates back to the 18th century, when Poole was one of England's busiest trading ports and ships sailed the globe with cargoes of cotton, silk, tea, cotton, spices and opium. Those privately owned vessels were armed like warships, equipped to fight off pirate attacks and privateers far from naval help. Now, it seems, one ocean at least is becoming lawless again.

Sailing from havens on Somalia's coast, young men with AK-47s, rocket-propelled grenades, grappling hooks and ladders have wreaked havoc with regional shipping over the past six years. Dozens of warships from the world's navies have failed to stem the attacks, leading a growing number of shipowners to turn to private security companies. It's a lucrative trade, and there's no shortage of applicants for the three-day "ship security officer" course run by former Royal Marine commandos John Twiss, Nick Williams and their company, Independent Maritime Security Associates (IMSA).

"We're probably training twice as many people as we were last year," 55-year-old Williams told Reuters in the pub's function room, which serves as a classroom. "If

[*] Copyright © 2011 by Thomson Reuters. All rights reserved. Reprinted by permission.

you look at the way things are going in the Indian Ocean, it's just getting worse. The work is there, and there are guys who want to do it."

But even these tough, no-nonsense men—confronted with a wheelchair-bound Reuters correspondent and a flight of stairs, they simply haul wheelchair and reporter aloft and carry them to the first floor—are far from blase about what they might face.

"The standard operating procedure for the pirates these days is to fire into the superstructure of the vessel to intimidate the master," Williams tells the group. "Some of these attacks now last upwards of 90 minutes. It takes a lot of bottle to hold your nerve during that."

The class would not be so popular if the world's navies had managed to fix the problem. Ships from the European Union, NATO, a separate U.S.-led coalition and newer powers such as South Korea, India, China and Russia have all sailed to the waters off Somalia in recent years. Loosely coordinated through meetings in Bahrain and a secure internet chatroom, they have managed to reduce attacks at choke-points in the Gulf of Aden, between Yemen and Africa. But the pirates have responded by shifting further out into the Indian Ocean, which naval commanders say is too big to police.

Pirate activity has risen steadily. The first three months of 2011 were the worst on record, the EU says, with 77 attacks and hijackings—up from only 36 in the same period of 2010. The pirates have started using hijacked vessels—including giant tankers the size of skyscrapers—as mother ships, so they can operate throughout the stormy monsoon season and far further out to sea than before.

The worsening situation, say experts, has made it almost inevitable that today's merchant ships will [bring] in their own armed protection. "Nation-states don't appear to have the ability or the enthusiasm to solve the root problem," says Nikolas Gvosdev, professor of national security studies at the U.S. Naval War College in Rhode Island. "That leaves the private sector having to manage effectively on its own."

In a world where power is fragmenting, this raises serious questions. Should shipping lines be allowed to arm their vessels? Does carrying ex-soldiers change the legal status of a merchant ship? Who's policing what companies do to defend themselves? And why are the world's most powerful nations unable or unwilling to prevent a handful of barely equipped young Somalis from commandeering their ships, leaving hired protection the only option?

MACHINE GUNS

It's difficult to estimate the number of private security contractors now working off Somalia, but most experts say it's as high as the mid-hundreds at any one time. Williams and Twiss say about 200 men have taken their courses so far. Several other companies offer similar services, but there is no particular legal requirement for contractors to have any training.

Most of the maritime private security firms are British, including several based in and around Poole—close by the main recruiting barracks of the Royal Marines and home to its elite Special Boat Squadron. With cuts to defense spending on the way, recruitment is brisk.

"The close-protection side of life in Iraq and Afghanistan seems to be winding down," said one student, a Royal Marine due to leave service in December who asked not to be named to avoid upsetting both his current commanders and potential future employers. "You can see the pirates are expanding their operations, so that looks like a good opportunity for us."

Pay is not as high as for much riskier jobs in Iraq and Afghanistan, but a security consultant working off Somalia can still expect to bring home around 6,000 pounds ($10,000) a month.

Until last year, security contractors—as most in the industry call themselves—usually acted as unarmed advisers, helping overstretched, undertrained crews keep watch for pirates, and ensuring captains held their nerve under attack. A ship's master was advised to stick to routes patrolled by naval forces, use razor wire and water cannon to prevent pirates from boarding and—crucially—keep the vessel moving.

Now, though, more and more ships carry their own weapons. Trawlers and other deep-sea fishing vessels routinely carry heavy machine guns. Before a ship enters port, industry insiders say, the arms are hidden or thrown overboard; that way, no-one gets caught breaking the law.

The shipping industry says it's taking that step extremely reluctantly. The International Maritime Organization (IMO), the United Nations body charged with ensuring the safety of shipping, advises against seafarers carrying weapons, but leaves the decision on whether they travel with specialist security personnel up to the state where a ship is registered.

"We spent three years advising against carrying armed security details," says Peter Hinchcliffe, a former British submarine commander who is now chairman of the London-based International Chamber of Shipping. "It's something I feel very uncomfortable about. But the situation has deteriorated to the extent that sometimes now there is just no choice, even though it is a legal minefield."

Several experts and military officers say there might now be at least one firefight between contractors and pirates every day, although many are never reported.

LEGAL GRAY AREA

"Right guys, the current IMO guidelines are against the carriage of weapons and you need to be aware of this," Williams tells his class. "But things are changing all the time. Legally speaking, it's complicated, to put it mildly. In Iraq, it is very clear. You work under the rules of the country. Here, there are many more grey areas."

Over the last two centuries, the use of military force at sea has become largely the preserve of states. The legal basis under which modern-day cargo ships—with their often multinational crews and ownership structures—can use lethal weaponry is far from clear, and the IMO guidelines have no weight in international law.

Williams tells his students that their best bet is to find a reputable security company that operates with clear rules of engagement—but that even then, it may be impossible to avoid a whole host of legal dangers.

"We are former servicemen, and as such are simple creatures, but you can guarantee the ambulance-chasers and human rights lawyers are sitting on the sidelines watching this," he says.

Some of his students say they would be happier carrying weapons—"it's kind of a comfort blanket, I suppose," says one Afghanistan veteran. Others worry. "I haven't made up my mind yet. There are arguments for and against," said a former policeman who now works as a private investigator—"mostly marital."

CONVENIENT?

The legal risks of bearing arms at sea are further complicated by the often complex ownership of modern merchant ships. Shipping companies routinely register vessels under flags of convenience, placing their legal ownership in jurisdictions such as Panama and Liberia where tax and other regulations are lenient. But in a case of self defense, the nationality of a ship's owners, its master and crew, and which ports it has passed through also have legal implications.

"There are multiple layers of law that might apply in any case," says John Drake, senior risk consultant with UK-based security firm AKE, another company operating in the Somali region—albeit one that refuses to carry weaponry and only operates unarmed teams. "The thing is no one wants to be the one to take responsibility for pulling together the legislation to clarify the situation."

Naval forces operating in the Horn of Africa say that makes their work harder as well, and is one reason—along with serious concerns over hostage safety—they have been reluctant to board captured ships even when they are being used to attack other vessels. "Who do you call when you have, say, a Mongolian ship with a Vietnamese crew?" asked one officer involved in international counterpiracy efforts. "Sometimes it stops us from acting."

Gvosdev, at the U.S. Naval War College, agrees, and says the complexities of ownership make states less keen to intervene. "There's a feeling that if companies are going to chase the flag of convenience for tax and other reasons, they can also take on responsibility for protecting themselves," he says.

But that, says Hinchcliffe at the International Chamber of Shipping, should not let navies dodge their responsibilities. Even if shipping companies register vessels in particular ports for financial advantage, he says they still contribute to the wider global economy and deserve protection.

"What they need to do is tackle the 'mother ship' problem," he said. "We know that it probably could not be done without at least some risk to the crews being held, but it is the only way of addressing the problem. Without it, the pirates will keep growing the area of operation—perhaps out beyond the bottom of India."

CITADEL HIDEOUT

How closely a ship is secured is most often determined by what it and its cargo are worth. High-value vessels such as seismic survey craft, drilling rigs and the occasional luxury yacht are usually well protected, and almost never taken.

In contrast, bulk carriers—big cargo vessels which are relatively easy to board—are typically already operating on squeezed margins, so are much less likely to carry special security personnel.

"It's a big, bad commercial world out there," says Twiss. He periodically still sails as a security contractor in the region to keep his skills up, and experienced his first pirate boarding just a few months ago.

In late 2010, the bulky former commando was leading an unarmed four-man security detail on a chemical tanker as it slowly made its way up the east African coast.

Before dawn one morning, a colleague spotted a small craft on the radar, apparently shadowing the tanker's movements. Shortly after first light, the men made out a white fishing boat. A smaller skiff was already heading toward them with young Somali men ready in the bows.

"The hairs on the back of your neck stand up," Twiss says. "You know it's going to be a long day."

As 7.62 mm AK-47 rounds slammed into their ship, Twiss and the captain abandoned the bridge, pausing only to send pre-set distress messages to the owner and international naval forces. They and the crew moved en masse to a secure space in the engine room from which they could still communicate and steer the ship— the "citadel," in anti-piracy jargon.

Temperatures were sweltering, the predominantly Filipino crew members terrified. But after several hours the pirates appeared to have fled—perhaps because of the impending arrival of a NATO warship. Twiss and his colleagues armed themselves with the largest spanners they could find to go room by room and check the Somalis had all gone.

Would Twiss have been happier if he and his team were carrying weapons?

"Oh God yes," he says. "The way things are going out there at the moment, you definitely need it. The problem was that in that case the flag state would not allow it."

LONG SHOT

Not everyone agrees. Some insurers are against ships carrying armed security staff. Many serving military officers say they are inherently uncomfortable with letting private guards use lethal force on the high seas. Some security companies, too, say heavy weaponry makes an already risky situation worse. They say the answer is having good advisers who ensure the ship follows best practice, help keep a constant lookout and reassure the captain during attacks.

Nonetheless, no vessel carrying armed guards has yet been pirated.

"It would be foolish of us to deny their success so far," says Wing Commander Paddy O'Kennedy, spokesman for the EU antipiracy task force EU NAVFOR. "But we do not endorse the practice and we do have concerns. We are worried that you will get an escalation of violence with the pirates and an arms race. We are also worried about how you guarantee quality of training. We know of cases where contractors have fired on fishing boats, and we are worried that innocent people could get killed."

Some in the industry even wonder if a special security effort is really necessary. There are around 35,000 ship voyages a year through the Indian Ocean, they point out: the vast majority are completely unarmed and make it through. One security veteran already working in the region said private contractors could spend months without ever seeing a pirate.

For now, insurers and most shipping companies seem willing to risk the occasional hit. Experts say piracy adds only slightly to the cost of shipments through the region. As long as cost remains negligible, world powers feel scant compulsion to take tougher action.

"The rate of suspicious approach is about 1 to 350, and hijacked is 1 to 950," Twiss tells the group. "If you were offered those odds in a betting shop you'd like to take them."

Williams takes a more personal approach to shipping firms who choose to do without security. "What they are doing is gambling with the lives of crews," he says.

There have been upwards of 600 crew held hostage at any given time this year, the shipping industry says, mainly sailors from places such as Malaysia, India and Vietnam. According to data from risk firm AKE, ships taken by Somali pirates are on average now held for 187 days, up from roughly 100 in early 2010.

In shipping, the saying goes, owners worry about protecting their vessels, cargoes and crew—in that order. The industry itself disputes this; some in the security business suspect one reason companies use armed guards is the risk that crew taken hostage might sue their employers for failing in their duty of care by not hiring enough protection.

Many of those recently released say they were mistreated, underfed, used as slave labor and sometimes even forced to join in attacks on other ships. When international naval forces approach, officers say hostages are often simply lined up on the deck with guns to their heads until the forces withdraw.

Sometimes—especially on ships carrying low-value cargoes—crews say owners seem willing to abandon them to their fate. Williams and Twiss tell the group in the pub that there are tales of oil tanker owners deliberately holding back ransom payments to ensure ships are held while the price of oil rises.

BROADER TREND

The growth in private security work is not limited to the Indian Ocean. When governments and organizations needed to get thousands of their citizens out of Libya in a hurry, many turned to private firms staffed mainly by ex-military people to organize and sometimes carry out evacuations.

And the demand isn't just coming from western states and companies. London-based consultancy firm Control Risks—one of the largest of a new breed of such firms providing services from IT security to advice on piracy to hostage negotiation—says it managed the evacuation of about 2,000 Chinese oil workers using hired commercial airliners.

"We are the child of globalization," says its chief executive Richard Fenning.

Increasingly, private firms provide data-crunching for intelligence agencies that need to go through millions of phone calls and e-mails to detect hints of militancy and dissent. They guard embassies, maintain tanks and aircraft. NATO forces in Afghanistan are heavily dependent on small Pakistani trucking firms hired to bring supplies across the Khyber pass.

In the Indian Ocean, several companies are even trying to raise funds to buy former naval patrol boats or converted commercial vessels to form a flotilla of small private armed escort ships. They would be the first private warships in more than 200 years—although not everyone is convinced the sums involved would make it viable. For some, that's a relief.

"There is no great enthusiasm for this privatization of what used to be the military," says Gvosdev at the U.S. Naval War College. "It's something that has happened as states no longer have the resources to do everything and have looked to do things cheaper. But clearly no one wants these private entities to have too much in the way of capabilities."

Such thoughts are far from the minds of those completing the ship security officer course in Poole. After a test and a curry buffet the students receive their pre-printed certificates and head off to an uncertain future. There are jokes and bluster, but these men may soon be out at sea, taking life-and-death decisions far from help.

"The last thing you want to do is open fire," says Williams. "But if it's three in the morning and you're standing watch on your own, what are you going to do?"

Nigeria[*]

The "Other" Maritime Piracy Hotbed

By Donna J. Nincic

The Journal of Ocean Technology, April–July 2009

INTRODUCTION

Although global attention is currently focused almost exclusively on maritime piracy in Somalia, as recently as 2004 Nigerian waters were declared "the most deadly in the world" due to the increasing intensity of attacks in the Niger Delta region. Since then, attacks in Nigerian waters have only increased. Although not at the level of frequency seen in the Horn of Africa, attacks in Nigeria tend to be more violent. In the last three years, more seafarers have been injured or have lost their lives in Nigerian waters than at the hands of Somali pirates.

Most of the pirate attacks are directed against smaller ships involved in oil exploration in Nigerian waters. These include supply and support vessels, barges, and small security vessels. Attacks on general merchant cargo ships are relatively rare. Piracy is especially common in the Niger Delta region, the centre of oil exploration and production activities in the country. The wealth represented by the region's oil industry is significant: Nigeria is the world's eighth largest exporter of crude oil, and one of the largest producers of highly-valued light sweet crude. The Gulf of Guinea region supplies more than 15% of the hydrocarbons imported by the United States, and by 2015 may supply more than 25%. Within the next 10 years, it may supply the bulk of US imports of sweet crude oil. This wealth, and the presence of a large number of foreign companies in the Delta, is a huge draw for those engaged in criminal activities.

---

[*] Article by Donna J. Nincic from the *Journal of Ocean Technology* (www.journalofoceantechnology.com). Reprinted with permission. All rights reserved.

NIGERIA PIRATE ATTACK STATISTICS

Pirate attacks worldwide are considered to be vastly under-reported, and Nigeria is no exception, particularly when it comes to attacks on fishing vessels. The Nigerian Maritime Security Task Force on Acts of Illegality in Nigerian Waters has reported at least 293 documented sea robberies and pirate attacks between 2003 and 2008 on the country's fishing vessels alone. Another source reports 100 attacks on fishing vessels in 2007 alone. And the Piracy Reporting Centre in Kuala Lumpur states it is aware of 100 unconfirmed attacks in 2008, in addition to the 40 confirmed attacks reported.

As noted previously, attacks in Nigeria have ranked among the most violent in recent years, especially when compared with the rest of the world.

Importantly, and pointing to some concern for the future, in the last two years, a mariner has had a significantly greater chance of being injured in a pirate attack in Nigeria than anywhere else in the world (see Figure 2).

SOME RECENT NOTABLE INCIDENTS

- April 21, 2009: Nigerian gunmen kidnap the master and chief engineer after attacking the product tanker Aleyna Mercan, operated by the Istanbul-based shipping company MRC, and on charter to the French oil company Total.
- February 24, 2009: Pirates attack the Russian oil tanker Khatanga, owned by Murmansk Maritime Shipping Company, 20 miles off the Nigerian coast. The ship managed to evade its attackers with no casualties or damage.
- February 6, 2009: Gunmen kill the Nigerian captain and wound another crew member on the security vessel M/V Red One while it was protecting the oil production facilities of Addax Petroleum, near Nigeria's Antan tanker loading terminal. Nigerian armed forces returned fire, repelling the attack, in their ongoing effort to protect offshore oil facilities. The captain and a crew member were killed in an exchange of gunfire with the pirates.
- January 21, 2009: Pirates attack the tanker MT Meredith carrying 4,000 tonnes of diesel and kidnap a Romanian crew member, who is released a day later. The engine and superstructure were badly damaged in the dynamite attack. Up until this point, while acts of piracy against vessels in support of the oil trade had become increasingly common, direct and successful attacks on oil tankers remained unusual.
- January 4, 2009: Pirates hijack the French ship Bourbon Leda with five Nigerians, two Ghanaians, one Cameroonian, and one Indonesian on board. It was freed January 7. This was the second time in two months a ship owned by the French company Bourbon was attacked in the region. The ship owner declined to say whether a ransom had been paid.

Attacks can occur both on the high seas as ships approach or leave Nigerian waters, and within the territorial seas of Nigeria itself, with most occurring within the 12 nm territorial sea limit. In 2008, nearly all attacks occurred within Nigeria's territorial waters, with one significant exception. In June 2008, pirates attacked Royal Dutch Shell's Bonga oil platform, located some 75 km offshore. As the pirates escaped, they seized a supply boat, capturing one United States oil worker in the incident. Up until that point, facilities that far from land had been thought to be outside the reach of the pirates. The attack provided a wake-up call, ending the sense of relative security among the offshore sites, which had felt themselves to be immune from attack. The attack on the facility forced Shell to halt production temporarily, cutting Nigeria's total oil output by one-tenth until production resumed.

The impact on Nigeria's economy and global energy production has been significant. As a result of these and other incidents, oil production in Nigeria has dropped 20% since 2006. Piracy and other illegal maritime activities have cost the Nigerian economy N25 billion (US $202 million) between 2005 and 2008.

A summary analysis of recent pirate attacks in Nigerian waters shows a number of disturbing trends:

- Pirate attacks are becoming more violent. As noted previously, a mariner stands a greater chance of being injured during a pirate attack in Nigerian waters than anywhere else in the world.
- Nigerian pirates are operating farther offshore, and are attacking larger targets as evidenced by the attacks on the Bonga oil facility, and the dynamite attack against the tanker M/V Meredith. While it is too soon to draw any firm conclusions based on only a few cases, the expansion of piracy farther into the Gulf of Guinea and against larger vessels must give rise for concern.
- Pirates in Nigeria seem to be adopting the successful techniques used by Somali pirates. Despite their differences (Somalia is a failed state, with a nonexistent government, its pirates operate in a vast area of over one million square miles of ocean; Nigerian pirates operate in the densely populated Lagos harbour and the vast Niger River delta region), piracy in West Africa is beginning to mirror piracy off the Horn of Africa. Nigerian pirates are increasingly using Somali tactics, including sophisticated weaponry, multiple speedboats for attacks, kidnapping the crew and/or cargo for ransom, and operations that extend farther and farther offshore. Local governments in the Niger Delta now keep a special fund to pay kidnappers; unlike in Somalia where the hostages are exclusively foreigners, victims of Nigerian kidnapping are often Nigerians themselves.
- The costs of maritime piracy and criminal activities against oil production facilities in Nigeria are felt globally.

WHO ARE THE NIGERIAN PIRATES?

Unlike Somalia, where the motives for piracy are exclusively financial, in Nigeria the reasons for "turning pirate" are more complex and are at least in part political. Nonetheless, the underlying motivations are rooted in the chronic unemployment situation within the country. Many of the pirates in Nigeria are believed to come from the some 150,000 former seafarers who have lost their jobs in recent years. Others are believed to be drawn from retired military personnel or those who have been dismissed from the Nigerian Navy. The high levels of unemployed youth in general are also a large pool of potential pirates. Massive unemployment, especially in the Delta region, has drawn young people into all sorts of maritime criminal activities, including bunkering, kidnapping and piracy.

POLITICALLY MOTIVATED PIRATES/MILITANTS

Some pirates—particularly those from the Movement for the Emancipation of the Niger Delta (MEND)—claim to be fighting for a fairer distribution of Nigeria's vast oil wealth, and as a protest to the social, economic, and environmental damage caused by oil production in the Delta. While the federal government of Nigeria and the oil companies split profits roughly 60-40, and the federal money is supposed to be disbursed to local authorities to fund various projects, this rarely occurs. As a result, destitution is rampant in the Delta region. Pollution from oil production facilities has decimated local fisheries and farmland, and gas flaring has caused chronic respiratory problems, especially among children. A 2006 report by a team of scientists from the United Kingdom, United States, and Nigeria called the Niger Delta "one of the five most severely petroleum damaged ecosystems in the world." By some estimates, 1.5 million tonnes of oil has been spilled in the Delta over the last 50 years, or the equivalent of one Exxon Valdez spill per year.

While the largest, most vocal, and best known of the groups protesting conditions in the Delta, MEND is by no means the only militant group operating in the region. Other political groups such as the Rumuekpe Youth Council and the Niger Delta People's Volunteer Force are now engaged in acts of militancy and piracy. Shortly after the attack on the M/V Meredith, the MEND actually issued a statement that the attackers were from an "affiliate" group, and that they (MEND) were working on the safe return of the abducted Romanian. In fact, a notable risk consultancy group estimates that the majority of the "politically" motivated attacks for which direct responsibility is claimed may actually be from groups other than MEND.

CRIMINAL GANGS

There are many armed groups in the Delta region that view kidnapping, extortion, and oil theft purely as a money-making endeavour, and are sometimes directed and/or protected by powerful and politically well-connected individuals. In a country where the US Agency for International Development estimates that most of the population lives on less than $1/day, kidnapping for ransom has become a lucrative business. Pirates are often young unemployed men who complain about the lack of job opportunities and admit they were enticed into pirate gangs by the promise of riches, fancy cars, luxury consumer goods, and weapons.

Despite these many motivations, according to Bergen Risk Solutions, the majority of attacks since January 2006 are increasingly believed to be motivated by criminal financial gain, and not undertaken for any political purpose.

THE HIGH COST OF MARITIME POLICY

Not only does maritime piracy in Nigeria have a significant impact on global energy prices, there are important—but less well known—impacts on the domestic economy. The local fishing industry has been disrupted, negative regional trade effects are being felt, and the increasing interconnection between bunkering and the arms trade threatens to increase the intensity of violence in the region.

LOCAL FISHERIES

Apart from the impact on the oil industry, a lesser-known impact is on the important local fishing economy. Fishing in Nigeria is the second highest non-oil export industry. Pirate attacks on fishing trawlers have reached the point that many fishing boat captains refuse to sail. The attacks range from minor harassment, to theft of fish cargoes, engines and other material on board, financial shakedowns, and to the killing of fishermen.

Of particular importance is the impact on the shrimp fishery. Tiger shrimp in particular are an important delicacy in world markets, and Nigerian waters supply a significant percentage to European and American consumers, as well as providing jobs in the local economy. As of March 2008, over 170 fishing trawlers were idle because fishing boats were afraid to put to sea, threatening approximately 50,000 jobs. All told, Nigeria stands to lose up to $600 million in export earnings due to the piracy threats to its fisheries.

In addition, due to the scarcity of fish, seafood prices have skyrocketed—more than doubling and even quadrupling in some instances—placing this important protein source out of the reach of the common person. Nigerian pirates are increasingly reported to have effectively taken over the coastal waters of the country; and similar piracy problems are reported among fishermen elsewhere in the African continent.

REGIONAL IMPACTS AND EFFECTS ON SHIPPERS

Nigeria accounts for over 60% of the total seaborne traffic for the 16 nations in the West Africa sub-region. Because cross-border trade is centred in Nigeria, challenges to the maritime sector have ripple effects throughout the entire sub-region. As warnings to mariners to be on their guard in and near Nigerian waters become more common, increases in shipping costs for Nigerian and Gulf of Guinea destinations are of increasing concern as shippers begin to factor higher insurance premiums into their pricing. Oil loading onto shipping vessels at some terminals is now restricted to only daylight hours, delaying shipments and further increasing prices.

BUNKERING

The illegal oil trade (bunkering) has funded arms procurement in the country, which is behind a wide range of criminal activities, including maritime piracy. While the Nigerian Navy has made some efforts to combat piracy, the bunkering proceeds have allowed the pirates to arm themselves with automatic weapons and rocket-propelled grenades, effectively outgunning the Navy. Illegal oil buyers and arms traders have flocked to the Nigerian coast hoping to benefit from the activities of pirate gangs. According to Asari Dokubo, leader of the Niger Delta People's Volunteer Force, a rebel group operating in the region, he has enough weapons at his command to equip some 2,000 men. Being so close to international waters, he says, makes it easy to acquire weapons.

A recent report commissioned by Royal Dutch Shell estimates that 10% of Nigeria's daily oil output (approximately 100,000 barrels) is stolen every day, worth approximately $1.5 million, and would buy enough weapons to sustain a fighting force for two months. Over the last 50 years, the amount of oil stolen or wasted has amounted to between $300 and $400 billion.

CONCLUDING REMARKS: POSSIBLE SOLUTIONS

Resolving the maritime piracy situation in Nigeria will be neither easy nor quick, but will have to involve two simultaneous approaches: 1) increasing the safety of all vessels operating in the area; and 2) dealing with the underlying causes of maritime piracy and related activities.

As in all cases where maritime criminal activities occur within a nation's territorial waters, it is the responsibility of the state to address the problem. The Nigerian

FIG. 1: MARITIME PIRATE ATTACKS IN NIGERIA: 2000–2008.	
2000	7
2001	20
2002	14
2003	39
2004	28
2005	16
2006	12
2007	42
2008	40
Total	**218**

Source: International Maritime Organization and International Maritime Bureau

Navy had come under repeated criticism from the international community for its failure to prevent maritime piracy in the Niger Delta and Gulf of Guinea. In February 2009, the Secretary General of the International Maritime Organization urged the Nigerian government to intervene and reduce piracy and attacks on vessels in the region. The Nigerian Minister of Transport, Ibrahim Bio, responded by noting Nigeria has created a new Niger Delta Ministry to address, inter alia, the problem of militancy and piracy in the region, and that the Action Plan adopted at a 2008 international conference on maritime piracy in the Delta was being implemented by the Nigerian government to bring it into compliance with international conventions.

The Nigerian Navy has been plagued by funding problems, lack of hardware and inadequate maintenance, training and discipline, as well as some confusion over its role in combating maritime piracy. For example, after the attack on the Bonga oil platform, one naval officer claimed it was not the responsibility of the Navy to provide security for the facility. Other nations have offered assistance to help address some of these problems. The United Kingdom has promised military training to help the Nigerian government address the piracy problem. Naval forces in Nigeria have been patrolling coastal waters in four ships donated by the United States Department of Defense with some success: As of 2004, more than 20 suspicious ships had been impounded, 90 people arrested who were accused of dealing in stolen crude, and at least 30 pirates killed in gun-battles.

Fishing and farming, the traditional economic activities in the region, are increasingly less viable, making piracy and all forms of criminal activity attractive options for youth with little economic future. Long term solutions to maritime piracy will require economic alternatives. There is discussion underway of training some of the unemployed youths at the Maritime Academy at Oron. This could have two positive effects: providing mariners who are equipped to deal with the maritime piracy problem and taking potential pirates off the streets and putting them to good work. While strengthening the anti-piracy efforts of the Nigerian Navy and addressing problems in its defense efforts will go a long way towards mitigating pirate attack incidents, the reality is that maritime piracy in Nigeria cannot be resolved without addressing the massive economic, environmental, social, and unemployment problems in the country, specifically within the Delta region.

Dr. DONNA NINCIC is Professor and Chair of the Department of Maritime Policy and Management at the California Maritime Academy, California State University. She received her doctorate in Political Science/International Relations from New York University, and has held previous positions at the University of California, Davis; the Hoover Institution; and the US Department of Defense. Dr. Nincic's research focuses on maritime security, particularly piracy and terrorism. Recent publications include "Sea Lane Security and US Maritime Trade" in Sam J. Tangredi, ed., Globalization and Maritime Power, Washington DC: National Defense University Press (2002); "The Challenge of Maritime Terrorism: Threat Identification, WMD, and Regime Response," Journal of Strategic Studies (August 2005); and "Maritime Security as Energy Security: Current Threats and Challenges," in Luft, G., and Konin, A., eds. Energy Security: Challenges for the 21-Century (2009). Her current research focuses on maritime piracy in Africa and Arctic maritime conflict.

FIG. 2: VIOLENCE AGAINST MARINERS: 2006–2008

	Injured			Killed		
	2006	2007	2008	2006	2007	2008
Bangladesh	3	3	1			
Ghana	1					
Gulf of Aden			2			3
Indonesia	1	1	2			
Iraq			1			
Liberia			3			
Madagascar			2			
Malaysia			4	1		
Nigeria	1 (6.7%)	15 (42.9%)	14 (43.8%)	3 (20%)	2 (40%)	0 (0%)
Philippines	1		9	5		7
Saudi Arabia	1			1		
Sierra Leone	1					
Somalia	2	6		1	2	1
South China Sea	3			4		
Tanzania			1			
Thailand					1	
Trinidad & Tobago					1	1
Venezuela	1		2			
Total	**15**	**35**	**32**	**15**	**5**	**11**

Source: International Maritime Bureau.

How Somalia's Fishermen Became Pirates*

By Ishaan Tharoor
Time, April 18, 2009

Amid the current media frenzy about Somali pirates, it's hard not to imagine them as characters in some dystopian Horn of Africa version of *Waterworld*. We see wily corsairs in ragged clothing swarming out of their elusive mother ships, chewing narcotic khat while thumbing GPS phones and grappling hooks. They are not desperate bandits, experts say, rather savvy opportunists in the most lawless corner of the planet. But the pirates have never been the only ones exploiting the vulnerabilities of this troubled failed state—and are, in part, a product of the rest of the world's neglect.

Ever since a civil war brought down Somalia's last functional government in 1991, the country's 3,330 km (2,000 miles) of coastline—the longest in continental Africa—has been pillaged by foreign vessels. A United Nations report in 2006 said that, in the absence of the country's at one time serviceable coastguard, Somali waters have become the site of an international "free for all," with fishing fleets from around the world illegally plundering Somali stocks and freezing out the country's own rudimentarily-equipped fishermen. According to another U.N. report, an estimated $300 million worth of seafood is stolen from the country's coastline each year. "In any context," says Gustavo Carvalho, a London-based researcher with Global Witness, an environmental NGO, "that is a staggering sum."

In the face of this, impoverished Somalis living by the sea have been forced over the years to defend their own fishing expeditions out of ports such as Eyl, Kismayo and Harardhere—all now considered to be pirate dens. Somali fishermen, whose industry was always small-scale, lacked the advanced boats and technologies of their interloping competitors, and also complained of being shot at by foreign fishermen with water cannons and firearms. "The first pirate gangs emerged in the '90s to protect against foreign trawlers," says Peter Lehr, lecturer in terrorism studies at Scotland's University of St. Andrews and editor of *Violence at Sea: Piracy in the Age of Global Terrorism*. The names of existing pirate fleets, such as the National

* Article by Ishaan Tharoor, from *Time*, April 18, 2009. Copyright © Time, Inc. Reprinted with permission.

Volunteer Coastguard of Somalia or Somali Marines, are testament to the pirates' initial motivations.

The waters they sought to protect, says Lehr, were "an El Dorado for fishing fleets of many nations." A 2006 study published in the journal *Science* predicted that the current rate of commercial fishing would virtually empty the world's oceanic stocks by 2050. Yet, Somalia's seas still offer a particularly fertile patch for tuna, sardines and mackerel, and other lucrative species of seafood, including lobsters and sharks. In other parts of the Indian Ocean region, such as the Persian Gulf, fishermen resort to dynamite and other extreme measures to pull in the kinds of catches that are still in abundance off the Horn of Africa.

High-seas trawlers from countries as far flung as South Korea, Japan and Spain have operated down the Somali coast, often illegally and without licenses, for the better part of two decades, the U.N. says. They often fly flags of convenience from sea-faring friendly nations like Belize and Bahrain, which further helps the ships skirt international regulations and evade censure from their home countries. Tsuma Charo of the Nairobi-based East African Seafarers Assistance Programme, which monitors Somali pirate attacks and liaises with the hostage takers and the captured crews, says "illegal trawling has fed the piracy problem." In the early days of Somali piracy, those who seized trawlers without licenses could count on a quick ransom payment, since the boat owners and companies backing those vessels didn't want to draw attention to their violation of international maritime law. This, Charo reckons, allowed the pirates to build up their tactical networks and whetted their appetite for bigger spoils.

Beyond illegal fishing, foreign ships have also long been accused by local fishermen of dumping toxic and nuclear waste off Somalia's shores. A 2005 United Nations Environmental Program report cited uranium radioactive and other hazardous deposits leading to a rash of respiratory ailments and skin diseases breaking out in villages along the Somali coast. According to the U.N., at the time of the report, it cost $2.50 per ton for a European company to dump these types of materials off the Horn of Africa, as opposed to $250 per ton to dispose of them cleanly in Europe.

Monitoring and combating any of these misdeeds is next to impossible—Somalia's current government can barely find its feet in the wake of the 2006 U.S.-backed Ethiopian invasion. And many Somalis, along with outside observers, suspect local officials in Mogadishu and in ports in semi-autonomous Puntland further north of accepting bribes from foreign fishermen as well as from pirate elders. U.N. monitors in 2005 and 2006 suggested an embargo on fish taken from Somali waters, but their proposals were shot down by members of the Security Council.

In the meantime, Somali piracy has metastasized into the country's only boom industry. Most of the pirates, observers say, are not former fishermen, but just poor folk seeking their fortune. Right now, they hold 18 cargo ships and some 300 sailors hostage—the work of a sophisticated and well-funded operation. A few pirates have offered testimony to the international press—a headline in Thursday's *Times* of London read, "They stole our lobsters: A Somali pirate tells his side of the story"—but Lehr and other Somali experts express their doubts. "Nowadays," Lehr says, "this sort of thing is just a cheap excuse." The legacy of nearly twenty years of inaction and abuse, though, is far more costly.

We're Firing Blanks in the War Against Piracy[*]

By Praveen Swami
The Daily Telegraph (London, U.K.), April 12, 2011

In the autumn of 1816, Admiral Lord Exmouth arrived off the port of Algiers with five ships of the line, and orders to use nothing but shot to negotiate with the city's pirates. In the battle that followed, the British lost 128 men, and their Dutch allies 13. But casualties among the enemy were monumentally greater, as Algiers's fleet was destroyed and its fortifications levelled. Even though the corsairs of the Barbary coast continued to prey on merchant ships until 1830, when the French occupied Algiers, their backbone was broken—and tens of thousands of lives that would have been lost to the slave trade were saved.

This week, it has emerged that 17 Somali pirates captured by HMS Cornwall in February were given meals, medical check-ups and cigarettes (or, in one case, a nicotine patch) before being set free after the captain was advised that Britain had no legal framework to prosecute them.

It seems incredible, yet it is symptomatic of a far graver problem. Ever since 2008, almost 30 navies have been jointly operating against Somali pirates in the Gulf of Aden and Indian Ocean—a level of international co-operation that has no precedent. Even Iran has a warship in the area. Yet little is being achieved. Jack Lang, the United Nations' special adviser on piracy, has admitted that nine out of 10 of the hundreds of pirates captured have been released because of legal issues.

The problem, however, is getting worse. Last year, the number of hostages taken rose to 1,065, up from 867 in 2009, 815 in 2008 and just 165 in 2007. Ships are being captured ever further from the Somali coast, and there are disturbing signs that the pirates have become more efficient. Even though the number of unsuccessful attacks fell from 170 in 2009 to 154 last year, successful attacks rose from 48 to 65. Figures published by the International Maritime Bureau show that 587 sailors are now being held, along with 28 ships. This year alone, 14 ships have been hijacked, and 250 hostages taken.

[*] Copyright © Telegraph Media Group Limited 2011. Reprinted with permission.

The strange thing, however, is the lack of concern. There's been none of the outcry we'd have seen if even a tenth of that number of pilots were being held at Mogadishu airport. It's hard to see why, given that 92 per cent of Britain's trade is conducted by sea, and piracy adds no small amount to the price of the fuel that heats our homes, the goods we export and the food we eat. Anna Bowden, a maritime expert, has estimated that the total cost to the world is as much as £7.5 billion a year—up to £2 billion in extra insurance premiums, another £2 billion or so to re-route ships through safer waters, £1.5 billion for security equipment, and some £1.25 billion to maintain international forces in the Indian Ocean.

Somalia's pirate cartels have their roots in a failed state: the country has had no government or law enforcement since 1991. Its administration, besieged by the powerful jihadist group al-Shabaab, has no influence outside Mogadishu, the capital. Communities, administrators and even less-than-scrupulous bankers have been seduced by the cash the cartels have brought into port towns such as Haradhere, Eyl, Garard and Ras Asir—£108 million last year. Earlier this month, for example, the Thai-owned Thor Nexus and its 27 crew, hijacked 350 miles off the coast of Oman on Christmas Day, were ransomed for £3 million; last year, £5.75 million was paid for a South Korean ship.

The central problem is that where nation states break down, international law just doesn't have a structure for dispensing large-scale justice. Kenya and the Seychelles have been hosting trials of pirates, but they simply can't cope with the numbers. Last year, a court in the United States handed down convictions in the first piracy trial the country had seen in two centuries. A subsequent trial, though, has been delayed until November because of issues over evidence. Similar problems have been seen in India, while South Korea fears that the five pirates it is now trying could even press a claim for asylum after completing their sentence.

On Monday, the UN Security Council agreed to set up special courts to try pirates, but there is no consensus on where they will operate and how prosecutions will be handled. And patience is running out. Last summer, Russian special forces stormed the Moscow University oil tanker, killing one of the 11 pirates holding the ship. The authorities claimed to have released the rest of the pirates, but then mysteriously reported that "they could not reach the coast and, apparently, have all died". Dmitry Medvedev, Russia's president, gave some indication of what that meant when he said the country would "have to do what our forefathers did when they met the pirates until the international community comes up with a legal way of prosecuting them". Ship-owners, for their part, have been deploying armed guards, who can charge up to $50,000 per voyage, and hardening defences for their crew.

Ultimately, however, no amount of warships and arrests are going to solve the problem. In March, the US government said a naval analysis had "estimated that 1,000 ships equipped with helicopters would be required to provide the same level of coverage in the Indian Ocean that is currently provided in the Gulf of Aden—an approach that is clearly infeasible".

That leaves just one option, which no one so far has wanted to take: punitive action against the pirates' bases on the Somali coast. As in 1816, the risks are considerable. But it is increasingly clear that the easier, softer way is leading nowhere.

6

The End of Seafood?
Overfishing Around the World

A fishing trawler cruises off the coast of Bretagne, France.

Courtesy of Axel Rouvin

Seafood displays like this one at a supermarket in Madrid, Spain, may become a thing of the past if certain researchers are correct about the danger our fishing practices pose to the health of the oceans.

Editor's Introduction

According to a famous proverb, if you give a man a fish, he'll eat for a day, but if you teach a man to fish, he'll eat for a lifetime. Some scientists would add a third part: Give man trawlers and helicopter-guided purse seines—giant nets used to maximize yield—and he'll deplete the oceans of fish, leaving none to eat for future generations.

That's what Boris Worm, a marine biologist at Dalhousie University in Halifax, Nova Scotia, warned of in 2006, when he released the study "Impacts of Biodiversity Loss on Ocean Ecosystem Services." Leading a team of 14 economists and ecologists, Worm found that in 2003 fishing yields had decreased by 10.6 million metric tons since 1994, the year the seafood catch is thought to have peaked. Most jarring was Worm's prediction that unless humanity changes its ways, seafood could cease to be a viable form of sustenance by 2048.

Scientific American writer David Biello highlights Worm's data and explains his methodology in "Overfishing Could Take Seafood Off the Menu by 2048," the article that opens this chapter. The short piece sets up the five longer ones that follow, all of which center on overfishing and how it affects consumers, fishermen, and marine ecosystems.

The next two entries in the chapter come from Michael Conathan's "Fish on Fridays" series for the Center for American Progress. In the first, "The End of Overfishing in America," Conathan cites the 2007 reauthorization of the Magnuson-Stevens Fishery Conservation and Management Act as a turning point in the fight against overfishing. The law was rewritten to mandate annual catch limits, or ACLs, and—heartened to hear the nation's 528 managed stocks would soon be in compliance—Conathan heralds the legislation as "the biggest national news story our fisheries have seen in years." Looking ahead to a year in which the National Marine Fisheries Service (NMFS) was gearing up to increase limits for 12 of the 20 species found in the New England groundfishery, Conathan salutes fishermen and fishery managers. "They are making the difficult choices," he contends. "They have endured tremendous hardships. And they are turning a critical corner to ensure a healthy, sustainable future for America's most historic profession."

In his subsequent column, "Maximizing the Value of America's Fisheries," Conathan looks at the second aim of the Magnuson-Stevens Act: achieving "optimum yield," a quantity that "will provide the greatest overall benefit to the Nation," as the law stipulates. One way to achieve optimum yield is "sector management," a system whereby fishermen trade shares of the total allowable catch, much like carbon polluters operating under a cap-and-trade plan. Reaction to sector management has been mixed, and while Conathan calls it a "work in progress" that is showing signs of helping, he sympathizes with those fishermen that are hampered by overly strict regulations and unable to catch all of the fish they're allowed to by law.

With "Time for a Sea Change," the following entry, *National Geographic* writer Paul Greenberg explains why charting overfishing isn't as simple as measuring total tons caught. Some fish, such as tuna, Greenberg observes, are "apex predators," meaning they are high up on the food chain and must consume vast quantities of lesser species in order to survive. "A pound of tuna represents roughly a hundred times the footprint of a pound of sardines," says Daniel Pauly of the University of British Columbia. Alongside National Geographic fellow Enric Sala, Pauly initiated a study called SeafoodPrint, which seeks to raise awareness about overfishing and pave the way for viable solutions. According to Pauly, the best way forward is for governments to mandate consumption targets and regulate fishing much as they have the fur and ivory industries.

Up next, in "Red Fish, Green Fish: What You Need to Know About Seafood Ratings," a piece for *E: The Environmental Magazine*, Jacqueline Church explains how consumers can make informed decisions about which fish to purchase. Overfishing isn't the only thing to consider, Church reports. Some fish are associated with habitat destruction, illegal fishing, and "by-catch," the term for fish and other wildlife inadvertently scooped up in fishing nets. In addition, Church maintains, nursing and pregnant women should avoid large fish, such as tuna and swordfish, which can contain high amounts of mercury and other pollutants known to cause neurological damage in infants.

The chapter ends with "Food: Something's Fishy," in which Matthew McClearn examines Canada's Marine Stewardship Council (MSC), a private charity that grants certifications to fisheries it deems sustainable. As consumers and supermarket chains increase their demand for sustainable seafood, MSC certification is becoming a necessity for suppliers. Obtaining the agency's seal of approval involves hiring environmental consultants, which is potentially problematic, since these outside evaluators have financial incentive to grant approval. Doing otherwise might make them less attractive to potential clients. In addition, the MSC has been accused of putting industry interests first. "How badly do you have to screw up before the MSC will remove your certification?" asks biologist Otto Langer. "That has yet to be seen."

Overfishing Could Take Seafood Off the Menu by 2048[*]

By David Biello
Scientific American, November 2, 2006

In 1994, seafood may have peaked. According to an analysis of 64 large marine ecosystems, which provide 83 percent of the world's seafood catch, global fishing yields have declined by 10.6 million metric tons since that year. And if that trend is not reversed, total collapse of all world fisheries should hit around 2048. "Unless we fundamentally change the way we manage all the oceans species together, as working ecosystems, then this century is the last century of wild seafood," notes marine biologist Stephen Palumbi of Stanford University.

Marine biologist Boris Worm of Dalhousie University in Halifax, Nova Scotia, gathered a team of 14 ecologists and economists, including Palumbi, to analyze global trends in fisheries. In addition to data from the U.N. Food and Agriculture Organization stretching back to 1950, the researchers examined 32 controlled experiments in various marine ecosystems, observations from 48 marine protected areas, and historical data on 12 coastal fisheries for the last 1,000 years. The latter study shows that among commercially important species alone, 91 percent have seen their abundance halved, 38 percent have nearly disappeared and 7 percent have gone extinct with most of this reduction happening since 1800. "We see an accelerating decline in coastal species over the last 1,000 years, resulting in the loss of biological filter capacity, nursery habitats and healthy fisheries," notes team member Heike Latze, also of Dalhousie.

And across all scales, from very small controlled studies of marine plots to those of entire ocean basins, maintaining biodiversity—the number of extant species across all forms of marine life—appeared key to preserving fisheries, water filtering and other so-called ecosystem services, though the correlation is not entirely clear. "Species are important not only for providing direct benefits in terms of fisheries but also providing natural infrastructure that supports fisheries," explains team member Emmett Duffy of the Virginia Institute of Marine Sciences. "Even the bugs and weeds make clear, measurable contributions to productive ecosystems."

[*] Reproduced with permission. Copyright © 2006 Scientific American, Inc. All rights reserved.

Although the trend is grim, the study of protected areas offers some hope that marine ecosystems can rebound, according to the paper presenting the analysis in the November 3 issue of *Science*. The 48 studied showed an overall increase of 23 percent in species diversity and a fourfold increase in available catch. "It's not a miracle. It's something that is do-able, it's just something that requires a big chunk of political will to do it," Worm observes. "We have a 1,000-, probably 10,000-year habit of taking the oceans for granted and moving from one species to the next, or replacing it with a technological fix like aquaculture. To me, the major roadblock is we have to change our perception of what the ocean is." Should we fail, we may lose the ocean's bounty entirely.

Fish on Fridays[*]

The End of Overfishing in America

By Michael Conathan
Center for American Progress, March 25, 2011

Eric Schwaab, the administrator of the National Marine Fisheries Service, or NMFS, stood before a crowd of fisheries experts on Monday at the Boston Seafood Show. Schwaab had made many forays to New England—home of some of the squeakiest wheels in our nation's fishing industry—since taking over the job about a year ago. But this time was different. He came bearing a remarkable message: We are witnessing the end of overfishing in U.S. waters.

One of the biggest changes to fisheries law in the 2007 reauthorization of the Magnuson-Stevens Fishery Conservation and Management Act was the imposition of strict annual catch limits, or ACLs, in fisheries experiencing overfishing beginning in 2010, and for all other fisheries in 2011, "at a level such that overfishing does not occur." Schwaab said the 2010 target of putting ACLs in place for all overfished fisheries was achieved, and "We are on track to meet this year's deadline of having [ACLs] in place, as required, for all 528 managed stocks and complexes comprising U.S. harvest."

Schwaab went on to call this accomplishment an "enormous milestone." Quite frankly, that is an even more enormous understatement.

The end of overfishing should be shouted from rooftops from New England to the Carolinas to the Gulf Coast to Alaska to the Pacific Island territories and back to NMFS's Silver Spring, Maryland headquarters. This is the biggest national news story our fisheries have seen in years.

So where are the headlines? A few stories trickled onto the pages of local New England newspapers. But even the *Boston Globe* didn't spare so much as a column inch. Prophetically, Schwaab alluded to the likelihood of radio silence during the second half of his remarks, in which he suggested the National Oceanic and At-

---

[*] Article by Michael Conathan from American Progress. Copyright © 2011. All rights reserved. Reprinted with permission.

mospheric Administration should "do a better job of getting out the word on the progress made."

Fisheries doomsayers have certainly been more successful at garnering attention. Dr. Boris Worm, a scientist at Dallhousie University in Canada, published a study in November 2006 that splashed across major media outlets worldwide. His study, "Impacts of Biodiversity Loss on Ocean Ecosystem Services," contained a message far more digestible than its title: Continuing the world's current rate of fishing would lead to the "global collapse" of fish populations by 2048.

Now that's a headline.

As panic ensued about the possibility of empty seafood menus, Dr. Ray Hilborn of the University of Washington penned "Faith-Based Fisheries." It was a sharp rebuke of not just Worm, but the entire scientific publishing community, which he accused of accepting "articles on fisheries not for their scientific merit, but for their publicity value."

This all sounds esoteric on the surface. In the elevated discourse of academia, however, Hilborn's words should have sparked nothing short of a Biggie-versus-Tupac-level throwdown.

Yet instead of Worm or Hilborn upping the ante with the academic journal iteration of "Hit 'Em Up"—Tupac's vitriolic rap widely credited with escalating the east coast/west coast hip-hop conflagration—a funny thing happened. The two scientists decided they had more in common than in opposition, so they sat down to work on a collaborative assessment of world fisheries.

Science published the result of their efforts, "Rebuilding Global Fisheries," in July 2009. It is a comprehensive assessment of 10 large ocean ecosystems with the most comprehensive catch data. The findings showed that fishing in half of the areas they studied was either already sustainable or showing significant progress toward sustainability and that "combined fisheries and conservation objectives can be achieved by merging diverse management actions, including catch restrictions, gear modification, and closed areas."

Not coincidentally, all of these practices are in place in the United States today to varying degrees.

Of course, an important distinction to draw here is the difference between the act of "overfishing" and the fact that some fish populations remain "overfished." Overfishing means taking more fish out of the ocean than natural reproduction rates can replace—think of it as withdrawing principal from an endowment instead of just the interest. A fish stock that is overfished is defined as being below an optimal population level. While the two conditions can be and often are interrelated, one can also exist without the other.

In effect, this is the difference between a household's budget and debt. Exceeding an annual budget is overspending. Overspending for multiple years will accumulate debt, which can be referred to as being in an "overspent" state. Even when overspending stops, the red ink doesn't magically turn black. The deficit remains. Many of our fisheries are still overfished (or overspent), but the first step in resolving that dilemma is halting overfishing.

We balance our fisheries budget by ending overfishing. Then we can deal with the deficit. NMFS's rebuilding plans establish catch limits that pay down the principal on the fishy debt we have accrued because in addition to ending overfishing, the law also requires that such limits rebuild fish populations to more productive levels within 10 years. Simultaneously, fishermen are already seeing some returns as a result of their sacrifices as fish stocks recover toward their rebuilding targets.

Schwaab touted Exhibit A in his statement: NMFS will increase catch limits for 12 of the 20 fish populations managed in the historic New England groundfishery for the new fishing year that begins on May 1. This includes haddock, flounders, and the iconic cod. This announcement follows decades of mismanagement that saw fishermen's opportunity to fish cut deeper and deeper until by 2009 the average groundfisherman was allowed to operate for fewer than three weeks a year.

As an independent indicator of New England's nascent success, the Monterey Bay Aquarium's Seafood Watch program shifted several groundfish species, including haddock and pollock, from the red "avoid" list to the yellow "good alternatives" list. And it even added line-caught haddock to the green "best choices" list.

Meanwhile, controversy continues to roil in New England ports about the implementation of a new regulatory system known as sector management that took effect in 2010. The next column in this series will delve deeper into the details of that saga. We must acknowledge, too, that reductions under the previous system, referred to as Days-at-Sea, took steps to begin reducing the overfishing that plagued the industry in the early 1990s.

After decades of decline—and thousands of pages of apocalyptic rhetoric—it's time to give our fishermen and our fisheries managers a little credit. They are making the difficult choices. They have endured tremendous hardships. And they are turning a critical corner to ensure a healthy, sustainable future for America's most historic profession.

MICHAEL CONATHAN *is Director of Ocean Programs at American Progress.*

Fish on Fridays[*]

Maximizing the Value of America's Fisheries

By Michael Conathan
Center for American Progress, April 8, 2011

> Conservation and management measures shall prevent overfishing while achieving, on
> a continuing basis, the optimum yield from each fishery for the United States fishing
> industry.
> —*National Standard (1) of the Magnuson Stevens Fishery Conservation and Management
> Act*

Two weeks ago, Fish on Fridays focused on an announcement by the National Marine Fisheries Service, or NMFS, that we have effectively declared an end to overfishing in America. The first of the 10 National Standards in the Magnuson-Stevens Act that governs our fisheries establishes this goal as a fundamental principle.

Yet the law doesn't stop there. It further mandates achieving "optimum yield," which is defined as the amount of fish that "will provide the greatest overall benefit to the Nation" while maintaining sustainable populations. This dual requirement implores managers to seek a careful balance between catching too many fish and catching too few.

Many of our fisheries are struggling to find this balance. But perhaps the New England groundfishery, arguably the most historic industry in the nation, is the best example. The fishery consists of 16 different species, including four different flounders, haddock, and the iconic cod. Overfishing was rampant in the 1980s and early 1990s in the groundfishery, technically known as the Northeast multispecies fishery. Now, with overfishing ended, one of the biggest problems facing today's groundfishery is—wait for it—*underfishing.*

The Magnuson Stevens Act was first enacted in 1976. Its primary goal was simply to force foreign fishermen out of U.S. waters. It wasn't until 1996 that Congress got serious about including conservation measures as part of our domestic

* Article by Michael Conathan from American Progress. Copyright © 2011. All rights reserved. Reprinted with permission.

fisheries regime with passage of the Sustainable Fisheries Act, which required all overfished fisheries to be rebuilt within 10 years.

By that time, it was too late for the New England groundfishery, which had already seen a precipitous decline in catch. The peak of the harvest came in the early 1980s, with an annual catch averaging slightly more than 173,000 metric tons from 1980 to 1983. But when Congress amended the law to impose rebuilding requirements in 1996 the catch amounted to just 47,000 metric tons, slightly over a quarter of what it had been 13 years prior.

As a result, fishery managers in New England imposed increasingly strict measures forcing fishermen to tighten their belts. While they resulted in only modest gains in many of the fish stocks, populations of a few fish, such as haddock and redfish, rebounded remarkably. Sure, this was great for the haddock, but the rapid growth raised questions about whether the ecosystem could be kept in balance. Would there be enough food or habitat for the rest of the species in a system with high quantities of haddock? Is it even biologically feasible to engineer the reconstruction of a natural order?

With these questions hanging in the balance, battles intensified among fishermen, regulators, and environmental groups—including multiple lawsuits. Meanwhile, despite the best efforts of fishery managers and the best hopes of the industry, overfishing on many species continued, even as fishermen couldn't come close to catching their legally allowed limit on healthier stocks, like haddock and redfish, because of limitations designed to protect the weaker species. Finally, in 2006 regulators and fishermen began developing a completely new management system.

After three and a half years of deliberations and debate, that system, known as "sector management," took effect in May 2010. Sector management is akin to a cap-and-trade system in which fishermen are allocated a percentage of the total allowable catch of each fish stock in the fishery. They are then permitted to trade their percentage with other permit holders. One key wrinkle is that instead of receiving this allocation as an individual quota, fishermen must first form cooperative organizations known as "sectors." A given sector then controls the sum of the allocation granted to each of its members.

Depending on who you ask, this development is either the death knell for America's first fishery, or its last, best hope. As fishermen approach the end of the first year of sector management, many feel they are being squeezed out, particularly in the traditional fishing ports of New Bedford and Gloucester.

New Bedford's Mayor Scott Lang has been one of the most vocal critics of sectors. Just this week he brought his New Bedford Fisheries Council to Washington to meet with lawmakers and describe the hardships he feels the system has imposed on the coastal economy of his city. According to his council, far fewer boats are fishing this year under sectors as effort is traded to a smaller number of vessels. And a fishery consolidated in fewer hands means fewer jobs.

Others, including sectors fishing from Cape Cod to Portland and Port Clyde, Maine, have seen benefits from the system. They believe it will provide a much stronger foundation for the future of their fishery. Sen. Olympia Snowe (R-ME) captured the feelings of many of her constituents in an op-ed piece in the *Portland Press Herald* in which she stated that initial data from the sector system is "promising" but for the system to work, "We must streamline regulations, because the fact is that cumbersome federal policies are costing thousands of jobs."

The clear bright side is that overfishing has ended in this fishery after decades of trying to staunch the trend. With less than a month remaining in the fishing year, none of the stocks managed under sectors is in danger of exceeding its annual catch limit.

As the problem of overfishing recedes, however, it is replaced by a new dilemma. Recall the words of National Standard (1) requiring both prevention of overfishing and achievement of the optimum yield. As the first goal is achieved, regulators must now turn their attention to the second by ensuring restrictions go as far as they possibly can to ensure fishermen are capable of catching the fish the law allows them to harvest.

New England groundfishermen caught barely a quarter of the total amount of fish they were legally able to harvest in 2008. A back-of-the-envelope calculation based on the value of fish actually brought to market means catching all the fish to which they were entitled would have equated to roughly an additional $300 million in value. At the same time, in 2009, the United States imported $13.1 billion worth of seafood or 84 percent of the total amount we consume—in nearly all cases from countries with less stringent environmental safeguards.

This year's early data shows that sector management has made some improvement in this area. But still, as of March 26, with just over a month left in the fishing year that ends on April 30, the only stock even close to its allowable harvest for the year was Gulf of Maine cod. Fishermen in sectors have caught about 80 percent of their allowable amount, according to NMFS's own data. Meanwhile, they have caught just 17 percent of their Georges Bank haddock—the single stock that accounts for more than half of the total available groundfish catch.

Fishermen have a legitimate beef when they complain that regulations are preventing them from catching fish that scientists say they should be able to catch. The law is clear on this point: Regulators must act as swiftly and decisively now to help fishermen catch more of the fish they are allowed to land as they did to impose restrictions when harvest levels were too high.

Sector management, like many fishery management plans, is a work in progress, and by allowing fishermen to trade their quota among groups, the hope is it will allow harvest of more of the healthier fish populations. As it evolves, it will be critical for regulators, industry members, and other stakeholders to understand that failure to strive for optimum yield from our fisheries is failure to adhere to the law. At a time when our economy is struggling to rebound, and every job is counted, regulators must minimize the waste in our system and stop leaving money at the bottom of the ocean.

MICHAEL CONATHAN *is Director of Ocean Programs at American Progress*

Time for a Sea Change[*]

By Paul Greenberg
National Geographic, October 2010

Just before dawn a seafood summit convenes near Honolulu Harbor. As two dozen or so buyers enter the United Fishing Agency warehouse, they don winter parkas over their aloha shirts to blunt the chill of the refrigeration. They flip open their cell phones, dial their clients in Tokyo, Los Angeles, Honolulu—wherever expensive fish are eaten—and wait.

Soon the big freight doors on the seaward side of the warehouse slide open, and a parade of marine carcasses on pallets begins. Tuna as big around as wagon wheels. Spearfish and swordfish, their bills sawed off, their bodies lined up like dull gray I beams. Thick-lipped opah with eyes the size of hockey pucks rimmed with gold. They all take their places in the hall.

Auctioneers drill core samples from the fish and lay the ribbons of flesh on the lifeless white bellies. Buyers finger these samples, trying to divine quality from color, clarity, texture, and fat content. As instructions come in over cell phones, bids are conveyed to the auctioneer through mysterious hand gestures. Little sheets of paper with indecipherable scribbling are slapped on a fish's flank when a sale is finalized. One by one fish are auctioned and sold to the highest bidder. In this way the marine wealth of the north-central Pacific is divided up among some of the world's most affluent purchasers.

Every year more than 170 billion pounds (77.9 million metric tons) of wild fish and shellfish are caught in the oceans—roughly three times the weight of every man, woman, and child in the United States. Fisheries managers call this overwhelming quantity of mass-hunted wildlife the world catch, and many maintain that this harvest has been relatively stable over the past decade. But an ongoing study conducted by Daniel Pauly, a fisheries scientist at the University of British Columbia, in conjunction with Enric Sala, a National Geographic fellow, suggests that the world catch is neither stable nor fairly divided among the nations of the world. In the study, called SeafoodPrint and supported by the Pew Charitable

[*] Copyright © 2010 National Geographic Society. (Paul Greenberg/National Geographic Stock).

Trusts and National Geographic, the researchers point the way to what they believe must be done to save the seas.

They hope the study will start by correcting a common misperception. The public imagines a nation's impact on the sea in terms of the raw tonnage of fish it catches. But that turns out to give a skewed picture of its real impact, or seafood print, on marine life. "The problem is, every fish is different," says Pauly. "A pound of tuna represents roughly a hundred times the footprint of a pound of sardines."

The reason for this discrepancy is that tuna are apex predators, meaning that they feed at the very top of the food chain. The largest tuna eat enormous amounts of fish, including intermediate-level predators like mackerel, which in turn feed on fish like anchovies, which prey on microscopic copepods. A large tuna must eat the equivalent of its body weight every ten days to stay alive, so a single thousand-pound tuna might need to eat as many as 15,000 smaller fish in a year. Such food chains are present throughout the world's ocean ecosystems, each with its own apex animal. Any large fish—a Pacific swordfish, an Atlantic mako shark, an Alaska king salmon, a Chilean sea bass—is likely to depend on several levels of a food chain.

To gain an accurate picture of how different nations have been using the resources of the sea, the SeafoodPrint researchers needed a way to compare all types of fish caught. They decided to do this by measuring the amount of "primary production"—those microscopic organisms at the bottom of the marine food web—required to make a pound of a given type of fish. They found that a pound of bluefin tuna, for example, might require a thousand pounds or more of primary production.

In assessing the true impact that nations have on the seas, the team needed to look not just at what a given nation caught but also at what the citizens of that nation ate. "A country can acquire primary production by fishing, or it can acquire it by trade," Pauly says. "It is the sheer power of wealthy nations to acquire primary production that is important."

Nations with money tend to buy a lot of fish, and a lot of the fish they buy are large apex predators like tuna. Japan catches less than five million metric tons of fish a year, a 29 percent drop from 1996 to 2006. But Japan consumes nine million metric tons a year, about 582 million metric tons in primary-production terms. Though the average Chinese consumer generally eats smaller fish than the average Japanese consumer does, China's massive population gives it the world's biggest seafood print, 694 million metric tons of primary production. The U.S., with both a large population and a tendency to eat apex fish, comes in third: 348.5 million metric tons of primary production. And the size of each of these nations' seafood prints is growing. What the study points to, Pauly argues, is that these quantities are not just extremely large but also fundamentally unsustainable.

Exactly how unsustainable can be seen in global analyses of seafood trade compiled by Wilf Swartz, an economist working on SeafoodPrint. Humanity's consumption of the ocean's primary production changed dramatically from the 1950s to the early 2000s. In the 1950s much less of the ocean was being fished to meet our needs. But as affluent nations increasingly demanded apex predators, they excceded the primary-production capacities of their exclusive economic zones, which extend up to 200 nautical miles from their coasts. As a result, more and more of the world's oceans had to be fished to keep supplies constant or growing.

Areas outside of these zones are known in nautical parlance as the high seas. These vast territories, the last global commons on Earth, are technically owned by nobody and everybody. The catch from high-seas areas has risen to nearly ten times what it was in 1950, from 1.6 million metric tons to around 13 million metric tons. A large part of that catch is high-level, high-value tuna, with its huge seafood print.

The wealthier nations that purchase most of the products of these fisheries are essentially privatizing them. Poorer countries simply cannot afford to bid for high-value species. Citizens in these nations can also lose out if their governments enter into fishing or trade agreements with wealthier nations. In these agreements local fish are sold abroad and denied to local citizens—those who arguably have the greatest need to eat them and the greatest right to claim them.

Although supermarkets in developed nations like the U.S. and Japan still abound with fish flesh, SeafoodPrint suggests that this abundance is largely illusory because it depends on these two troubling phenomena: broader and broader swaths of the high seas transformed from fallow commons into heavily exploited, monopolized fishing grounds; and poor nations' seafood wealth spirited away by the highest bidder.

Humanity's demand for seafood has now driven fishing fleets into every virgin fishing ground in the world. There are no new grounds left to exploit. But even this isn't enough. An unprecedented buildup of fishing capacity threatens to outstrip seafood supplies in all fishing grounds, old and new. A report by the World Bank and the Food and Agriculture Organization (FAO) of the United Nations recently concluded that the ocean doesn't have nearly enough fish left to support the current onslaught. Indeed, the report suggests that even if we had half as many boats, hooks, and nets as we do now, we would still end up catching too many fish.

Some scientists, looking at the same data, see a different picture than Daniel Pauly does. Ray Hilborn, a fisheries scientist at the University of Washington, doesn't think the situation is so dire. "Daniel is fond of showing a graph that suggests that 60 to 70 percent of the world's fish stocks are overexploited or collapsed," he says. "The FAO's analysis and independent work I have done suggests that the number is more like 30 percent." Increased pressure on seafood shouldn't come as a surprise, he adds, since the goal of the global fishing industry is to fully exploit fish populations, though without damaging their long-term viability.

Many nations, meanwhile, are trying to compensate for the world's growing seafood deficit by farming or ranching high-level predators such as salmon and tuna, which helps maintain the illusion of abundance in the marketplace. But there's a big problem with that approach: Nearly all farmed fish consume meal and oil derived from smaller fish. This is another way that SeafoodPrint might prove useful. If researchers can tabulate the ecological value of wild fish consumed on fish farms, they could eventually show the true impact of aquaculture.

Given such tools, policymakers might be in a better position to establish who is taking what from the sea and whether that is just and sustainable. As a global study, SeafoodPrint makes clear that rich nations have grossly underestimated their impacts. If that doesn't change, the abundance of fish in our markets could drop off quickly. Most likely the wealthy could still enjoy salmon and tuna and swordfish. But middle-class fish-eaters might find their seafood options considerably diminished, if not eliminated altogether.

What then is SeafoodPrint's long-range potential? Could some version of it guide a conservation agreement in which nations are given a global allowance of oceanic primary production and fined or forced to mend their ways if they exceed it?

"That would be nice, wouldn't it?" Pauly says. He points out that we already know several ways to shrink our impact on the seas: reduce the world's fishing fleets by 50 percent, establish large no-catch zones, limit the use of wild fish as feed in fish-farming. Unfortunately, the seafood industry has often blocked the road to reform.

SeafoodPrint could also give consumers a map around that roadblock—a way to plot the course toward healthy, abundant oceans. Today there are dozens of sustainable-seafood campaigns, each of which offers suggestions for eating lower on the marine food chain. These include buying farmed tilapia instead of farmed salmon, because tilapia are largely herbivorous and eat less fish meal when farmed; choosing trap-caught black cod over long-lined Chilean sea bass, because fewer unwanted fish are killed in the process of the harvest; and avoiding eating giant predators like Atlantic bluefin tuna altogether, because their numbers are simply too low to allow any harvest at all.

The problem, say conservationists, is that the oceans have reached a critical point. Simply changing our diets is no longer sufficient if fish are to recover and multiply in the years ahead. What Pauly and other conservation biologists now believe is that suggestions must be transformed into obligations. If treaties can establish seafood-consumption targets for every nation, they argue, citizens could hold their governments responsible for meeting those targets. Comparable strategies have worked to great effect in terrestrial ecosystems, for trade items such as furs or ivory. The ocean deserves a similar effort, they say.

"Barely one percent of the ocean is now protected, compared with 12 percent of the land," Enric Sala adds, "and only a fraction of that is fully protected." That's why National Geographic is partnering with governments, businesses, conservation organizations, and citizens to promote marine reserves and help reduce the impact of fishing around the globe.

In the end, neither Pauly nor Sala nor the rest of the SeafoodPrint team wants to destroy the fishing industry, eliminate aquaculture, or ban fish eating. What they do want to change is business as usual. They want to let people know that today's fishing and fish-farming practices are not sustainable and that the people who advocate maintaining the status quo are failing to consider the ecological and economic ramifications. By accurately measuring the impacts nations have on the sea, SeafoodPrint may lay the groundwork for effective change, making possible the rebuilding of the ocean's dwindling wealth. Such a course, Pauly believes, could give the nations of the world the capability, in the not too distant future, to equitably share a truly bountiful, resurrected ocean, rather than greedily fight over the scraps that remain in the wake of a collapse.

Red Fish, Green Fish[*]

What You Need to Know About Seafood Ratings

By Jacqueline Church
E: The Environmental Magazine, May 1, 2011

With bigger fish high in mercury content, and fish and other water-dwelling species of all kinds struggling for survival as a result of overfishing, anyone watching his or her health—or concerned about the environment—might be tempted to forgo fish altogether. Unlike so many other food choices—organic versus non-organic, fresh versus processed—deciding which fish to select requires a lot of specific knowledge before determining if it's one to choose or to avoid. We need to know how a fish was raised, or where it was caught, and the survival status of a particular species which changes as fish populations diminish and rebound.

Thankfully, there are a series of new tools to help us become better fish buyers.

WALLET CARDS, APPS AND SITES

Wallet cards are probably the best-known consumer tool for making ecologically sound fish choices, with smartphone apps a close second. Aimed at maintaining or restoring diminishing fish stocks, these little cards have lofty goals. Using simple color coding, wallet cards break choices into three categories:

- **Green:** "Best Choice." Fish stocks are abundant and well-managed; Fish is caught or farmed in responsible ways.
- **Yellow:** "Good Alternative." There are concerns with how the fish is caught or farmed, or known habitat destruction.
- **Red:** "Avoid." Biomass needs time to recover or changes are needed in how the fish is farmed or caught.

Of course, beyond this basic guide, there's a lot to know about what's happening to fish and why we should be concerned.

* Copyright © 2011 *E: The Environmental Magazine*. Reprinted with permission. All rights reserved.

UNDERSTANDING SEAFOOD RATINGS

Five main factors generally go into rating seafood:

1. Overfishing: Overfishing happens when the biomass of a species becomes critically low or if a species is fished faster than it can reproduce to replenish stock. Haddock in the Northeast was for many years on the "avoid" (red) or "good alternative" (yellow) list depending on catch method. Better management beginning in 1995 ended overfishing, allowing the species to recover. Choose hook-and-line caught haddock (green) when possible.

2. By-catch: By-catch is the unintended discarded dead or dying fish and other marine life. Fishers are allowed nine pounds of discard to every one pound of intended catch—a plainly unsustainable ratio. Ask about by-catch reduction equipment information especially for shrimp. Pacific halibut fishermen adopted fly-fishing streamers and catch-shares to dramatically reduce the destruction of seabirds and turtles from their longlines and to protect the fishery from overfishing. Look for wild-caught Alaskan halibut (green).

3. Habitat destruction: This comes from destructive fishing methods such as bottom trawling—a practice that's not unlike clear-cutting a forest to catch a few deer. Whole habitats are mowed down by large, heavy rolling bars paving the way for nets pulling up the ground-dwelling fish and everything else around it. Some trawlers have modified equipment to create less damage to the ocean floor.

The vast majority of imported shrimp is farmed in environmentally destructive conditions. All shrimp imported in the U.S. from Thailand is farmed. Only about 25% come from recirculating systems which do not release untreated waste into the environment. Choose U.S. wild caught shrimp if you can get information about by-catch reduction or imported Thai shrimp if it is from a recirculating farm.

4. Aquaculture/farmed fish: At least half of the seafood we eat is aquaculture-raised. And some fish farms use more fish for feed than they produce. Pressure is mounting for internationally recognized, environmentally sound aquaculture standards.

U.S. farmed catfish and barramundi are both good examples of environmentally sound aquaculture. The best farmed fish involves land-based, recirculating tanks and fish feed with a high portion of plant matter.

5. Illegal, Unreported and Unregulated (IUU) Fishing: Prior to 2010, IUU fishing accounted for 19% of world seafood catch, with an estimated worth of $13.5 billion. Some international discussions have begun to address improved traceability.

Bluefin tuna ("avoid") is near collapse thanks to well-documented illegal fishing. Chilean seabass also comes from waters with high rates of illegal fishing. Avoid it altogether or choose only Marine Stewardship Council-certified Chilean seabass.

FURTHER CONSIDERATIONS

Nursing or pregnant? Steer clear of large fish like tuna and swordfish, which have the highest quantities of pollutants like mercury and PCBs (polychlorinated biphenyls), substances that can impair neurological development in infants.

And sustainability can also include economic and social goals. Is the fishery from which your purchase comes managed in a way that sustains fish and local fishing communities? Many people choose to participate in community supported fisheries programs to support their local economy and local families.

Before you head to the store or out to dinner, take a few minutes to familiarize yourself with the many tools now available. You'll find that making healthy and informed seafood decisions is well within reach—as close as your phone or your wallet.

JACQUELINE CHURCH *is a freelance food, wine and spirits writer with a focus on sustainability issues. She's online at http://jacquelinechurch.com.*

Food*

Something's Fishy

By Matthew McClearn
Canadian Business, April 8, 2011

You mightn't think a fish classified as a "slimehead" would prove appetizing, yet orange roughy's mild flavour makes it a popular dish baked, broiled or fried. Shoppers seeking it at Loblaw supermarkets this summer, though, might have been sorely disappointed: where the deep-sea fish is normally displayed, they may have encountered an empty stainless steel tray—with a note inside suggesting they consider tilapia or sole instead. The problem is that bottom trawling has devastated the species—certain Australian stocks, harvested only since the 1990s, have dwindled by an estimated 90%. To protect the pittance that remains, Loblaw has stopped selling it.

The empty trays are perhaps the most visible evidence of a sea change underway behind the scenes at Canada's largest grocer and fishmonger. Last year, Loblaw promised that all seafood sold on its shelves—canned, frozen, fresh, wild and farmed—will come from sustainable sources by the end of 2013. That includes not only in-house brands like President's Choice, but also national brands like High Liner. Implications extend well beyond the obvious: half of Loblaw's product categories, including pet food, fertilizer and dairy products, contain seafood ingredients. And the policy will apply at all its banners coast to coast, among them Loblaws, Zehrs, Atlantic Superstore and Provigo. "We're very concerned that seafood is in dramatic shortage," says Paul Uys, Loblaw's vice-president of sustainable seafood. "Certain species, such as orange roughy and Chilean sea bass, are increasingly difficult to come by—and prices are obviously increasing."

Loblaw's definition of sustainability owes much to its partner, the Marine Stewardship Council (MSC). One of the oldest international eco-certifications, MSC offers a widely recognized blue check mark. Its promise: any seafood bearing its logo has not been overfished, nor harvested in ways that harm ocean ecosystems.

* Reprinted with permission from Canadian Business, v. 83, no. 15. Copyright © 2010 Canadian Business. All rights reserved.

Already popular in Europe and gaining steam in the U.S., the MSC is taking the world by storm—and with other Canadian retailers including Metro, Sobeys, and Walmart also seeking certified products, it's coming to a supermarket near you.

A wide variety of logos, such as those for fad diets like Atkins and South Beach, have been shown to increase food sales. Yet arguments over credibility inevitably surface, and the MSC's check mark is no exception. Its certification of B.C. sockeye salmon this summer is just the latest in a series of controversial decisions. Several long-term MSC supporters now worry that the organization has become corrupted by commercial interests and may only accelerate the depletion of the world's oceans. "This was something that was created as a bridge between conservation and supplying people and markets in a responsible fashion," says Daniel Pauly, an internationally recognized marine biologist involved in the certifier's creation. "And now it is at the forefront of stupid exploitation and destruction."

Overfishing is but one of many forces that can ravage fish populations, and is not always among the most significant. But consider the following: between 1950 and the mid-1980s, the estimated global catch of marine fish rose fourfold from 19 million tonnes to 80 million, a level at which it has hovered ever since. During that time, average annual consumption per human rose from 10 kilograms to 16 kg—and the number of rumbling stomachs increased considerably. The math points to aquatic Armageddon.

The modern fishing arsenal includes fish aggregating devices, GPS and bird radars that can detect flocks congregating around schooling fish. Research from Dalhousie University suggests that given just 15 years, a modern industrialized fishery can reduce the biomass of large predatory fish communities by 80%. Little wonder, then, that the UN Food and Agriculture Organization claims more than four-fifths of the world's fish stocks are harvested at or beyond sustainable limits. Populations of cod, flounder, hake and halibut have fallen before our awesome harvesting machine.

Governments the world over share responsibility for fishery collapses. The federal Department of Fisheries and Oceans, for example, presided over the collapse of Atlantic cod stocks in the 1980s. "DFO has not done its job vis-a-vis the Canadian people," says Pauly, a professor at the University of British Columbia. "It saw its mission as responding to the short-term interest of the industry that was exploiting these stocks."

Food giant Unilever and an NGO, the World Wildlife Fund, believed market forces could do better. They partnered during the late 1990s to found the MSC, which promised that henceforth, shoppers could turn the tide on overfishing by choosing products bearing its blue logo. Pauly was an early supporter, joining other scientists in helping develop its criteria. Among other things, the MSC seeks proof that wild fish populations can endure current levels of exploitation, and that the fishery is not laying waste to other species or ecosystems.

Promptly spun off as an independent charity, the MSC is now run by a London-based secretariat. Applicants must hire an accredited consultant to score fisheries against the MSC's requirements. Certificates are valid for five years, subject to annual audits. For distributors and retailers, the MSC offers a three-year "chain of custody" certification, which requires that they maintain inventory control systems allowing them to trace product all the way back to its source.

Although there are competing initiatives, none can match the MSC's growing cachet among supermarkets and consumers. Earlier this year, the WWF published a study by Accenture, the accounting firm. Accenture found that while MSC wasn't perfect, it was the best of all certification schemes examined, earning a stellar score of 95%. High Liner Foods, a Nova Scotian seafood marketer, says the MSC "has emerged as the most credible organization in this field."

Meanwhile, provincial governments in B.C. and Nova Scotia help fund eco-certifications, which can cost between $100,000 and $500,000. DFO is aligning its own sustainability plans to complement the MSC's. Last year, federal Fisheries Minister Gail Shea assured reporters her department was doing everything it could to help fisheries get certified, saying, "the cost of not doing it would be, well, we can't even talk about that."

Here's why: uncertified fisheries might find themselves shut out of lucrative export markets as the movement gains momentum. Canada exports 85% of the seafood it harvests every year (by value). Little wonder, then, that haddock, swordfish, shrimp, lobster, scallop and yellowtail flounder fisheries are among the 17 Canadian fisheries under assessment. A dozen have already achieved certification. And with more applications arriving monthly, it's a feeding frenzy.

B.C.'s salmon fishermen and processors know the cost of being behind the curve— their tardiness handed a competitive advantage to Alaskan competitors, who achieved MSC certification a decade ago. "It certainly closed off markets to us," says Christina Burridge, a project consultant with the Canadian Pacific Sustainable Fisheries Society (formerly the B.C. Salmon Marketing Council). "The markets that are prepared to pay the most for fish are also those that are most conscious of sustainability issues." So that same year, in 2000, her employer began its own bid for certification. Burridge spearheaded it. It proved the longest, hardest-fought MSC certification ever. And it cost about $500,000—double the initial estimate.

The chief problem is that some B.C. sockeye species are in trouble. Each year four-year-old sockeye swim up the Fraser River in a spectacular bid to return to the freshwater streams where they hatched four years earlier. There they spawn and die, their bloated corpses testifying to nature's almost Shakespearean cruelty. The number of returning individuals offers vital clues about the species' health and helps determine how much fishing will be allowed—and is therefore subject to much scrutiny and speculation. Poor returns in 2007 and 2009 resulted in moratoriums, and fishing is greatly reduced from generations past. Last year, between 11 and 13 million were expected to return up the Fraser, but just 1.3 million were counted— a cataclysm that prompted Prime Minister Stephen Harper to establish a judicial inquiry—the latest in a series of such initiatives stretching back decades. But this year proved once again how little we understand the species: returns proved bountiful beyond all expectations. The Pacific Salmon Commission estimates 30 million headed up the Fraser, the most since 1913.

Concern over sockeye populations was already acute in 2000 when Burridge's employer hired Scientific Certification Systems Inc. to conduct a pre-assessment of four areas (the Fraser, Skeena and Nass watersheds, and Barkley Sound) that comprise substantially all commercial sockeye fishing in B.C. This confidential process is the only stage during which there seems to exist genuine risk of failure. Burridge says SCS determined that certification was likely possible, but would require changes to fisheries practices. Full assessment is a more transparent process that involved input from recalcitrant NGOs like the David Suzuki Foundation and Sierra Club. It typically takes three years, but the biological and political complexities of sockeye contributed to reams of contradictory research and heated arguments. Frustrated by the lack of progress, the Marketing Council replaced SCS with another independent certifier, Tavel Certification, in 2008.

At long last, Tavel released a 600-page report in January giving a green light. Statistically, this was inevitable: of the 200-plus fisheries that have entered the public certification process to date, only two have suffered rejection. Indeed, one wonders what would motivate an independent certifier to do that, given the impact that might have on its ability to attract future customers.

The Watershed Watch Salmon Society's response to the sockeye certification reveals the MSC's often complicated relationship with conservation groups. The society supported the Skeena, Barkley and Nass certifications. "We think it will improve DFO's ability to manage the salmon," says executive director Craig Orr. Fraser sockeye was another matter entirely. "The evidence is just so strong that the fish are not doing well" on the Fraser, Orr contends. "The bar has been set too low on certification."

Fish are not officially threatened or endangered until designated so by a recognized body. Last year, the International Union for the Conservation of Nature (IUCN) controversially placed all Pacific sockeye on its list of threatened species, listing overfishing as a "key threat" to populations. The MSC, however, disagrees: it claims "there is general agreement that commercial fishing pressure is not the cause" of recent poor runs. And it also maintains that any well-managed fishery should be able to gain certification, regardless of the status of the underlying species. Its representatives point to sockeye moratoriums as evidence DFO properly regulates Fraser sockeye. Fisheries biologist Otto Langer finds that explanation ludicrous. "You simply must have fish to have a sustainable fishery!" he exclaims. Opponents of Fraser sockeye certification, including the Watershed Watch Salmon Society, availed themselves of the MSC's last-ditch option: they mounted an official objection under MSC rules. It was futile. "No objections have ever been successful," says Orr. "That takes wind out of your sails, but we felt we had to try." The certificate was issued on July 30, and expires in five years.

When Burridge's client first applied a decade ago, the MSC's check mark might have given them a leg up on competitors. Today, a fishery's survival may depend on it. Burridge says it will take some months before certified product reaches the

market, and that can't happen too soon. "It is virtually impossible to sell uncertified salmon to the northern European markets," she says. "And we are beginning
to see it in North America, with companies like Loblaw."

Paul Uys has spent more time aboard commercial airliners since Loblaw made
its commitment in May 2009. As vice-president of sustainable seafood, part of his
job involves working with suppliers. "Galen and myself have just been to St. John's
earlier this week," he said during a phone interview from California. "We met with
the top seafood suppliers on the East Coast." ("Galen" is none other than Galen
Weston Jr., Loblaw's executive chairman.)

Suppliers cannot afford to blow off these meetings. The company vows to drop
suppliers that cannot or will not meet its new requirements. That message was not
well-received when Loblaw first began hunting for certified products about four
years ago. "We had vendors who just put their hands up in horror," he recalls.

While major suppliers are now on board, smaller ones are struggling with the
costs and paperwork. "What we're looking for is in some ways quite onerous for
them," Uys admits. Even national brands face a daunting challenge: last year, just
20% of High Liner's wild-caught seafood came from certified fisheries—a level
that exposes the company to considerable commercial risk.

With so many retailers chasing so few certified products, price increases pose a
genuine (albeit as yet unrealized) threat. Even Uys wonders aloud whether Loblaw
can fully meet its own deadline. "We do face challenges," he concedes. "How much
seafood can we get? Where will we get it?" But Loblaw's stable of certified products
(now numbering 20) is growing rapidly. They're exclusively canned and frozen, but
the chain hopes to begin offering certified fresh product at its counters next year.

Better labelling may also result. A startling portion of seafood packaging—some
estimates say as much as one-third—contain incorrect or misleading information.
Pauly's research has found that while fishers mislabel seafood (particularly if they're
poaching), profit-seeking distributors and retailers are the prime culprits. For the
past year, the Metro grocery chain has been telling suppliers it will soon demand
more detailed labels. "We feel very strongly that in a couple of years, customers will
be looking for the origin of the product, how it was caught, and the scientific name
of the species," says Marie-Claude Bacon, director of corporate affairs.

As critical intermediaries between fisheries and consumers, supermarkets are
uniquely situated to influence supply chains. The level of commitment varies
among retailers; Greenpeace, which has rated supermarkets on seafood sustainability for several years, ranks B.C.'s Overweitea the top performer, followed by
Loblaw. (Overweitea was also the first ever to get a passing grade—albeit barely—
from Greenpeace.) It accuses some retailers, such as Costco Wholesale, with making few discernible efforts.

Unveiling a sustainable seafood policy is not without peril, though. None of the
four species Loblaw has delisted to date (Chilean sea bass, orange roughy, skate
and shark) were top sellers, but each gives customers reason to shop elsewhere—a
risk supermarkets are struggling to mitigate. Metro, which plans to delist several
species in September, will monitor sales closely to ensure customers are respond-

ing positively. "There's no way we're going to lose money over this," vows Bacon. "We're in business to sell products to our customers, products that they want and are looking for . . . Without our customers we're nothing."

Protecting troubled fish species requires resolve—something many government regulators demonstrably lack. With human appetite growing and stocks dwindling, additional moratoriums will likely be necessary so as to avoid collapses. The MSC has yet to prove its own mettle. "How badly do you have to screw up before the MSC will remove your certification?" asks Langer. "That has yet to be seen."

Some worry that over time, the MSC has become corrupted by the same forces that caused government regulation to fail: bowing to short-term commercial interests. The Walton Family Foundation, the philanthropic instrument of Walmart's founding coterie, is now its largest financial supporter. Says Beth Hunter, oceans coordinator at Greenpeace: "There's a concern that in the rush to sell all of those MSC products that Walmart has signed up to sell, they're going to be pushing fisheries that aren't sustainable to be certified, and pushing [them] to produce at levels they shouldn't be."

UBC's Pauly concedes that the MSC is improving business practices—for example, its insistence of traceability makes product mislabelling more difficult. But as for its prime objective of conservation, he believes it has failed. "When it starts certifying fisheries that are very much in question, then you can ask yourself whether the MSC has lost its way," he says. Langer's relationship with the MSC is similarly complicated. Like Pauly, he also believes the organization has proven a positive force, and argues its market-based approach offers more promise than relying on government. Langer's perspective is broad: he worked for DFO for decades, and served on the MSC's stakeholder advisory committee for nine years. But recently he began to feel his concerns were being ignored. The Fraser sockeye certification was the final straw—he resigned from the MSC's panel immediately afterward. "How do you manage a fishery sustainably when you can't even determine how many fish are out there?" he marvels. "Now's a good time to pull the plug."

Bibliography

Books

Achenbach, Joel. *A Hole at the Bottom of the Sea: The Race to Kill the BP Oil Gusher.* New York: Simon & Schuster, 2011.

Anderson, Alun. *After the Ice: Life, Death, and Geopolitics in the New Arctic.* Washington, D.C.: Smithsonian Books, 2009.

Burnett, John. *Dangerous Waters.* New York: Plume, 2002.

Byers, Michael. *Who Owns the Arctic? Understanding Sovereignty Disputes in the North.* Vancouver: Douglas & McIntyre, 2009.

Churchill, R. R., and A. V. Lowe. *The Law of the Sea* (3rd edition). Huntington, N.Y.: Juris Publishing, Inc., 1999.

Clover, Charles. *The End of the Line: How Overfishing Is Changing the World and What We Eat.* Berkeley, Calif.: University of California Press, 2008.

Danson, Ted, and Michael D'Orso. *Oceana: Our Endangered Oceans and What We Can Do to Save Them.* New York: Rodale, 2011.

de Rothschild, David. *Plastiki: Across the Pacific on Plastic: An Adventure to Save Our Oceans.* San Francisco, Calif.: Chronicle, 2009.

Earle, Sylvia. *The World Is Blue: How Our Fate and the Ocean's Are One.* Washington, D.C.: National Geographic Society, 2009.

Ebbesmeyer, Curtis, and Eric Scigliano. *Flotsametrics and the Floating World: How One Man's Obsession with Runaway Sneakers and Rubber Ducks Revolutionized Ocean Science.* New York: HarperCollins, 2009.

Eichstaedt, Peter. *Pirate State: Inside Somalia's Terrorism at Sea.* Chicago: Lawrence Hill Books, 2010.

Ellis, Richard. *The Empty Ocean.* Washington, D.C.: Island Press, 2003.

Emmerson, Charles. *The Future History of the Arctic*. New York: PublicAffairs, 2010.

Fujita, Rod. *Heal the Ocean: Solutions for Saving Our Seas*. Gabriola Island, B.C.: New Society Publishers, 2003.

Grescoe, Taras. *Bottomfeeder: How to Eat Ethically in a World of Vanishing Seafood*. New York: Bloomsbury USA, 2008.

Henderson, Bonnie. *Strand: An Odyssey of Pacific Ocean Debris*. Corvallis, Ore.: University of Oregon Press, 2008.

Howard, Roger. *Arctic Gold Rush: The New Race for Tomorrow's Natural Resources*. New York: Continuum, 2009.

Juhasz, Antonia. *Black Tide: The Devastating Impact of the Gulf Oil Spill*. Hoboken, N.J.: John Wiley & Sons, Inc., 2011.

Mitchell, Alanna. *Seasick: Ocean Change and the Extinction of Life on Earth*. Chicago, Ill.: University of Chicago Press, 2009.

Moody, Skye. *Washed Up: The Curious Journeys of Flotsam and Jetsam*. Seattle: Sasquatch Books, 2006.

Murphy, Martin N. *Somalia, the New Barbary? Piracy and Islam in the Horn of Africa*. New York: Columbia University Press, 2011.

Payne, John C. *Piracy Today: Fighting Villainy on the High Seas*. Dobbs Ferry, N.Y.: Sheridan House, Inc., 2010.

Reed, Stanley, and Alison Fitzgerald. *In Too Deep: BP and the Drilling Race That Took It Down*. Hoboken, N.J.: John Wiley & Sons, Inc., 2011.

Russell, Denise. *Who Rules the Waves?: Piracy, Overfishing and Mining the Ocean*. New York: Pluto Press, 2010.

Safina, Carl. *A Sea in Flames: The Deepwater Horizon Oil Blowout*. New York: Crown Publishing Group, 2011.

Sale, Richard, and Eugene Potapov. *The Scramble for the Arctic: Ownership, Exploitation and Conflict in the Far North*. London, U.K.: Frances Lincoln Ltd., 2010.

Sohn, Louis B., et al. *The Law of the Sea in a Nutshell* (2nd edition). St. Paul, Minn.: West Publishing Co., 2010.

RestoreTheGulf.gov

www.restorethegulf.gov

This "official federal portal for the Deepwater BP oil spill response and recovery" reports on how the April 2010 disaster continues to affect humans and wildlife, offering updates on drinking water, fishing regulations, air monitoring, and other related issues. In addition to providing fact sheets, news updates, and relevant links, the site explains how individuals and businesses harmed by the oil spill can go about filing claims for compensation.

Natural Resources Defense Council (NRDC): Sustainable Seafood Guide

http://www.nrdc.org/oceans/seafoodguide/

According to the NRDC, consumers looking to purchase safe, environmentally friendly seafood should follow seven basic rules. The list can be found in the "Quick Tips" section of this Web site, which also features a breakdown of which fish are "usually OK," "sometimes OK," and "never OK" to buy. The NRDC also provides links to recipes that incorporate sustainable seafood and a search engine that enables visitors to find fresh-food retailers in their communities.

Web Sites

Readers seeking additional information on the politics of the oceans and related subjects may wish to consult the following Web sites, all of which were operational as of this writing.

The United Nations Law of the Sea Treaty Information Center

www.unlawoftheseatreaty.org

Maintained by the National Center for Public Policy Research, this Web site provides a wealth of information regarding the Law of the Sea Treaty (LOST), an international agreement adopted by the United Nations (UN) in 1982. In addition to reading the treaty in its entirety, visitors are able to peruse news updates, research papers, and opinions related to the treaty, which the United States has yet to put before the Senate for ratification. There are also links to other policy organizations that have weighed in on the pros and cons of LOST.

Oceans Beyond Piracy

http://oceansbeyondpiracy.org/about

Sponsored by the One Earth Future Foundation, a nonprofit organization (NPO) founded in 2007, Oceans Beyond Piracy "seeks to develop a global response to maritime piracy that deals comprehensively with deterrence, suppression, and prosecution of piracy while building the foundation for a longer-term solution," according to this official Web site. The site outlines the cost of piracy and efforts to thwart pirates around the world, and offers links to relevant news stories, research papers, and government documents.

5 Gyres

http://5gyres.org

Alongside partners Pangaea Explorations and the Algalita Marine Research Foundation, 5 Gyres sails through Earth's five major gyres, or convergence zones, where ocean currents meet and collect debris—much of it plastic—discarded by humans. By submitting research papers to peer-reviewed publications, raising public awareness, promoting cleanup efforts, and advocating for the use of more environmentally friendly materials in consumer products, 5 Gyres aims to "eliminate the accumulation of plastic pollution in the 5 subtropical gyres." The Web site features links to research papers and information on how to get involved.

Additional Periodical Articles with Abstracts

More information about the politics of the oceans and related topics can be found in the following articles. Readers interested in additional material may consult the *Readers' Guide to Periodical Literature* and other H.W. Wilson publications.

The Future of Space Could Be LOST. Greg Allison. *Ad Astra* v. 21 p41 Fall 2009.

The UN Law of the Sea Treaty places road blocks in the way of future resource development on the open seas, setting a precedent that will likely impede the development of space as well, Allison writes. President Reagan rejected the treaty in 1982 because of the nature of its rules for developing the resources of the unclaimed ocean and the seabeds beneath it: the UN declares them to be "the common heritage of mankind." Unclaimed parts of the ocean are, in practice, community property, owned by everybody but subject to a new UN bureaucracy called the International Seabed Authority (ISA). The writer discusses what might happen if the same regulations were applied to the resources of space in the next 10 to 20 years.

The Third United Nations Law of the Sea Treaty and the Piracy Question. Dorothy A. Nyakwaka. *Africa Insight* v. 40 pp74–84 September 2010.

The international crime of piracy was believed to have largely disappeared in modern times, or at least to have reduced to levels that would not demand international attention. However, contrary to that belief, piracy has become endemic, particularly off the coast of Somalia and the East African coast in general, Nyakwaka writes. Somalia has not had a stable government since 1991, and this has partly contributed to the piracy problem off the East African coast. The Law of the Sea defines piracy in various ways and has been used to tackle the problem in East Africa. The writer focuses on the evolution of piracy, its definition as provided by the Law of the Sea, the implications of piracy on the coast, and finally solutions to the problem.

Blinded by Ecoporn. Mark Meisner. *Alternatives Journal* v. 36 p7 2010.

Photographer Chris Jordan's series "Midway: Message from the Gyre" is a collection of photos of dead albatross chicks from the Midway Atoll National Wildlife Refuge in the North Pacific Ocean. By some counts, tens of thousands of birds have died, but it is how they died that is affecting, Meisner writes. As Jordan's pictures make clear, the birds succumbed because they ingested all manner of plastic debris that their parents had scooped up in good faith from the ocean surface, mistaking it for food. The writer argues that these photos accurately reflect what humanity is doing to its fellow creatures and are more effective than previous depictions of animal endangerment that people have developed a tolerance for.

Terrorism and Piracy: The New Alliance. Tara Helfman and Dan O'Shea. *Commentary* v. 131 pp30–34 February 2011.

Over 600 foreign nationals remain in captivity in Somalia. Since most are crew members on commercial merchant ships, the authors write, the price of their freedom will most assuredly be extremely high. Even more worrying, Helfman and O'Shea contend, is the growing body of evidence that these pirate ransoms might be funding the next generation of Islamic militants in Africa. In 2008, Somali pirate militias were alleged to have extorted up to $150 million in ransom payments. The authors suggest that the total of ransoms paid last year will surely dwarf those of previous years, adding that Somali pirates succeed due to the trifecta of location, opportunity, and profits. For the Somali kidnappers, the authors note, piracy is a low-risk, high-reward enterprise made possible by multiple unprotected, slow-moving commercial vessels.

Oceans of Trouble. Kathiann M. Kowalski. *Current Health Teens* v. 37 pp16–19 October 2010.

The April explosion of the *Deepwater Horizon* oil rig in the Gulf of Mexico sent millions of gallons of oil into the gulf, threatening the health of ocean plants and animals as well as humans. An enormous oil slick flowed into marshes and onto beaches, and the oil coated sea birds and harmed sea turtles, fish, and other marine life. In addition, fishing areas were closed to prevent contaminated seafood entering the food chain, and petroleum chemicals evaporated into the air, causing breathing hazards locally. Kowalski discusses the potential threat posed by the chemicals in crude oil to people and animals.

Student Wins Environment Prize. *Current Science* v. 95 p14 September 18, 2009.

High school student Jordan Steeves was appalled to learn about the discarded plastic, 100 million tons of it, swirling around the Pacific Ocean. This litter kills animals and disrupts marine ecology—and can last up to 1,000 years. To help stem the tide of permanent plastic on the ocean surface, the writer of this article reports, Steeves invented a water bottle that is 75% paper and only 25% plastic and that will degrade in under five years. His high school chemistry teacher urged him to enter it in a contest sponsored by Washington State University and he won first prize. Now a college student, Steeves is hoping to market his bottles.

A New Approach to Oceans. Mark J. Spalding. *E: the Environmental Magazine* v. 22 pp15–17 March/April 2011.

Human activities have taken a heavy toll on the world's oceans, which face a range of threats, including overfishing, habitat destruction, the effects of climate change, and growing toxin levels in animals, Spalding writes. The U.S. ocean governance system is ill equipped for these challenges, the writer suggests, because it is fragmented. According to Spalding, it requires a logical framework, an integrated decision-making process, and a joint vision of man's relationship to the oceans now and in the future. Although touted as a means of achieving integrated ocean governance, the writer adds, marine spatial planning is not the solution. It is a tool for producing maps of ocean usage, and it is hoped that it can bring together ocean users, avoiding conflicts while sustaining the ecosystem. Marine spatial planning is not, however, a governance strategy and does not establish a system for determining use that prioritizes the needs of marine species, according to Spalding.

Saving Our Seas. Haris Livas-Dawes. *The Ecologist* v. 38 pp18–19 September 2008.

Short-term political thinking could prove disastrous for the seas around the U.K., according to Livas-Dawes. In response to concerns about the threats that pollution, over-exploitation, and overfishing pose to the oceans, the U.K. government has published a draft Marine Bill that calls for the protection of the sea over a network of sites covering 14–20 percent of U.K. seas. The draft bill is, however, inadequate, the author writes, and Marinet—the marine arm of Friends of the Earth—has responded to it with a submission to MPs presenting the scientific evidence in favor of a bill that places a duty on the secretary of state to establish an ecologically coherent network of Highly Protected Marine Reserves covering at least 30 percent of U.K. seas out to 200 nautical miles. Resuscitation of the seas is too important for anything less than such long-term investment in the marine environment, the author concludes.

The Sea Around the Philippines: Governance and Management for a Complex Coastal Ecosystem. Pepito R. Fernandez. *Environment* v. 51 pp36–51 May/June 2009.

The archipelago of the Philippines illustrates the problems associated with the governing and management of a complex coastal ecosystem, Fernandez writes. The waters around the country's central islands are home to the most diverse marine ecosystem in the world; however, overfishing and environmental degradation mean that this ecosystem is also one of the most threatened. Coastal governance and management structures throughout the islands have been amended in the last three decades to deal with the problems. However, the writer posits, much remains to be done to address poverty among coastal communities, declining capture fishery production, and fragile socioecological conditions.

A Whale Tale: Using Blubber Biopsies to Characterize Pacific Ocean Pollutant. Angela Spivey. *Environmental Health Perspectives*, v. 119 pA133 March 2011.

The writer reports on a new large-scale monitoring study by Godard-Codding et al. of whether analysis of dermal CYP1A1 expression and organic pollutants in sperm whales could show ocean-wide geographical trends in chemical exposure. The researchers analyzed eight sex-specific pooled samples for burdens of polycyclic aromatic hydrocarbons, hexachlorobenzene, polychlorinated biphenyls, and the pesticide DDT, and compared them with CYP1A1 immunohistochemistry scores estimated for the pooled samples. The study identified regional differences in CYP1A1 expression, providing a baseline for this known biomarker of exposure to organic pollutants.

Sushinomics. Daniel Pauly. *Foreign Policy* pp36–37 March/April 2009.

The enormous global demand for seafood has resulted in overfishing, Pauly writes, adding that catches leveled off after 1990, as fish were unable to reproduce quickly enough to keep up with demand, with illegal and unreported fishing contributing hugely to the depletion of the oceans. Three species of bluefin tuna, for example, will take decades to recover from near extinction, Pauly reports, and that is only if consumption stops immediately. The author presents statistics on global overfishing.

Bush Trying to Revive Law of Sea Treaty. Phyllis Schlafly. *Human Events* v. 63 p1, 6 May 21, 2007.

LOST created the International Seabed Authority (ISA), giving it total jurisdiction over all the oceans and everything in them, including the ocean floor with "all" its riches ("solid, liquid or gaseous mineral resources"), along with the power to regulate seven-tenths of the world's surface, Schlafly writes. The real purpose of the taxing power is to compel the United States to pay billions of private-enterprise dollars to the ISA bureaucrats, the author opines, who can then transfer our wealth to Socialist, anti-American nations (euphemistically called "developing countries") ruled by corrupt dictators.

It's a Pirate's Life for Some: The Development of an Illegal Industry in Response to an Unjust Global Power Dynamic. Elliot Anderson. *Indiana Journal of Global Legal Studies* v. 17 pp319–339 Summer 2010.

Anderson discusses the domestic and international economic effects of the recent surge of piracy off the coast of Somalia and uses Somali piracy as a method of exploring conflicting ideological conditions that arise from globalization. In exploring the underlying motivations for this trend, the writer identifies a dichotomy between primary needs satisfaction within underdeveloped nations and the satisfaction of secondary interests in developed nations. Anderson also explains how globalization may be exacerbating the turn toward piracy. The writer first discusses the recent rise in piracy and then explores how the contemporary history of Somalia has engendered the upsurge. Next, he considers how piracy has influenced the economy of coastal Somalia, followed by a look at the ideological intersection between primary domestic interests and secondary global interests. Finally, Anderson explores some of the international implications of the rise of piracy in Africa, and whether further expansion is a possibility.

Clearing the Water: Oil Slick Detection Systems. Edward Short. *The Journal of Ocean Technology* v. 6 pp25–29 2011.

A number of oil slick systems that are responsible for cleaning different oil spills are discussed. These slick detection systems include the Norwegian Clean Seas Association for Operating Companies, the European Maritime Safety Agency, and the Rutter Oil Spill Detection system with its Sigma S6.

Lounging on the Deep Green Sea. Steve Collins. *The Journal of Ocean Technology* v. 5 pp1–6 2010.

Cruise ships have adopted efficient environmental technology and best-management practices and are leading the maritime community on issues of air and water pollution prevention, Collins writes. According to the author, large cruise ships produce large amounts of waste, but volume does not constitute pollution or prevent pollution; it is the failure or strength of waste management practices and procedures. Cruise vessels continually study where waste is produced and work with vendors to reduce the amount of waste coming aboard using waste minimization, Collins observes, adding that cruise ships regularly recycle more than 20 kinds of waste generated on board and work with vendors in dozens of countries.

Hostile Takeovers. Matthew Power. *Lapham's Quarterly* v. 2 pp194–196+ Spring 2009.

Much to the alarm of the maritime shipping trade, which carries 90 percent of global commerce, 2008 was the year of the pirate, Power writes. Pirate attacks off the Horn of Africa tripled in 2008, as Somalis in wooden ships stalked the shipping lanes of the Gulf of Aden, through which 20,000 merchant ships and 7 percent of the world's oil supply travel annually. Armed with little more than modified ladders, Kalashnikovs, and a total absence of fear, according to Power, Somali pirates attacked at least 100 ships and succeeded in taking over at least 40. After lengthy negotiations, they managed to negotiate as much as $150 million in ransom, a particularly huge sum in a failed state where per capita GDP is $600, from ship owners around the globe. Piracy has existed off the Horn of Africa for millennia, Power adds, but 2008's attacks were more coordinated, numerous, and bold than any previously recorded.

Sick Bay. Bill Sharpsteen. *Los Angeles Magazine* v. 55 pp70–75, 110+ January 2010.

In Los Angeles, everything that is flushed down the toilet has gone into the ocean, Sharpsteen contends. For decades, the city has barely treated the stuff it pumped into the Pacific, and this has helped make Los Angeles's coastal waters some of the dirtiest in the United States, according to the author. Sharpsteen discusses the campaign of Howard Bennett, a teacher from Culver City High, to clean up the ocean. A sidebar includes statistics on the chemicals that pollute the sea and their adverse affects on people and the environment.

Why Are We Setting Pirates Free? Philippe Gohier. *Maclean's* v. 122 p36 May 4, 2009.

The increasing number of incidents in which pirates are being caught on the high seas has raised the issue of who has jurisdiction over their trial. According to some, the crucial factor is whether a particular country's navy is defending its own citizens or the citizens of another country, but according to Michael Byers, a professor of global politics and international law at the University of British Columbia, the UN Convention on the Law of the Sea and a UN Security Council resolution adopted last June provide ample legal authority for arresting pirates, no matter whom they're attacking. Byers suspects that some Western countries have been unwilling to charge pirates not because it's illegal, but because "bringing a dozen Somali teenagers back to Canada for prosecution wouldn't actually address the root cause of the problem," Gohier reports.

The Arctic Killers. Marek Kohn. *New Statesman* v. 136 pp24–26 August 13, 2007.

Kohn discusses the threats facing the fragile arctic environment around the Svalbard archipelago, far to the north of Norway. Industrialization is already obvious in the region, and Russia—which has the right of access to this Norwegian territory under the Spitsbergen Treaty of 1920—intends to use its fields of oil and gas to project global influence. In fact, the encroachment of industry into the permafrost is well under way right across the Arctic Circle, one of the most sensitive environments on the planet, Kohn reports. Although some of the effects of climate change in the arctic remain unclear, what is indisputable, the writer maintains, is that the arctic sea ice is being reduced by around 8 percent per decade.

Plastic Particles Permeate the Atlantic. Dave Lawrence. *Oceanus* v. 48 pp18–21 December 2010.

In two significant studies published in August 2010, scientists at the Sea Education Association (SEA) and Woods Hole Oceanographic Institution found that plastic debris is widespread across the North Atlantic, chiefly in particles measured in millimeters, Lawrence reports. The scientists based their studies on ocean debris collected by SEA students since 1984—a data set of roughly 64,000 pieces of plastic. Lawrence discusses the scientists' findings.

Message in a Bottle. Arnie Cooper. *Popular Science* v. 274 pp30–31 February 2009.

In this article, Cooper interviews David de Rothschild, who is sailing from San Francisco to Sydney, Australia, in a boat made of recycled plastic to highlight the problem of ocean debris. As founder of the nonprofit educational organization Adventure Ecology, de Rothschild sees the *Plastiki*, a 60-foot catamaran, as the perfect way to promote new uses for recycled plastic. At the time this piece was published, he and a crew of scientists had plans to sail to environmental hotspots including the northern reaches of the "Great Pacific Garbage Patch," the supposedly Canada-size, 100-million-ton accumulation of mostly plastic refuse trapped in a vortex of ocean currents in the middle of the Pacific. In the interview, de Rothschild talks about the refuse problem and his plan to help clean it up.

Sharing the Catch, Conserving the Fish. David Festa, et al. *Science and Technology* v. 24 pp75–84 Winter 2008.

An approach in which fishermen are given a share in, and responsibility for, a fishery's total allowable catch could mitigate the problem of overfishing, the authors write. Since the introduction of modern U.S. fisheries regulations in 1976, the government has attempted to achieve conservation by controlling how fishermen fish, but success has been elusive and 94 of 230 U.S. fish stocks are known to be unsustainably exploited, according to the writers. Different varieties of programs that incorporate a right to share have been implemented around the world for over 30 years and have the central feature of fishermen, individually or in cooperatives, being assigned a percentage share of either the total allowable catch or the fishing concessions in a given area, the authors add. A study of share programs that have been implemented in the U.S. and British Columbia has shown improved management outcomes in 5 key areas: overharvesting, bycatch and habitat destruction, economics, safety, and fisherman-manager cooperation, the authors report.

Oceans Yield Huge Haul of Plastic. Sid Perkins. *Science News* v. 177 p8 March 27, 2010.

Oceans may hold more fine plastic flotsam than scientists thought, Giora Proskurowksi of the Sea Education Association in Woods Hole, Massachusetts, reported in February 2010 at the American Geophysical Union Ocean Sciences Meeting in Portland, Oregon. Most of these objects are the size of fingernail clippings or smaller and are the wave-shattered remnants of items, such as rubbish, abandoned fishing gear, floats from fishing nets, and scientific instruments, Perkins reports. Debris floats to the surface on calm days, where it can be readily collected by fine mesh nets that scientists tow behind their boats. However, when winds roil the seas, Perkins writes, wave action mixes the tiny plastic bits down as much as 20 meters below the surface.

Styrofoam Degrades in Seawater, Leaving Tiny Contaminants Behind. Rachel Ehrenberg. *Science News* v. 176 p9 September 12, 2009.

Ehrenberg discusses a study suggesting styrene units are fouling the Pacific Ocean. Researchers reported in August 2009 that the chemical building blocks of foamed polystyrene have been detected in areas of the Pacific Ocean and that laboratory experiments demonstrate that the plastic degrades at seawater temperatures. Bill Henry of the Long Marine Laboratory at the University of California, Santa Cruz, says that the researchers' reports are important because they provide some of the first evidence of polystyrene as a potential contaminant to wildlife that is more on the molecular level. The new work adds to a growing body of evidence that plastics break down in water into pieces too small to see, Ehrenberg reports.

The Great Haddock Revival. Kirsten Weir. *The Scientist* v. 23 pp40–46 July 2009.

Another day of fishing has begun, Weir declares. Since the 17th century, fishing has been an integral part of New England's economy and culture. According to the law governing the nation's fisheries, conservation and management efforts must prevent overfishing while achieving a continuous optimum yield from each fishery.

A Generation-Scale Disaster in the Gulf. Douglas N. Rader. *USA Today* (Periodical) v. 139 p16 August 2010.

As Rader reports, two factors magnify the effect of the Gulf oil spill on marine and coastal ecosystems: the depth and location of the broken wellhead. Oil rising through more than 5,000 feet of water affects the entire water column. Oil pollution near the bottom, or descending from the plume, pollutes ancient deepwater coral reefs; surface oil threatens not just sea turtles and migratory birds but also billions of smaller unseen plants and animals that form the foundation of ocean food networks; and oil in the middle depths threatens the abundant life of the "deep scattering layer," including prey for diving whales, dolphins, tunas, sharks, and billfish. Moreover, Rader writes, the well is situated very close to world-class coastal ecosystems inshore and ocean current systems offshore, leading to a situation in which none of the key elements of the marine ecosystems is immune from damage.

Why We Need the Oceans—And Why They Need Us. David Rockefeller, Jr. *USA Today* (Periodical) v. 138 pp20–21 May 2010.

Around the Americas is a partnership between Sailors for the Sea and the Pacific Science Center, a Seattle-based not-for-profit institution that has created an entire curriculum for K–8 students on ocean studies. Rockefeller outlines his experiences sailing around Cape Horn and exploring the archipelago of Chile's Pacific Coast during the Around the Americas expedition, and he explains how he was inspired to launch the initiative by his desire to protect the oceans against degradation by human activity.

Index

About the Editor

Were he less prone to seasickness, **KENNETH PARTRIDGE** might have realized his childhood dream of becoming a pirate. Instead, the land-loving Connecticut native settled for writing and editing, joining the H. W. Wilson Company in 2007. A Boston University graduate, Partridge moonlights as a freelance rock journalist, and his work has appeared in such publications as the *Village Voice*, *USA Today*, the *Hartford Courant*, and *M Magazine*, as well as online at AOL Music's Spinner.com and MTV Hive. He's been known to wear an eye patch while walking the streets of Brooklyn, New York, where he lives with his wife.